T0329982

The Economics of Knowledge Production

NEW HORIZONS IN THE ECONOMICS OF INNOVATION

General Editor: Christopher Freeman, *Emeritus Professor of Science Policy, SPRU – Science and Technology Policy Research, University of Sussex, UK*

Technical innovation is vital to the competitive performance of firms and of nations and for the sustained growth of the world economy. The economics of innovation is an area that has expanded dramatically in recent years and this major series, edited by one of the most distinguished scholars in the field, contributes to the debate and advances in research in this most important area.

The main emphasis is on the development and application of new ideas. The series provides a forum for original research in technology, innovation systems and management, industrial organization, technological collaboration, knowledge and innovation, research and development, evolutionary theory and industrial strategy. International in its approach, the series includes some of the best theoretical and empirical work from both well-established researchers and the new generation of scholars.

Titles in the series include:

Foundations of the Economics of Innovation
Theory, Measurement and Practice
Hariolf Grupp

Industrial Organisation and Innovation
An International Study of the Software Industry
Salvatore Torrisi

The Theory of Innovation
Entrepreneurs, Technology and Strategy
Jon Sundbo

The Emergence and Growth of Biotechnology
Experiences in Industrialised and Developing Countries
Rohini Acharya

Knowledge and Investment
The Sources of Innovation in Industry
Rinaldo Evangelista

Learning and Innovation in Economic Development
Linsu Kim

The Economics of Knowledge Production
Funding and the Structure of University Research
Aldo Geuna

Innovation and Research Policies
An International Comparative Analysis
Paul Diederen, Paul Stoneman, Otto Toivanen and Arjan Wolters

The Economics of Knowledge Production

Funding and the Structure of
University Research

Aldo Geuna

SPRU, University of Sussex, UK

NEW HORIZONS IN THE ECONOMICS OF INNOVATION

Edward Elgar

Cheltenham, UK • Northampton, MA, USA

© Aldo Geuna 1999

All rights reserved. No part of this publication may be reproduced, stored in a retrieval system or transmitted in any form or by any means, electronic, mechanical, or photo-copying, recording, or otherwise without the prior permission of the publisher.

Published by
Edward Elgar Publishing Limited
Glensanda House
Montpellier Parade
Cheltenham
Glos GL50 1UA
UK

Edward Elgar Publishing, Inc.
136 West Street
Suite 202
Northampton
Massachusetts 01060
USA

A catalogue record for this book is available from the British Library

Library of Congress Cataloging in Publication Data

Geuna, Aldo, 1965–
    The economics of knowledge production: funding and the structure
of university research / Aldo Geuna.
    (New horizons in the economics of innovation
series)
    Includes bibliographical references.
    1. Research—Europe. 2. Science and state—Europe.
3. Universities and colleges—Europe. I. Title. II. Series: New
horizons in the economics of innovation.
Q180.E9G48   1999
507'.204—dc21   99–18524
                                                                             CIP

ISBN: 1-84064-028-6

ISBN 13: 978-1-84064-028-1

Printed and bound by CPI Group (UK) Ltd, Croydon, CR0 4YY

Contents

Figures

Tables

ix

Abbreviations and acronyms

B-E	BRITE-EURAM
B-E I	BRITE-EURAM I
B-E II	BRITE-EURAM II
BID	Bi-discipline
BIG	Big Companies
BRITE	Basic Research in Industrial Technologies for Europe
CEC	Commission of the European Communities
DEA	Data Envelopment Analysis
DG XII	Directorate-General Science, Research and Development
EU	European Union
EURAM	European Research on Advanced Materials
HEFC	Higher Education Funding Council
HEIs	Higher Education Institutions
IC	Institutions Count
ISCED	International Standard Classification for Education
ISI	Institute for Scientific Information
LDs	Large Departments
MECUs	Millions of ECUs
MOD	Mono-discipline
MUD	Multi-discipline
PC	Participation Count
PCFC	Polytechnics and Colleges Funding Council
PSIs	Post Secondary Institutions
RAE	Research Assessment Exercise
R&D	Research and Development
REC	Public or Private Research Centres
RTD	Research and Technological Development
SCI	Science Citation Index
SF	Second Framework
SMDs	Small and Medium Departments
SMEs	Small and Medium Enterprises
TF	Third Framework
UFC	Universities Funding Council

Preface

This book takes a fresh and illuminating approach to a subject whose importance for sustaining modern industrial development and improvements in economic welfare over the long run is now widely acknowledged. Almost forty years ago, Simon Kuznets remarked that the epoch of modern economic growth has been characterised by, and come increasingly to rest upon, the scientific expansion and systematic exploitation of 'useful knowledge.' That perspective has more recently been sharpened by an appreciation of the possibilities being created by rapid advances in information and communications technologies, giving rise to the conceptualisation of 'the knowledge-based economy' – a mode of production and social organisation in which a central, strategic place is occupied by the means of generating new knowledge and the institutional arrangements that enable individuals and societies more fully to appropriate its material benefits. Indeed, the policy importance that should be accorded to institutional arrangements and incentive structures in this area also constitutes one of the main messages to have emerged from the recent economic literature on 'endogenous growth theory.'

Of course, it would be hard to imagine anything that we would recognise as an economic regime that did not rest upon some 'knowledge-base.' Yet, that currently fashionable phrase is meant to convey a rather more complicated notion, namely, that the economically advanced societies have entered an epoch in which much greater strategic importance attaches to private and public sector decisions purposely affecting resource allocation in the spheres of research and development, the formation of intangible 'human capital' through educational and training activities, and the management and control of access to information and expertise. From this it follows that for policy makers in knowledge-driven spheres of public and private endeavour to proceed on the basis of only casual understandings, uninformed by systematic empirical inquiries into the processes that now impinge upon the growth of the accessible knowledge-base, no longer can be thought satisfactory – if ever it was. Effective measures for the promotion of competitiveness and long-term economic growth through innovation in any society must rest upon a clear picture of the ways in which it generates, distributes and exploits scientific and technological information and know-how.

Today there is wide recognition and acknowledgement that complex and dynamic interdependencies link the progress of basic research with the development of more effective technologies, and, equally, that inquiry into particular questions of practical application may open up lines of systematic investigation that yield knowledge of a fundamental nature. Government policy-makers, along with science administrators, university leaders, and business managers in an increasing number of sectors have become concerned, in one way or another, with the promotion of innovation through the managed production of knowledge. A growing number of individual researchers in science and engineering fields, especially those having an entrepreneurial bent, are coming to share the same concerns. Understanding the social norms and economic incentives that govern the behaviour of individuals, scientific research teams, and entire institutions within this system is essential for intelligent decision-making and effective research management; it is no less necessary for evaluating and improving public policies and institutional rules governing the macro-level organisation of research, training and development activities and the allocation of resources to that sphere.

Aldo Geuna's research findings directly address the increasingly insistent need for greater knowledge about key parts of the knowledge-driven economy. His book therefore will be seen to be of timely importance, no less for its novel extension and empirical application to this subject of the analytical approach associated with the 'new economics of science' than for the new substantive findings it contains. The latter shed new light on many dimensions of European research universities' remarkable growth during the post-WWII era, the shifting patterns of funding for university-based research, the networks of collaboration among these institutions and their sub-units that have emerged under the auspices of EC-sponsored research programmes, and the development of closer university–industry research relationships. Although the volume is written from the dominant perspective of economics, it is manifestly trans-disciplinary in its approach to questions that are of no less interest to educators, university administrators, and organisational sociologists.

The general conceptual orientation of the 'new economics of science' literature to which this work makes a significant contribution, has been developed through the fusion of insights from two distinct perspectives within the social sciences. One of these points of departure is found in modern industrial organisation analyses of the behaviour of agents in games of incomplete information, where the problems of asymmetric information, agency and reputation formation are seen as central, and as being compounded by other problems peculiar to the production and distribution of knowledge – a 'commodity' that has some of the attributes of a pure public good. But, rather than simply treating the generic problems of knowledge production, Dr Geuna's studies exhibit what might be described as the touchstone of research in the new economics of science genre: explicit and detailed attention is paid to the implications of the institutional settings, and particularly to the differentiation between publicly-funded academic and non-academic organisations, on the one hand, and private sector research activities, on the other. Therefore, complementing the insights he draws from industrial organisation economics, his approach integrates the well-known contributions of Robert K. Merton and his students in the sociology of scientific institutions, while taking notice of some of the perspectives developed by the more recent sociology of scientific knowledge movement.

Dr Geuna's research explores quite new terrain, however, in pioneering quantitative analyses of the formal collaborative arrangements into which Europe's research universities (and other institutions) have been drawn. He has adopted a regional systems perspective in order to examine the patterns of institutional participation and performance in the 'research networks' that were organised formally within the context of the publicly-funded cooperative R&D programmes of the European Economic Community and the European Union. This proves most fruitful in shedding new light upon the opposing forces at work in these programmes, some reinforcing pre-existing stratification and divergence, and others tending to promote greater national convergence of scientific and technological research capabilities within Western Europe.

These findings carry the analysis of the economics of university-based research well beyond the labour economists' concentration on incentives affecting the micro-level behaviours of members of scientific research communities and, equally, beyond the exclusive concern with internal allocative issues that often preoccupies studies of the relationship between university governance and budget management. In thus shifting analytical attention upwards, from the level of the individual scientist and the research group to that of the *institutional* participants involved in formal collaborative arrangements spanning a range of public and private non-profit scientific research entities, Dr Geuna's book provides a direct parallel with the industrial organisation economics literature devoted to describing the proliferation of inter-firm agreements and R&D collaborations involving private corporations, and analysing the determinants of company participation.

University–industry research collaborations are the other principal type of inter-organisational relationship affecting knowledge production, whose recent growth, causes, and likely consequences are considered in this volume. In the advanced economies of the West, and the newly industrialised countries alike, new and closer links have been forged during the past two decades between spheres of knowledge production that formerly had been regarded as substantially insulated, if not isolated, from each other. Following what was internationally perceived to be a US government policy shift during the 1980s to encourage the commercial exploitation of university-based research, national and regional policy in Europe and elsewhere has sought to bring the worlds of the academy and institute, on the one hand, and that of the commercially oriented corporate research laboratory on the other, closer together. Formation of successful partnerships to effect the 'transfer' of new science and engineering knowledge to industry has gained increasing weight among the competitive performance criteria that are now more and more regularly consulted for the purposes of allocating funding among universities. Not surprisingly, the responses from financially hard-pressed university administrators in search of new sources of funding from businesses and governments have been generally receptive to the new rhetoric of 'wealth creation' as a societal goal for which their institutions should be seen to be striving. Most research universities in the US and western Europe have embraced corporate involvements in a growing web of multi-party cooperative undertakings with business enterprises, including ventures that typically feature contractual arrangements for the assignment to the latter parties of control over the intellectual property that is expected to result.

In one sense it can be said that there really is nothing new about the involvement of scientists and engineers in 'contexts of application' that could be described as heterogeneous, transdisciplinary, organisationally diverse and built upon multiple criteria of quality control rather than the strict, discipline-rooted criteria of the academy. Europe has a long history, reaching back at least to the latter part of the seventeenth century, of participation by private, ostensibly independent, scientists and university-based scholars in undertakings of that sort, which aimed to exploit new scientific knowledge for practical purposes of commercial gain to the projectors. Nevertheless, there is something new in the current advocacy of such ventures as innovative modes of team-based research that, because they better suit the R&D requirements of modern businesses, should receive encouragement wherever possible, even at the expense of support for universities' more traditional, discipline-based styles of research. There is indeed a significant degree of discontinuity from past experience also in the recent trend toward *contractual corporate participation* by research universities in commercially oriented research collaborations with industry, and acceptance of the limitations that such involvements frequently impose upon the distribution of new knowledge by, and among, faculty and student members of the institution.

Parallel to the emerging view of university instruction as production of 'human capital', and the growing orientation to encourage market competition in the supply of such services, the new narrow instrumentalism of 'wealth creation' has tended to promote a gradual re-conceptualisation of the modern research university as simply one among a number of institutional components in a 'managed' national or regional system of innovation. Against that tendency, this book's examination of the impacts of the shifting rationale for public patronage, the ways in which that has been reflected in altered patterns of public funding and incentives affecting universities in Europe, and the likely consequences, explicitly recognises the broader set of societal missions that universities historically have fulfilled, and the connections among them.

The nexus of functions that have been supported by universities in, and on behalf of, *open* societies is indeed extensive and multifarious. Included within the core are the peer-evaluation and validation of additions to the knowledge-base, their further codification and transmission to students and scholars at large, the provision of research conditions that help to insulate the conduct of inquiry from the manifestly distorting pressures that external economic and political interests otherwise would bring to bear, and the maintenance of institutional protections for the expression of independent judgement and, moreover, unpopularly heterodox opinion. Not all of these 'purposes' can be said to have been served in equal measure by all universities, nor can it be supposed that individual institutions have been unwavering over time in their performance with regard to any one of those functions. The acknowledged legitimacy of all those aspects of 'the university's mission', however, remains a unique, perhaps a defining attribute of these remarkable organisations, and is the fundamental basis of the university's continuing claim to society's patronage and protection of its autonomous character.

Dr Geuna's discussion of the possible unintended consequences of the recent shifts that have been taking place in the rationale for public funding of Europe's research universities directs our attention to the problematic aspects of increased concentration of public research resources in a small number of institutions, heightened incentives for short-term contractually specified investigations, encroachment of tightening information controls demanded by proprietary research organisations upon the sphere of free dissemination of knowledge characteristic of academic communities engaged in open science, and still other sources for concern. In this respect, his book offers an appropriate and timely warning about the leverage that competition for marginal resources can exert upon the internal priorities and incentives that shape organisational cultures. What may appear to be minor procedural modifications facilitating an organisation's immediate exploitation of new opportunities, can turn out to exert a disproportionally powerful impact upon the values and behaviours of the people who are undergoing training and remain in the formative stages of their careers within the institution. Ill-considered responses to transient circumstances may, in that way, produce unforeseen and unwanted changes in the future institutional character and performance of today's research universities.

Paul A. David
All Souls College, Oxford
and Stanford University

Acknowledgements

This book is the result of a pre-existent interest in the evolution of the university system as well as a series of events that have shaped its development in the last five years. It could not have been possible without the stimuli, discussions and comments of Cristiano Antonelli, Paul David and Ed Steinmueller.

Most of the research for this book has been carried out at MERIT, Maastricht University, although I completed it during my fellowship at BETA, Université Louis Pasteur (Strasbourg I). I would like to express my gratitude to all the people working in these two research centres for their direct and indirect support. Particular thanks for their comments and advice go to: Anthony Arundel, Robin Cowan, Karin Kamp, Marc Ledoux, Patrick Llerena, Ivo de Loo, Stéphane Malo, Myriam Mariani, Benoit Simon, Luc Soete, Bart Verspagen, Katy Wakelin and Thomas Ziesemer.

Of course, other people outside MERIT and BETA have also contributed to the realisation of this book. I am particularly obliged to: Giuseppe Catalano, Alfonso Gambardella, Walter Garcia-Fontes, Diana Hicks, the colleagues at the Center for Higher Education Policy Studies (CHEPS) and various officials of the Commission of the European Communities.

In the course of the past few years, different institutions have financially supported my research. I gratefully acknowledge the postgraduate fellowship of the Politecnico di Milano and the TMR Marie Curie fellowship of the Commission of the European Communities. Part of the research was financed via the Human Capital and Mobility Programme of the Commission of the European Communities and the STOA programme of the European Parliament.

Writing a book is a very long process and sometimes you just do not see the end any more. In such moments, but also in moments of happiness, the presence of Clarien, Karin, Katy, Marcello, and Stéphane has been extremely important for me.

1. Introduction

Attributing an economic significance to knowledge is not a novel idea. In 1776, Adam Smith wrote that 'A man educated at the expense of much labour and time to any of those employments which require extraordinary dexterity and skill, may be compared to one of those expensive machines' (p. 118, Book I), thereby laying a basis for what was to eventually become known as 'human capital'. Since then various scholars have built on this notion.[1] In particular, during the 1960s human capital theories gained intellectual pre-eminence and political influence. Starting in the same period, but from a different perspective, the comprehensive work of Fritz Machlup on the production and distribution of knowledge[2] offered insights and stimulated a wave of academic studies on the economic significance of knowledge.[3] The relevance of knowledge and learning in the process of economic development has been analysed from two perspectives. On the one hand, human competence, as well as the process of acquisition and the use of it, are considered to be at the core of economic development throughout history. On the other hand, the production, distribution and use of knowledge is seen as the paradigm for modern economic growth.[4]

By the 1980s and early 1990s, the central relevance of knowledge in the process of economic development had become widely recognised. Both neoclassical endogenous growth models and recent approaches of the economics of science and technological change have thus used the concepts of production and distribution of knowledge to explain economic growth. Conceptualisations such as the knowledge-based economy, the learning economy and more generally the knowledge-based society have all sprung from the cross-fertilisation of economics, history and sociology. Common to all the studies, albeit at different levels, is the concern with the 'sites' where knowledge is created and from which it is transmitted.[5] The main institutional sites where scientific and technological knowledge are generated are universities, firms, public research agencies, and private research centres. Due to the presence of externalities and spillovers, as well as to the development of specific transfer mechanisms, the knowledge created at a specific site in the system tends to percolate,[6] although neither immediately nor completely, to other sites and to interact with learning processes that are taking place elsewhere in the system.[7]

1.1   THE CONTEXT OF THE RESEARCH

While the study of the production and use of knowledge in industries has developed giving rise to disciplines such as the economics of technological change and the economics of innovation,[8] the economic analysis of the process of knowledge production in the university is still in its infancy. In his original work on American universities, Veblen (1918) proposed economic explanations of the institutional behaviour of universities, focusing particularly on the introduction of business principles into university policy. After this seminal work, the understanding of the behaviour of universities has been mainly of concern to sociologists and historians. From the 1960s onwards, economists, with the development of human capital theories, again focused their research effort on the university. But, despite this new interest, it was mainly the educational aspects that were taken into account, leaving aside the analysis of the overall behaviour of the institution. While this research endeavour led to the development of the economics of education, it did not equally promote the development of the economics of university-based research.[9]

In the same period, the two articles of Nelson (1959) and Arrow (1962) laid some of the foundations of the economics of science. Together these two papers have underscored the fact that, due to the properties of non-excludability and non-rivalry in consumption characterising scientific knowledge, the creator cannot fully appropriate the knowledge produced. Moreover, as the marginal costs of duplicating scientific knowledge are very low, scientific knowledge can be characterised as a 'public good'. Furthermore, it is argued that, due to the 'public good' nature of scientific knowledge, the producer cannot capture the benefits stemming from the production of new knowledge and therefore market forces remain inadequate in delivering the socially optimal level of scientific research. As a result of this market failure, private investment is socially insufficient and the state has a legitimate role in taking responsibility for the support of an important part of scientific research.

The economics of science[10] was concerned mainly with the analysis of the behaviour of the individual researcher, considering only marginally the issues related to the institution where the research is carried out (Dasgupta and David, 1987). Throughout the 1980s and 1990s, attention has increasingly been devoted to the institutional analysis. On the one hand, different works developed within the framework of the 'national systems of innovation'[11] analysed the role played by universities and their relation with the other producers and users of knowledge within national or regional systems. On the other hand, a number of studies focused on the understanding of university behaviour,[12] giving rise to what can be defined as the 'economics of university'. Most of them originate from, and refer to, an Anglo-American context. Recently, especially in countries such as the USA, the United Kingdom and Australia, market forces and government simulated market actions (via performance-based funding systems) have significantly influenced the behaviour of universities (Massy, 1996). These changes towards a stronger market orientation of the higher education systems stimulated the development of scholarly works on the economics of university.

The university systems of the highly industrialised countries are going through a period of profound modification. Although the changes vary from country to country, they are driven by the same forces and have similar overall aims. After the Second World War the various higher education systems witnessed an impressive growth in the numbers of students and staff, and in the levels of expenditures. For example, the number of students in the EU countries increased from about one million in 1960 to *circa* nine million in 1990. In the same period, the gross enrolment ratio – that is, total enrolment, regardless of age, divided by the population of the age group 20–24 grew from less than 10 per cent to around 30 per cent, depending on the EU country.[13] This rapid growth was also connected with a rise in society's expectations for economic returns. These two phenomena have led to counteracting pressures on the institutional organisation and roles played by the university. Examples of the tensions characterising contemporary universities are: (1) incompatibility between the demands of elite and mass higher education; (2) friction between curiosity-driven research enterprise and targeted research; (3) the different impact of private and public financing; and (4) conflicts between the free advancement of the knowledge frontier and research driven by the needs of the society. From the early 1980s onwards, policies and priorities of universities have been increasingly influenced both by the quest for relevance of university research to national needs and by the pressure for accountability and cost reduction.

One of the most pertinent indications of the ongoing change can be found in the increased interactions between university and industry. During the 1980s the share of higher education expenditure on research and development (HERD) financed by business enterprises showed positive growth rates in all the EU countries.[14] Although industrial funding of university research showed an indication of stabilisation (and in some cases of decrease) during the first part of the 1990s, its share of total HERD was about 6 per cent in 1995. Universities contribute to knowledge inputs of industry in three major ways. First, industry receives inputs from universities in the form of trained individuals. Although these individuals may require further training, university education lays the foundations for the following more specialised industrial training.[15] Second, knowledge produced at universities and disseminated through publications is used as input in the process of knowledge creation that takes place in industry. Third, universities are increasingly involved in co-operative research and development (R&D) projects with industry. Although these collaborations are of various types,[16] they are all characterised by an exchange of knowledge among participants, with the university usually in the role of the most important supplier of knowledge. The intensification of interactions between university and industry owes much to the following four interrelated factors: (1) the development of science such as molecular biology, material science and computer science[17] characterised by high levels of applicability and shorter time between the phase of exploratory research and the possibility of industrial development spurring the interactions between industry and university; (2) an increasing budget stringency, forcing universities to seek external sources of income, and thereby encouraging them to carry out research work financed by industry; (3) the growing scientific and technological content of industrial production and certain forms of services such as health care making university knowledge more valuable to industry; (4) policies aiming at raising the economic returns of public financed research stimulating the interaction between university and industry with the goal of increasing the transfer of knowledge from the university.

The governmental push for increasing co-operation between university and industry is just one of the outcomes of the process of re-examination and modification of the rationale for resource allocation to universities and, in particular, to university research.[18] The model of university research funding developed after the Second World War related academic quality to the level of funding. The increase in public funding was grounded on the premise that the proportional rise of academic quality (for both teaching and research) would foster the welfare of society. Crucial to this view are the following two assumptions. First, the transfer of knowledge from basic research to commercialisation is seen as a linear process. In this linear model, basic research (mainly carried out at the university) leads to applied research and development and then to commercialisation.[19] Second, knowledge is a public good with important positive externalities and hence there is the need for public funding to reach a socially optimum level of investment.[20]

In the post-Second World War rationale, resource allocation to universities, as compared to other public-funded sectors such as health care, was mainly based on an *ex-ante* judgement of research promises and thereby was influenced by the priorities of the academic community. Two main reasons justified the self-determination of priorities by the university community. First, as the research output (and the value of education) is difficult to measure the people in the best position to evaluate it are the practitioners, that is the academic staff. Second, the strong conviction that the internal social organisation of the university was the most appropriate means for managing university activities supported the claim of autonomy in the definition and control of university behaviour.

On the basis of these premises the post-Second World War rationale for resource allocation to universities relied on a research funding approach whereby the government was funding the research that was considered by the academic community most worthy – that is, through the peer review process. In return, scientists were producing new knowledge that, due to its 'public good' nature, would enter into other knowledge production processes within and outside the university.

A more direct intervention of government in the guidance of the research enterprise in universities started in the mid 1970s. From the early 1980s onwards a transition from the post-Second World War rationale for scientific funding to what can be referred to as the 'competitive approach' to university research behaviour and funding took place. As pointed out above, governments have put increasing pressures on universities to focus their research on national economic priorities. Moreover, funding of science has shifted from a period of continuous budgetary expansion to one of constant or shrinking budgets.[21] Policies aimed at concentration and selectivity of research funds and, more generally, at a higher level of accountability and cost reduction have been implemented. What lies behind such resource allocation policies is the assumption that it is possible to implement an *ex-post* evaluation of university performance via market forces or simulated market actions. In this framework consumers, such as students, governments and other organisations, buy the services supplied by universities giving in this way a direct evaluation of their output.

In Europe the UK system based on *ex-post* institutional accountability for performance quality is a clear example of the new market steering approach. Although direct competition is not permitted, government attempts to simulate market actions by adjusting its demand for university services in relation to absolute or relative institutional performance[22] (Massy, 1996). Other European countries, such as The Netherlands, have started to implement similar approaches to university funding.[23] National policies aimed at concentration and selectivity of research funds may be further reinforced by the European Union (EU) research actions. The four Framework Programmes of the Commission of the European Communities for the support of R&D co-operative projects, discussed later in this book,[24] have been characterised by a highly competitive approach to research funding. Universities have increasingly taken part in these R&D co-operative projects, becoming in the Fourth Framework Programme the largest single type of institution both in terms of the number of times they have participated in an EU-funded R&D co-operative project and in terms of funds received.

A debate on the advantages and drawbacks of the new rationale for resource allocation to universities is currently taking place primarily in the fields of science and technology policy, and higher education studies.[25] One of the aspects that merits special attention is the analysis of the intended and unintended consequences[26] of the market approach on the medium- to long-term horizon. In particular, the absence of a systematic understanding of the operation of the university as an economic and social institution raises the possibility that unintended consequences may flow from the ongoing changes.

1.2   RESEARCH QUESTIONS AND OVERVIEW OF THE BOOK

The universities of the EU countries in the early 1990s are the subjects of inquiry in this book. The impacts of the changes in the rationale for university funding on university research behaviour, and on the structure of the university system, are the specific questions to be studied. Considerable attention will be paid to the changing opportunities and constraints facing European universities. The first part of this work formulates a behavioural approach to university research, and an historical characterisation of the 'European University' as the typical unit. On the basis of these, Part II analyses the relationships between the allocation of funds and the organisation and development of university research activity, whereas Part III is devoted to the detailed study of EU-funded university research.

The overall aim of this book is to investigate the unintended consequences of the changes in the rationale for resource allocation to universities. In particular, the existence and the impact of unintended consequences on the policies and priorities of universities are studied. In doing so, two other related subjects of a specific nature will be addressed. First, the connections between resource allocation and scientific research productivity are examined. This analysis is carried out both for the total population of universities in the EU countries and, in a more detailed way, for the 'old' universities of the UK. Particular attention is given to the understanding of the possible influences of an increased dependence on industrial funding upon the conduct of university research. Second, competitive research funding is influenced by the existence of cumulative and self-reinforcement phenomena and, in particular, by the Matthew effect.[27] The impact of these phenomena is studied for the participation of universities in EU-funded R&D co-operative projects.

The book is thus organised into four main parts. The first proposes a theoretical and historical framework for the analysis of European universities. The second considers the relationships between allocation of funds and university scientific research productivity. The third analyses different aspects of EU funding of university research. Finally, the fourth part presents the overall conclusions of the book.

Part I consists of two chapters. The first, Chapter 2, considers universities as socioeconomic organisations influenced by opportunities and constraints. These non-profit organisations have a multiplicity of objectives and decision-makers that cannot be reduced to a unique objective function. Hence a utility-maximising approach cannot be used to study their behaviour. One way to study their behaviour is to analyse the response of the institution to environmental changes. The chapter presents an economic approach to university research behaviour that focuses on how constraints and opportunities imposed by the regulatory framework and market conditions shape the behaviour of the organisation. The analysis of the relationships between inputs and outputs, and more specifically between diversified funding sources and research outputs, provides insights relevant for the understanding of university research behaviour. The approach is further developed in the second section where the implications for university research behaviour of the changes in the rationale for university research funding are analysed. The objectives, research allocation mechanisms and implicit assumptions of the competitive approach to university behaviour and funding are examined. This analysis underscores the importance of considering the possibility that the existence of diversified non-coordinated competitive funding sources, supporting different incentive settings and constraints, gives rise to unintended outcomes some of which may have perverse long-term consequences.

Chapter 3 presents an historical analysis of European universities. Focusing on universities' contributions to social purpose and on the governance and organisation of the institution, it describes the path of evolution of the typical institution, delineating the presence of continuity within change. It shows that the historical evolution of the European universities has led to the creation of routines and expectations that may influence their capacities and possibilities of responding to current changes. The aim of the chapter is to develop a systematic empirical grounding for taking the 'European University' as the unit of analysis in the book.

Part II considers the relationships between resource allocation and scientific research productivity of universities at different levels of detail. It is divided into two chapters. The first, Chapter 4, provides a description of the total population of universities in the EU countries in the period 1981–95. It begins with an aggregate analysis of the research funding structure of higher education institutions and of the scientific publications' output.[28] Next, focusing on the universities active in 1992, a methodology is developed for describing the university system in terms of its main characteristics, such as size of the university and research output. Here the objective is to identify the existence of well-defined clusters of institutions that have similar features. The analysis of the characteristics of the institutions included in the different groups points to a clear polarisation of the university system. Two extreme configurations have thus been identified. One accounts for the new postwar universities of small size with low research output and low scientific research productivity. The other includes institutions founded early that are large in size, high in research output and high in scientific research productivity.

Chapter 4 forms a background for the succeeding chapter, which considers the same issues within the context of a single country's university system, permitting a more detailed specification of both the funding patterns and research outputs. Chapter 5 is devoted to the analysis of the changing relationships between the allocation of funds and research output for the 'old' UK universities in the period 1989–93, that is, the institutions other than the former polytechnics. After a description of the evolution of the funding structure of UK universities, the methodology developed in the previous chapter is applied to the data pertaining to the initial and terminal years of the period considered in order to examine the impact on university research output of the intervening changes in the funding structure. Particular attention is given to the movements of institutions among the different clusters. By considering the changes in the scientific research productivity and in the funding structure of the universities that changed their profile of research activity and other characteristics, the existence of distinctive relationships between funding and research output is explored. Chapter 5 also considers in some detail the specific impact of an increased industrial funding on the conduct of university research.

Part III analyses several specific aspects of EU funding of university research. The participation of universities in research networks formed through EU-funded R&D co-operative projects is a central subject in the analysis, which is carried out in the two chapters of Part III at different levels of detail. The first of them, Chapter 6, considers the participation of universities in projects financed under the first three Framework Programmes of the European Commission. After an overview of the main characteristics of the research and technological development (RTD) programmes financed by the European Commission, an interpretative hypothesis is put forward, explaining the participation in EU-funded R&D projects in terms of information signalling and cumulative and self-reinforcement mechanisms. The hypothesis is then tested using the data-set for the total population of universities in the EU countries in 1992, which was introduced in Chapter 4. An econometric model is developed to test for the relevance of university size, scientific research productivity, and other fixed factors on two independent variables: (1) the probability that a university will join an EU-funded R&D co-operative project; (2) the number of times a university will participate in such co-operative projects. The results indicate that the probability of taking part in an EU-funded R&D project depends primarily on the scientific research productivity of the university. The main factors explaining the frequency of university participation include scientific research productivity, size, and differences among countries and scientific fields.

Chapter 7 extends the analysis to the interactions between EU and national university research funding. The chapter is focused on the participation of UK institutions into the two BRITE-EURAM programmes funded in the Second and

Third Framework Programmes. The relationships between EU and national university funding are studied considering both the deliberate action of government in response to EU funding and the unintended consequences related to the existence of two overlapping sources of funds. Sixteen departments accounting for 55 per cent of the participation of 'old' universities in the BRITE-EURAM programmes have been surveyed. The questionnaire has been complemented with interviews with heads of departments. The survey addresses the changes in the funding structure of departments in the period 1990–93 and the situation in 1994. The aim of the survey and interviews is to identify the presence (or absence) of positive or negative dependence between EU and national sources of funds in terms of cumulative and self reinforcement phenomena and substitution effects. Chapter 7 also presents a detailed analysis of both institutional participation and network structure of the BRITE-EURAM programmes.

Finally, in Part IV, Chapter 8 presents the overall conclusions of the book. This last chapter offers a synthesis of the themes discussed throughout the book. It also supplies a discussion of the overall implications of the competitive approach to university behaviour and funding on the medium- to long-term horizon. On the basis of this further avenues of research are put forward.

NOTES

1. See, among others, Becker (1962a, 1975) and Schultz (1960). For a recent critical analysis see Griliches (1996).
2. The breadth of Machlup's approach can be appreciated when one reads the definition of knowing and knowledge he has given in the preface of *Knowledge: Its Creation, Distribution, and Economic Significance*: 'my concept of knowing and knowledge are unusually wide. I do not confine myself to scientific or technological or verified or practical or intellectual knowledge. Anything that people think they know I include in the universe of knowledge' (1982, p. xiii).
3. See, among others, Elliason et al. (1990), von Hippel (1988) and Lundvall (1992). For a recent analysis of the so-called knowledge-based economy see Foray and Lundvall (1996).
4. For the original exposition of this argument see Kuznets (1966).
5. Transmitted is used with a broad connotation meaning both the transfer and distribution of knowledge inside and outside the 'site' of production.
6. There does not exist a preordained sequence in the percolation. The process can be depicted as an interchange of knowledge among the various sites and not as a one way transmission.
7. There exists a large body of literature dealing with the analysis of the diffusion of knowledge across different institutions. See, among others, Arora and Gambardella (1990), Cohen and Levinthal (1989), von Hippel (1988), Jaffe (1989), Mansfield (1991, 1995), Nelson and Rosenberg (1994), Pavitt (1993) and Rosenberg (1994).
8. For an overview of the main themes of the economics of innovation and technological change see Dosi *et al.* (1988) and Freeman and Soete (1997).
9. See Blaug (1970) for an introduction to the economics of education and a review of the literature.
10. For a critical presentation of the main thematic of the economics of science see the two recent survey articles of Stephan (1996) and Diamond (1996), and the survey on the new economics of science by David, Foray and Steinmueller (1998). For examples of current research see the special issue of the *Revue d'Economie Industrielle* edited by Callon and Foray (1997).
11. For the conceptualisation of the 'national systems of innovation' see Freeman (1987), Lundvall (1992), Nelson (1993) and Edquist (1997).

12. For examples of recent studies see Adams and Griliches (1996), Baldwin (1996), Cave, Dodsworth and Thompson (1992), Garvin (1980), Geuna (1997, 1998a), Hare and Wyatt (1988, 1992), Hoenack and Collins (1990), James (1986, 1990), Johnes (1988, 1992, 1997), Mansfield and Lee (1996), and Massy (1996).
13. For the analysis of the expansion and diversification of the higher education system of the EU countries see Section 3.3.
14. For the analysis of the financial sources of higher education expenditures on research and development in the EU countries in the 1980s and 1990s see Section 4.1.
15. It is not uncommon that training and retraining of the workforce is realised in collaboration with universities. Increasingly, universities are supplying highly specialised teaching services focused on industrial needs.
16. A large body of literature has been devoted to the analysis of university–industry co-operations. For the analysis of the different types of linkages see, among others, Blume (1987), Malerba *et al.* (1991) and OECD (1990a, 1984). For a recent survey including the analysis of the use of public research by industry at the European level, see Arundel (1995). For an analysis focused on the US context see, among others, Etzkowitz (1997), Geiger van de Paal and Soete (1993), Mansfield and Lee (1996) and Nelson and Rosenberg (1994).
17. See Blume (1990) for an analysis of the characteristics of what he defines transfer sciences.
18. For a recent analysis of public funding of university basic research see Wood (1995).
19. For a clear analysis of governmental expectations from scientific research generated by the successful use of scientific discoveries made during the war see Geiger (1993, Chapter 1 and Chapter 2). For an early formulation of the rationale used to justify the public support of science see Bush (1945).
20. As education is characterised by positive externalities a similar reasoning is also applicable.
21. See Ziman (1994) for the analysis of science in a 'steady state'. See Section 4.1 for the analysis of values and intensities of HERD in the EU countries in the 1980s and 1990s. Among the industrialised countries Japan is the only one that has committed itself to increase in a substantial way the relative level of public funding for university-based scientific research.
22. A series of administrative measures has had to be created to enable the evaluation of performance.
23. For the description of the changes in the Dutch higher education system see Maassen, Goedegebuure and Westerheijden (1993) and Van Vught (1991, 1997). Van Vught (1997), for instance, suggests that the new government strategy towards higher education in The Netherlands is the outcome of both government planing and market-coordination.
24. See Chapter 6 and Chapter 7 for the analysis of university participation in EU Framework Programmes.
25. For examples of works analysing the crisis of the postwar rationale for public support of science see Dill (1997), Guston and Keniston (1994), Shapley and Roy (1985), Slaughter and Rhoades (1996), Sommer (1995), Vavakova (1998) Ziman (1994). The debate transcends the academic circle, as illustrated by the recent survey in *The Economist* (1997).
26. For a recent analysis of the intended and unintended consequences of the new market steering approach for the Australian higher education see Meek and Wood (1997).
27. For the original definition of the Matthew effect in the sociology of science see Merton (1968), where he referred to the following passage of the gospel according to St. Matthew: 'For unto everyone that hath shall be given, and he shall have abundance; but from him that hath not shall be taken away even that he hath' (Matthew 13: 12). Merton (1968, 1973) and some of his students, see for example Cole and Cole (1973) and Zuckerman (1977), suggested that the organisation and resource allocation structure of science tend to reward successful individuals and groups with access to means that increase their probability of being successful in the future. For an early analysis of the relationships between scientific productivity and cumulative effect see de Solla Price (1963, 1976). For an economic analysis of the Matthew effect and its implications for resource allocation see Dasgupta and David (1987, 1994), David (1994) and Arora and Gambardella (1997). For the implications of the Matthew effect on the university status see Trow (1984).
28. Appendix 1: Research Performance Indicators provides a detailed analysis of the drawbacks characterising research output indicators.

PART I

A Theoretical and Historical Approach

2.   The economics of university research behaviour

The analysis of university behaviour has been mainly the concern of scholars in the field of social studies of science. Economic approaches to explain university behaviour have been developed only recently. From the early 1960s onwards, on the basis of human capital theories, the economics literature focused on specific features and contributions of higher education. Nonetheless, this research endeavour was mainly concerned with the analysis of student demand, with the study of the rate of return to and redistributive effects of higher education, and with cost and economies of scale in higher education.[1] University behaviour and its determinants were only marginally considered.[2] From the 1980s onwards an increasing number of economists have focused their research efforts on the understanding of university behaviour and on the process of knowledge production in the university.[3]

Universities are socioeconomic organisations whose economic behaviour is influenced by external opportunities and constraints. Like other non-profit organisations, they have a multiplicity of objectives depending on the tasks they accomplish, the organisation they have, and their status as public or private institutions.[4] The definition of the overall objectives of universities is an arduous task. Also, reducing the complexity of the university to a stylised model involves considering at least three main groups of actors shaping the definition of the objectives. They are: the government, which finances a large part of the university budget; the academic staff, who produce the various outputs of the institution; and the administrative personnel who, together with the academic staff, manage the university. The relationships among these three main actors are characterised by principal–agent type of situations which shape the definition of university objectives. Thus, the overall objectives of universities are defined by the interactions between the social goals determined by government, the aims of university academic staff and the aims of university administrative personnel. Moreover some objectives are socially but not economically relevant, nonetheless they are important in driving university behaviour. Therefore, a 'closed' definition of the multiple, and sometimes conflicting, objectives of the university in a general objective function is inappropriate.

This chapter develops an economic approach to university behaviour paying particular attention to university research. Here the focus is mainly on the university as a producer of knowledge; educational aspects are only considered in relation to research. Even in this more limited domain, university behaviour is the result of the interaction between the multiple, and sometimes conflicting, objectives of the institution and external constraints and opportunities imposed by the regulatory framework and market conditions. The behaviour of European universities is studied by examining their response to changes in their environment. In particular, the implications for university research behaviour of the new rationale for resource allocation based on an *ex-post* evaluation of university research performance via market forces or simulated market actions are analysed.

The chapter is divided into three sections. The first, after a brief review of the utility-maximising approach to university behaviour, sets out the framework employed in the book to analyse university research behaviour (Section 2.1). In Section 2.2 the framework is further developed considering the unintended consequences of the competitive approach to university research behaviour and funding. Finally, Section 2.3 explains how the proposed approach to the analysis of university behaviour is employed in the subsequent parts of the book.

2.1   MODELLING APPROACHES TO UNIVERSITY BEHAVIOUR

Universities are social and economic organisations. They are social institutions as regards the norms, incentives and organisational structure on which their behaviour is based.[5] They are economic organisations in so far as they are organisations that transform a set of inputs into outputs with value added depending on costs and revenues. Depending on the different importance given to the social and economic aspects of the organisation, university behaviour has been analysed from three broad perspectives. First, models of university behaviour focusing on the organisational features of the institution[6] have been developed using a sociological approach. Second, historical accounts of the social evolution of the university have been carried out on the basis of an institutional perspective. They have studied how the structure and governance of universities have changed in response to modifications in their external environment.[7] Finally, works with an economic perspective have modelled university behaviour as the result of purposive actions shaped by the competitive environment. The utility maximising approach has been used to analyse the economic features of universities and the behavioural implications of different cost and revenue structures.[8]

The analysis conducted here focuses on university economic behaviour. After discussing the main limitations of the utility-maximising approach to university behaviour, an alternative approach that relies also on the institutional perspective will be presented.

2.1.1   The Utility-Maximising Approach

Like other economic organisations, universities are influenced by opportunities and constraints. However, unlike business institutions they do not have stockholders claiming for the surplus generated by the organisation. Universities do not distribute a monetary residual, like other non-profit organisations they do not follow a profit-maximising rule, but tend to spend all revenues within the organisation.[9] On the basis of the non-profit behaviour several recent contributions to the literature have employed the framework of utility maximisation to explain different aspects of university behaviour. For example, James (1990), building on her previous works,[10] models the university as a non-profit organisation maximising an objective function for the entire institution. She assumes that faculty and administrators have an 'identical team-objective function (which can therefore be termed the institution's objective) and, moreover, that everyone is affected in similar ways by its arguments'. Hence, the university maximises an objective function subject to the break-even constraint that all the resources generated are used in the production of teaching and research. She considers prestige and faculty-worker satisfaction as the overall objectives of the university. These can be expressed in terms of intermediate objectives. She assumes that research, graduate training, undergraduate training, student quality and teaching load enter into the university's objective function. The objective function depends positively on research, the presence of graduate students and student quality because these increase the prestige of the university. Similarly, high student quality and small classes (especially graduate classes) increase the satisfaction of faculty. Finally, the revenues of the university depend on the number of students (especially undergraduate) accepted.

A utility-maximising approach to university behaviour, such as the one proposed by James, rests on three main assumptions. First, the multiple, and sometimes conflicting, objectives of the university are reduced to an overall objective function. Faculty and administrators have an identical team-objective function and are affected in similar ways by all outputs. Moreover, it is assumed that there are no conflicts between government goals and university aims, so that the latter are perfectly consistent with the former. Second, it is assumed that the university is facing a competitive market for education and research. Third, to develop a marginal analysis it is assumed that the system under study is in long-run equilibrium.

These assumptions are questionable, even for the purposes of approximating institutional behaviour. Assuming that faculty and administrators have a common objective function and that this objective function is consistent with the social goals imposed upon the university is an oversimplification for the following reasons.

First, the growth of universities in the postwar period brought a process of bureaucratisation of the organisation.[11] Contemporary universities are complex organisations run by administrators with participation from faculty. The increased diversification of the services provided by universities, such as the transfer of technology and patenting of innovations, has further augmented the relevance of the management staff. In this context assuming that the prestige enjoyed by the organisation, as is usually done, is its overall aim does not recognise that faculty members and administrators have different and conflicting preferences and goals. For example, while the former are affected by academic reputation, the latter are influenced by the growth of the organisation and thus they have a preference for income-generating activities.

Second, different and conflicting objectives also characterise faculty members. Due to the zero-sum nature of the allocation process across departments or centres, and due to the existence of negative externalities and free-rider situations – that is, the action of a department raises the cost associated to another department – the objectives of university units can be conflicting (James, 1990; Massy, 1996). With the increased commercialisation of university research the existence of different priorities among faculty members is becoming more evident at two different levels. On the one hand, a divide is forming between researchers in more utilitarian disciplines and scholars of the less marketable disciplines, such as the humanities. Faculty members are affected by different incentive structures and consequently they are forming different preference profiles. On the other hand, a new academic figure is developing, that of faculty members mainly involved in research contracts. These research scientists are primarily involved in sponsored research and they are not responsible for graduate and undergraduate education. Hence, the goals of research scientists may be different from those of other members of the faculty (Cohen and Florida, 1996).[12]

Third, as will be discussed in Section 2.2.1, new purposes for higher education have been defined in the last ten years – for example to produce knowledge that serves the need of the economy. Universities are reacting to these changes by adapting their behaviour to the new needs. Nonetheless, due to the presence of routines and expectations in the behaviour of the university, the adaptation requires a significant amount of time and the outcomes are not secure. Hence, particularly in a period of evolution in the role that the university is supposed to accomplish in society, the objectives of the organisation may diverge from those of the funding agency (the government).

The second assumption on which the utility-maximising approach to university behaviour rests is the existence of a competitive market for education and research. While this assumption may be an approximation for the university system of the US, it does not hold in the European context. Although recent years have witnessed the first steps in the development of quasi-markets[13] for education and research, the university systems of the EU countries tend to be characterised, on the one hand, by low levels of market competition for education, and, on the other hand, by increasing market competition for university research.[14]

Finally, the ongoing changes in the structure and organisation of European universities are sufficiently relevant and the adjustment times are sufficiently lengthy – for example time required to change the composition of tenure faculty – that it is highly unlikely that the system under study is in equilibrium. Hence, marginal analysis is not the most appropriate tool for examining the changes.

The intrinsic shortcomings of the utility-maximising approach to university behaviour, especially when applied to a context different from that of the US, affect the use of its predictions. On the one hand, some insights, such as the presence of cross-subsidisation among revenue-generating activities and utility-generating activities, allow a better understanding of university behaviour. On the other hand, however, the identification of a mix of inputs and outputs maximising a single objective function for the organisation is not useful for analysing the behaviour of institutions that do not have a clearly defined objective function and are also going through a period of profound change. Some of the shortcomings of the utility-maximising approach, such as the presence of heterogeneous actors in the organisation, could be handled by more complex models (for example principal–agent types of model). However, due to the lack of knowledge on university behaviour and objectives, this type of modelling would fail to express the complexity of the organisation.

2.1.2 An Industrial Economics Perspective on University Behaviour

The focus here is on European universities.[15] The large majority of universities in the EU countries are public organisations, financed in large part by the state, with approximately pre-defined pay scales, and student costs almost completely covered by the state. These characteristics differentiate them from many universities in the US, particularly the private institutions.[16] The behaviour of European universities can be better understood as the result of the interaction between the multiple, and sometimes conflicting, objectives of the various professional groupings within the organisation (the academic and business branches of the administration, the faculty members of various departments and research centres) and the changing constraints and opportunities externally imposed by the regulatory framework and market conditions. Shifting alignments of constituencies within, as well as outside, the university shape both the process and the outcomes of university decision making.

Moreover, there is no well-defined 'bottom line' in the operation of the non-profit university, whether it is public or privately funded; university outputs are only valued subsequent to their production and, even then, in a highly approximate way by the array of communities of interest – that is, the state apparatus, the tax-paying public, the academic professions, the graduates, industrial sponsors and clients, and so on. Hence, university decision-takers in the pursuit of manageable processes and viable outcomes are especially likely to adopt simple decision making procedures and operating rules. These procedures and rules are the result of interactions among the incentive structures of the various actors taking part in university production and university organisation. In turn, the incentive structures are affected by the external environment and by the internal resource allocation mechanisms.

Given this general description of university behaviour, two research paths can be followed. Neither proceeds on the assumption that the organisation is usefully characterised as a consistent utility-maximising 'agent'. The first examines the response of universities to changes in the regulatory framework and market conditions, focusing on the effect of alteration in the relevant incentives and constraints governing their behaviour; the second studies internal resource allocation mechanisms that affect the profile of the institution, recognising that there is structural heterogeneity within the population of institutions of higher education. These two approaches together provide the basis on which to develop an empirically implementable theory of university operation.

At this stage, it is important to clarify whether the subject of analysis is the single institution, or the ensemble of institutions whose behaviour could be characterised by some distributional statistics. In the first case, the theoretical framework to be used would be the one of the representative agent. However, even if the shortcomings of the utility-maximising approach to university behaviour described above were not important, the diverse characteristics and activities pursued by universities and the existence of sub-markets in which universities operate heavily constrain the usefulness of the representative agent approach.[17] In the second case, where the ensemble is explained but not the individual institution, a statistical mechanical approach could be applied to account for the behaviour of a distribution of universities in the same space (described by ranges of variables such as teachers per student, researchers per student, size of faculty, and so on).[18] This framework, focusing on population averages, acknowledges the high level of heterogeneity within the university system. It accounts for the dynamic of the system *via* well-specified details at the micro level such as the existence of a heterogeneous opportunity set or diversified response capabilities. Thus, it seems to be the most suited framework to develop a theory of university operation and, in particular, of its response to environmental changes.

This book does not tackle the task of elaborating a formal model along such lines.[19] Instead, it will draw from an informal exploration of this approach some general insights that can guide empirical inquiry. One practical reason for proceeding in this way resides in the prohibitive data requirements needed to test a full structural model of university behaviour, especially one that considers the distinct actors and internal conflicts through whose resolution university actions emerge. At present, the available statistics on resource allocation and the cost structure of European universities do not allow for the implementation of empirical studies at the level that would be required to test detailed behavioural hypotheses.

2.1.3   Diversified Funding Sources and University Research Structure

How can the response of universities to modifications in their environment be analysed? A study of the relationship between inputs and outputs can offer insights about the response of the university to changes in the regulatory framework and market conditions. It must be acknowledged, however, that defining and measuring university inputs and outputs is not a trivial task. First of all, the definition of an input or an output is controversial. For example, in some cases research incomes are included among the inputs while in other cases they are part of the outputs.[20] Also, assuming that it is possible to identify university inputs and outputs, the measurement has to take into account both their quantity and their quality. The value measurement is especially difficult for the outputs because, due to their non-market characteristics, prices cannot be used as a measure of the value that the consumer associates with the purchased good.

To reduce the degree of complexity this study focuses only on university research production. The main limitation of this partial analysis is that it will make it difficult to assess the indirect effects of behavioural changes in the production of research. For example, questions such as whether a rise in research quality is a complement to or a substitute for educational quality cannot be evaluated here. Nonetheless, considering only university research production allows one to use available statistics as partial indicators of inputs and outputs. The relationship between inputs and outputs can be expressed in terms of research productivity – that is, the ratio of output to input. Clearly, given the multiplicity of research inputs and outputs, and their qualitative and multidimensional character, research productivity represents only an approximation of the relationship between inputs and outputs.

The sociology of science and more recently scholars from the fields of science and technology studies, bibliometric studies, and the new economics of science have developed theoretical and empirical studies on scientific research productivity.

Starting with the works of Lotka (1926) and de Solla Price (1963), most of these investigations focused on the scientific research productivity of the individual scientist considering the research productivity of the department or research centre only in a few cases.[21] However, there is no overall agreement on which indicator (set of indicators) is best suited for measuring the quantity, impact, quality, and utility of the research.[22] Publication counts, citations analysis and peer review are the three methods that are usually applied to evaluate research performance.[23] Each has its own limitations. For example, publication counts are mainly a measure of the quantity of the research; citations analysis requires a costly and time-consuming methodology that, at the current level of development, is not optimal for the analysis of university research productivity; peer review is based on a subjective and not very systematic judgement of the research output.

Despite the above limitations it is important to assess the response of available measures of research productivity to changes in the university environment. In particular, while most of the literature has examined scientific research productivity at the level of the individual researcher or at the level of the department, here the subject of analysis is the entire institution.[24] New incentives, originating from the changes in the regulatory framework and market conditions, affect the behaviour of the university in general, and its scientific research productivity in particular. The focus at the institutional level endorses the use of less detailed output indicators than those employed at the level of the individual researcher or at the level of the department. However, when considering the institution as a whole, it is possible to have an account of the modification in the inputs that is a direct consequence of the environmental changes. Hence, even using incomplete research output indicators, the scientific research productivity of the university can be expressed in different ways depending on the inputs considered.

Among the various inputs, a crucial role is played by the competitive and non-competitive research funding sources. The changes in the regulatory framework and the consequent increase of competition in the market for university research have given rise to the development of a funding system for university research based on diversified competitive funding sources. On top of the less competitive general government research funds,[25] universities receive an important share of their research funding through competitive sources. A substantial advance in current understanding of university behaviour can be made by considering the impact of diversified funding sources for university research on the research subsystem engaged by this funding. The diversified funding sources can complement or substitute for each other; in both cases they affect the outputs and the incentive structure of the university, thus determining its behaviour. In addition, a detailed analysis of the relationships between diversified funding sources and output indicators allows one to obtain insights that help in understanding the whole university system.

This approach to the analysis of the response of the university to changes in its environment allows one to analyse three main issues. First, the push towards more competitive university research funding may cause, among other possible consequences, an increase in scientific agglomeration and a shorter time horizon for the evaluation of the research output. Both phenomena are characterised by an unclear balance between advantages and disadvantages. Second, the existence of competitive research funding sources may give rise to diverse incentive structures that, due to their conflicting character, may induce distortions in university research behaviour. Third, the existence of important cumulative and self-reinforcement phenomena in the process of scientific production may be exacerbated by the increasingly competitive character of university research funding and by the existence of non-coordinated competitive funding sources. In general, the ongoing changes in the university environment are characterised by important indirect effects and it is highly unlikely that these were ever intended by policy makers. The next section discusses in more detail these issues in relation to the re-examination and modification of the rationale for resource allocation to universities.

2.2 RESOURCE ALLOCATION TO UNIVERSITY RESEARCH

This section will analyse the implications for university behaviour of the changes in the rationale for university research funding. In particular, it will highlight how the existence of diversified competitive funding sources supporting different incentive settings and constraints may have important unintended consequences. The objectives, resource allocation mechanisms, and the implicit assumptions of the new rationale will be analysed. On the basis of this analysis, it will be shown that the potential advantages of the competitive approach may be counterbalanced by long-term disadvantages arising from unintended outcomes of the new rationale.

University income can be subdivided into four main sources: general government grants or general university funds, direct government funds, internal funds and the sale of academic services. By far the most important sources of university funds in Europe are the two government sources. Depending on the country the responsibility for the public funding of universities is attributed to different levels of government. It can be mainly the responsibility of the central government (Austria, Finland, Denmark, France, Italy, Ireland, The Netherlands, UK), mainly of the regional government (Belgium, Germany), or shared between the central and regional government (Spain) (OECD, 1995). Chapter 4 shows the subdivision of sources of financing of higher education expenditures in R&D. For most of the countries considered, government funds are responsible for more than three-quarters of total expenditure. Only Greece, Ireland and the UK have lower shares of about 60 per cent in 1995.

General government funds to universities are funnelled through three different channels: (1) incremental funding, (2) formula funding, and (3) contractual funding.[26] In the first, funds are allocated on the basis of historical expenditures with incremental resources made available for the development of new activities. This funding mechanism has been the dominant one in the expanding university systems until the early 1980s (OECD, 1990b). In formula funding the budget of the institution is determined by some form of assessment of the actual institutional expenditures per student enrolled or expected to be enrolled. These funds are combined with general research funds according to a ratio of government funding for teaching compared to research, for example a 60:40 split. Research funds can also be determined by a formula system that allows the distribution of the funds in a selective way on the basis of the research record. Contractual funding is applied via tender schemes. Public funding agencies issue targets in terms of student numbers or research and the various institutions apply to obtain the funds to carry out the specified tasks. There are different forms of contracting depending on the existence of fixed limits for the availability of funds, and on the level of specification for the activity. In the case of limited funds and tightly specified targets the universities have to compete with each other for the resources.

Although in the various EU countries there exists a high level of diversity in the mix of the different funding systems, the most recent years have seen an increasing reliance upon formula and contractual funding (OECD, 1990b). This move towards an indirect control of university behaviour via financial incentives is the result of the process of re-examination and modification of the rationale for resource allocation to universities.

The new rationale for university research funding can be referred to as the competitive approach to university research behaviour and funding. Two main features characterise a competitive approach to university research funding. First, the university is required to support aims that are intended to enhance national economic development and to strengthen competitiveness. Second, to obtain this result, and to increase the short-term efficiency of the institution, the government makes increasing use of competitive mechanisms for resource allocation, developing a market-oriented approach to university research funding. Each of these two points is discussed below.

2.2.1   The Role of the University in the New Rationale

A new governmental vision of the role of the university characterises the competitive approach to university research funding. Although the various

European nations have some differences in their views, the following can be considered the principal social goals for the university system as defined by governments:[27]

1. To reproduce the existing levels of knowledge.
2. To improve the critical reasoning capabilities and specific skills of individuals:
   (a) as an input into their public and private work activity;
   (b) as an input into the development of a democratic, civilised, inclusive society.
3. To increase the knowledge base:
   (a) pursuing knowledge for its own sake;
   (b) pursuing knowledge and its application for the creation of wealth.
4. To serve specific training and more general research support needs of the knowledge-based economy at the local, regional and national levels.

The first two aims correspond to the traditional role of the university as an institution for the preservation and the transmission, through education, of knowledge, culture and social values. The third social goal, although referring to the traditional role of the university as a site where knowledge is produced through scholarship and research, defines the action of the university in a broader sense. Scholarship and research should be pursued at the university for the production of knowledge for its own sake and for the production of a stock of useful knowledge that might be applied at other sites to produce benefits for society. Moreover, university research should also aim at the direct production of applied knowledge for the creation of wealth. Finally, the fourth social goal attributes a new role to the university. Universities are seen as direct actors in the process of economic development. In this new role, the university has to satisfy the knowledge needs, in terms of teaching and research, for economic development at the local, regional and national levels.[28]

Two streams of thought are at the basis of the new governmental vision of the role of the university. Both of them are highly criticised; however, the analysis of the debate is beyond the scope of this chapter. On the one hand, on the basis of the *laissez-faire* philosophy, and due to the process of globalisation and the resulting increased international competition, a large number of politicians and industrialists began perceiving the contribution of universities to wealth creation and national competitiveness as insufficient. In this view, public funding of university research has to give more concrete and direct returns. Hence, university research would have to reflect more the scientific and technological needs of the society, and universities would have to co-operate with firms, becoming the suppliers of applied knowledge, which can be readily transformed into innovations that increase the competitiveness of national industries.[29]

On the other hand, the increased complexity of scientific research and the development of cross-field research, for example information technologies and molecular biology, underscores the relevance of knowledge production based on cross-disciplinary and cross-institutional collaborations. On the basis of this observation, it has been claimed that the nature of the scientific investigation process is changing from the search for new knowledge in a single discipline to a search process that cuts across disciplines, institutions and methods. In this highly controversial view of a changing process of scientific discovery[30] the university ceases to be the leading player in the process of knowledge creation and becomes only one of the possible sites where knowledge is produced (Gibbons et al., 1994). In this view, the structure of the university is not suited to the new process of scientific discovery and, therefore, without radical structural changes, it cannot claim the current level of public resources.

Before turning to an analysis of the mechanisms for resource allocation used by the competitive approach to university research funding, one more observation on the role of the university is required. Also if one accepts the idea of a changing process of knowledge creation this does not imply that the university no longer plays a crucial role. A process of knowledge production characterised by an increasing number of actors, and by blurred boundaries between them, still needs to have a formal or informal institution where knowledge is certified. If a transfer of knowledge among the various sites has to be achieved there is a need for validating the knowledge that is flowing. In the so-called new nature of scientific investigation, private actors have an important role in the generation of knowledge. If this is the case, there will be an increased propensity to extract private benefit and consequently a higher level of secrecy. In this context, a university characterised by a traditional incentive structure that favours the open disclosure of new knowledge and its verification would stand as the best-suited site for the certification of knowledge produced in other more private environments. This is not a novel role for the university. In the early nineteenth century the renewal of the university was characterised by the reception of the methodologies and social organisation of the scientific research carried out in the eighteenth-century societies and academies.[31] One of the crucial roles played by, for example, the Royal Society and the Académie Royale des Sciences was the one of institutional sites where new knowledge was confronted and verified. The renewed universities also took over this aspect of the social organisation of scientific research.

If social welfare rises with an increase in the production and diffusion of knowledge, there is a need for knowledge certification. In this way, verified knowledge can diffuse more effectively and enter into other processes of production of fundamental and applied knowledge. In the absence of certification the 'quality' of knowledge must be ascertained more directly, which raises transaction costs and moral hazard risks.[32] Thus, in a more diffuse knowledge production process the university, with its traditional incentive structure that favours the open disclosure of new knowledge and its verification, plays a crucial role as a site for knowledge certification.

2.2.2 The Competitive Approach

The competitive approach to university research funding is based on using financial incentives to control university research behaviour indirectly. Quasi-market incentive schemes are applied to succeed in drawing university research behaviour toward the accomplishment of new objectives and to increase the short-term efficiency of the institution. Policies are implemented to increase the concentration and selectivity of research funds and, more generally, to improve accountability and reduce costs. Although direct competition is not permitted, the government attempts to simulate market actions by adjusting its demand for university services in response to absolute or relative institutional performance[33] (Massy, 1996).

The clearest example of the competitive approach is the market-steering model developed in the UK. To implement this model two paths are followed. First, due to budget constraints and competition for funds from other public funded sectors, the overall contribution from the government to the total research incomes of universities is reduced or maintained unchanged in nominal terms.[34] This strategy is pursued not only to stimulate cost-minimising behaviour in the universities, but also to create incentives for the development of research activities that could find funding support from nongovernmental sources such as firms and foundations. Second, a reallocation between government sources of funds is implemented with a decrease of general university funds and an increase of direct government funds. A larger allocation of resources through specific grants allows the government to develop policies aimed at a more purpose-directed allocation of research effort, and at the creation of quasi-market incentive structures that permit indirect control of university research behaviour.

Other European countries, such as The Netherlands, have started to implement similar approaches to university funding. Van Vught (1997), for instance, suggests that the new government strategy towards higher education in The Netherlands is the outcome of both government planning and market-coordination. In other countries, such as France and Italy, government proposals for changing the organisation of the higher education system are currently under discussion.[35]

National policies aimed at concentration and selectivity of research funds may be further reinforced by the research actions of the EU. The four Framework Programmes of the Commission of the European Communities for the support of R&D co-operative projects have been characterised by a highly competitive approach to research funding. Universities have increasingly taken part in these

R&D co-operative projects becoming, in the Fourth Framework Programme, the largest single type of institution both in terms of the number of times they participated in an EU-funded R&D co-operative project and in terms of funds received.[36]

Bearing in mind national differences, the core of the new resource allocation system resides in an *ex-post* evaluation of university research performance via market forces or simulated market actions. First, most of the non-government sources of university research funding, especially industrial funding, are characterised by a high level of competition and by a continuous short-term evaluation of research outputs. Second, direct government funds are allocated through competitive mechanisms, such as tenders with specific targets and limited budgets, on the basis of the past performance of the applicants, who are subject to repeated evaluation of the outputs. Finally, an increasing share of general university funds is granted through simulated market actions such as the case of limited research funding allocated to the universities in proportion to their previous research performance.

The competitive approach to university research funding stands on the following main assumptions. First, it is possible to evaluate the quality of the research output correctly. Second, it is possible to identify the most promising research avenues. Third, cost reductions can be obtained without lowering the quality of the output. Fourth, due to the existence of scale and scope economies, the concentration of scientific capabilities increases the research output of the system. Fifth, the administrative costs for both government and universities linked to the implementation of a competitive system are low compared to the cost savings.

2.2.3   The Unintended Consequences of the New Rationale

It is not the aim of this section to discuss each one of the five assumptions on which the competitive rationale for university funding stands. Instead, this section explores whether or not the negative unintended consequences of the new rationale might prevail in the long run over its predicted advantages. More specifically, the analysis focuses on the long-term implications of competitive public funding and of increased industrial funding of university research. The following four issues are examined: (1) increased concentration of resources, (2) disproportionate incentives for a short-term foreseeable research endeavour, (3) changing incentive structures, and (4) exacerbation of the impact of cumulative and self reinforcement phenomena and, in particular, of the Matthew effect.

Increased concentration of resources
One of the aims of the allocation of government funds via the simulation of market conditions is to obtain a higher concentration and selectivity of research

funds which permits the exploitation of economies of scale and scope present in the research production process, and to orient the research towards the needs of society.

First of all, it is important to notice that the existence of scale and scope economies in university production is an assumption that lacks strong empirical evidence. Indeed, the literature concerned with scale and scope economies in university production offers a blurred picture. There are two main approaches. The first one evaluates economies of scale and scope for the joint production of teaching and research using econometric cost function estimates (Cohn, Rhine and Santos, 1989; Johnes, 1997).[37] The second studies the relationship between size and research performance applying statistical-descriptive tools (Martin et al., 1993; Johnston, 1994). Neither of the approaches provides unequivocal answers. While there is some general consensus on the existence of scale economies in teaching and administration, when research production is included the empirical evidence in favour of scale and scope economies is more mixed, with cases in which department size and scientific research productivity have no or weak negative correlation.

Furthermore, uncoordinated multiple sources of research funding could result in negative unintended consequences that could offset the potential positive effects of the market-oriented approach. This could occur both at the national level, due to the existence of diversified competitive national sources of funds, and at the European level, due to the existence of national and EU funding sources. For example, due to its competitive character, industrial funding will tend to be mainly funnelled towards the top universities, which, via simulated market actions, also receive the largest share of public funding.[38] In the UK, 33 per cent of the total university research income from industry was accounted for by only 6 per cent of the institutions (seven institutions) in 1996–97 (HEFCE, 1998). On the other hand, multiple sources of funding may help to offset the danger of scientific sclerosis in established ideas that can occur when only one agency in a monopsony position allocates funds relying on an established group of peer reviewers.

An overlapping of industrial funding with increasingly selective public funding may create an increased concentration of resources. The following are the unintended consequences that can result from this situation. First, the trends towards increasingly selective funding will reduce the availability of non-competitive public funds that is, funds allocated in a proportional way. The allocation of resources on a basis other than merit enables human resources and research organisations to develop and express their potential in ways of their own choice, and hence allows the public agency to collect information about research potential. Distributive allocation of funds offers the possibility to researchers and research organisations of unknown 'quality' to perform research. Their success or not in producing relevant results from the research funded in this way is a source of information on their capabilities that can be used in future allocation of funds by the funding agency. The scientific capabilities of a researcher (or research organisation) tend to be uncertain in the early phase of her/his career. Acknowledging this situation, the Social Science and Humanities Research Council of Canada (SSHRCC) weights the proposal more heavily than the CV in the evaluation of research applications coming from young scientists (the reverse of the normal evaluation). Competitive allocation mechanisms that concentrate the funds in a few highly productive institutions produce less observable experience with research performance by other institutions and individuals. Thus, the selective funding approach, although efficient in the short term (the most productive universities/research organisations are the ones that receive the largest share of money), could have negative long-run effects for society by preventing new scientists who have bright ideas but work in low graded institutions from developing their potential. Indeed, only a reduced fraction of human resources and research institutions are able to express their quality, leaving unknown research potentials unexploited.

Second, the local positive externalities and scale and scope economies connected with the geographical concentration of scientific capabilities and the localisation of a large part of research in a few universities could be offset by the negative externalities imposed on the universities that are marginalised by this process. For example, the currency of knowledge that researchers have at an institution with scarce or no resources to carry on fundamental research will tend to become stale or obsolete, preventing them from teaching and carrying out targeted research in an effective way for social needs (Dresch, 1995).

Third, quasi-market allocation mechanisms for public funding and an increased industry funding of university research pushes universities to price their services at marginal cost. Consequently, average costs are not covered for universities with excess capacity and, more in general, the costs of the institutional and research infrastructure, such as the library, are only partially covered depending on the share of overheads. Moreover, universities are not prepared to account for the real opportunity costs of the involvement of their scarce resources in contract research for industry. When they are fixing the price for a contract Professors calculate marginal cost without, or only marginally, including opportunity costs. Industrial contracts enlarge the dimension of their laboratory with an increase in the number of junior staff, but they rarely cover the costs for the involvement of senior faculty, or the increasing organisational costs and the use of the infrastructure that is only marginally covered by the overheads. The adaptation to the new funding system requires a process of learning that may take several years.[39] Hence, contract research for industry may result in a form of public subsidy for particular industries for the type of research that firms would otherwise have had to finance on a full-cost basis. This situation is particularly important for universities with very low research receipts from the government that are pushed to rely more heavily on industry funding. Being in a weak financial situation, they find themselves in an asymmetric bargaining relationship with industry. This in turn could result in a large amount of these universities' research resources being tied up in routine contract work for industry. Researchers, technicians and the scientific instrumentation of these universities are thus employed to develop a type of research that mainly gives private returns to firms.

Disproportionate incentives for short-term research
The push towards tighter interactions between university and industry, with the aim of possibly fostering state economic development, and the use of *ex-post* evaluations of university research performance via market forces or simulated market actions, could create disproportionate incentives for a short-term foreseeable research endeavour. In fact, university research is impelled to respond to the short-term concerns of industry and, in addition, the *ex-post* evaluation approach tends to focus on the recent quantifiable outputs of the institution, without taking into account work in progress or plans for long-term projects. As a result, the following unintended consequences may arise. First, projects with a long-term horizon will be less likely to be performed. The competitive approach creates disincentives for researchers to be engaged in this type of project as they do not present quantifiable outputs at the time of evaluation. Hence, with this incentive structure, application-oriented short-term research will substitute for long-term research in the university research activity portfolio, dismantling what was the core activity and the source of comparative advantage for the university. Second, given the resource allocation mechanisms, industrial funding and public funding based on *ex-post* evaluation of university research performance will not provide the research funds for screening new scientific paradigms and developing new risky research programmes. The lack of incentives for path breaking, and consequently more risky, research decreases the probability of scientific innovation,[40] potentially reducing the new knowledge base from which new technological innovations can emerge.

Conflicting incentive structures
Different competitive research-funding sources create diverse incentive structures. University researchers and, in general, university institutions face different incentives and constraints depending on the source of funds upon which they rely. However, the research activities carried out at the university cannot be easily allocated to the sources of funds, hence university behaviour is the result of interactions among the various incentives and constraints. In the case in which the incentive structures lead to conflicting behaviours, for example relative to the secrecy and applicability of research results, tensions would characterise the

organisation of university research (David, Mowery and Steinmueller, 1994). Moreover, in certain cases the impact of the various incentive structures is proportional to the support provided, while in others it can be more or less important. In the former instance, university behaviour is driven towards accomplishing diverse aims depending on the weight of the various incomes in the total research budget of the university. In the latter instance, the incentives associated with a subsidiary source of funds may dominate university research behaviour, distorting the role played by the university and thus reducing the social benefits of the allocation of public resources to university research. This case is more probable when general government research funds are fully utilised. In fact, new research activities should be supported by other competitive funds, hence the incentive structure stimulated by these funds may have an impact on university research behaviour disproportionate to the amount of resources supplied (OECD, 1990b).

Cumulative and self reinforcement phenomena
The increased competitive character of university research funding, and the existence of diversified non-coordinated competitive funding sources, may exacerbate the importance of the cumulative and self-reinforcement phenomena present in the process of scientific production. Since the seminal work of Merton on the Matthew effect (1968), it has been recognised that the organisation and resource allocation structure of science tends to reward successful individuals and groups with access to means that increase their probability of being successful in the future. The new economics of science[41] has elaborated this concept in terms of path-dependence and self-reinforcing mechanisms.[42] The reputation of a researcher (group) derives in some measure from prior success, but this may be due to good luck and not to 'real' innate abilities. On the one hand, a lucky researcher may have an early success that feeds the subsequent performances putting her on a high productivity path. On the other hand, an unlucky but possibly talented researcher may have problems in seeing her work published, leading to decreasing means for further research and to reducing self-motivation that will drive her onto a low productivity path. The same mechanisms are applicable to groups as well as individuals.

In this situation, competitive allocation mechanisms based on *ex-post* accountability not only give a biased evaluation of real talent but also, due to their mechanistic accounting, tend to reinforce the virtuous and vicious circles described above. Moreover, the existence of diversified non-coordinated sources may further reinforce the cumulative process.[43] In fact, on the one hand, the concentration of public funding in a few institutions because of competitive resource allocation augments the probability of attracting other competitive research funds for these universities and, on the other hand, decreases the attractiveness of the less supported institutions to external providers of funds.

As pointed out above, this latter type of university will be pushed to carry out routine contract research to attract money from industry. This in turn may lead to a reduction in the quality of scientific output, which will further reduce the probability of attracting research funds targeted to high-quality research.

2.3   EMPIRICAL IMPLICATIONS

The available empirical economic studies of the university research subsystem have been mainly based on the utility-maximising model. Consequently their analysis focuses principally on the identification of the most efficient combination of inputs and outputs. The approach to university research behaviour developed in this chapter puts particular emphasis on the incentives and constraints created by the changing funding rationale. To test the behavioural hypotheses presented above requires time-series data at the institutional level that are not available at the cross-country level in Europe. Nonetheless some of the implications of these hypotheses can be tested by using cross-section data at a specific moment of time, while others can be verified for a single country or a particular type of competitive funding. The empirical studies presented in Part II and Part III are, thus, an attempt to evaluate the presence and importance of the unintended consequences resulting from the competitive approach to university behaviour and funding.

As pointed out above, the various EU countries implement different approaches to public university research funding, forming a continuum of possible funding configurations. On the one hand, countries such as the UK tend to rely more heavily on mission-oriented policies (selective policies), on the other hand, in countries such as Italy, proportional allocation policies (distributive policies) are still dominant. Nonetheless, the most recent years have witnessed an increasing orientation of public policies towards the competitive approach in all the EU countries. The UK system based on an *ex-post* institutional accounting for performance quality is the university system with the most evident market orientation, and hence may serve as a model for emulation by other European systems.

Throughout the book, the UK university funding system will be used as the reference case for two main reasons. First, the insights from the British experience can allow an evaluation of the intended and unintended consequences of the new competitive approach to university behaviour and funding that, although preliminary and limited, can offer valuable lessons for the shaping of the funding system in all the EU countries. Second, the availability of panel data on the funding structure and on the scientific research output for the 'old' British universities allows one to test specific behavioural hypotheses.[44]

One of the most important mechanisms on which the competitive research funding approach is based is the use of contractual funding via tender schemes. European universities compete for research contracts at the national and EU level. In the course of the four Framework Programmes of the Commission of the European Communities for the support of R&D co-operative projects, universities have increasingly taken part in these projects. In a context of reducing public funding of university research the existence of a new competitive source of funds may have important effects on the research activities of European universities. The analysis of university participation in co-operative R&D projects funded by the European Commission, and the interactions of this funding source with national sources, allows one to study how universities respond to diversified non-co-ordinated competitive sources of research funds.[45]

NOTES

1. For an introduction to the economics of education see Blaug (1970). For an analysis of educational benefits see, among others, Carnoy and Marenbach (1975) and Hansen (1970). For a survey of the studies on costs and economies of scale in higher education see Brinkman and Leslie (1986) and Hoenack (1990). For recent studies of economies of scale and scope in higher education institutions see, for example, Cohn, Rhine and Santos (1989) and Glass, McKillop and Hyndman (1995).

2. For examples of early works considering university behaviour and university production see Culyer (1970), James (1978) and Nerlove (1972).

3. See, among others, Adams and Griliches (1996), Baldwin (1996), Cave, Dodsworth and Thompson (1992), Garvin (1980), Geuna (1997, 1998a), Hare and Wyatt (1988, 1992), Hoenack and Collins (1990), James (1986, 1990), Johnes (1988, 1992, 1997), Mansfield and Lee (1996), and Massy (1996).

4. European universities are in the large majority public institutions; hence the framework developed here will devote particular attention to the behaviour of public universities.

5. See Chapter 3 for an historical account of European universities that highlights the evolution of norms, incentives and organisational structure characterising these institutions along their history.

6. Four main organisational models have been proposed: (1) the collegial model; (2) the bureaucratic model; (3) the political model; and (4) the organised anarchy model (Garvin, 1980).

7. See, among others, Geiger (1985, 1993), Kerr (1995) and Wittrock (1993).

8. For an early utility-maximising view of the university see Culyer (1970). For a prestige-maximising view of the university see Garvin (1980); for a multi-product (teaching and research) utility-maximising approach see Hare and Wyatt (1992) and James (1990); for a utility-maximising approach focused on university administrators see Kesselring and Strein (1986).

9. Given the non-profit character of the university the net revenue of the institution cannot be claimed either by the stockholders or by its workers. However, like employees in a managerial firm (see, for example, Williamson, 1967) academic staff may extract rents through discretionary expenditure or shirking (Cave, Dodsworth and Thompson, 1992).

10. See James (1978, 1986) for a theoretical and empirical analysis, mainly focused on instruction, of the non-profit behaviour of public and private universities and colleges. See also James and Neuberger (1981) for a view of the university department as a non-profit labour co-operative. For a review of the economics of non-profit organisations see James and Rose-Ackerman (1986).

11. See Gornitzka, Kyvik and Larsen (1998) for the analysis of the bureaucratisation of universities. For the administrative, organisational and structural changes following the expansion of the

university sector in the European countries in the 1960s and 1970s see, for example, Daalder and Shils (1982). See also Gellert (1993) and Neave and Van Vught (1991) for an analysis of the most recent changes.

12. Carnegie Mellon University has recognised this new academic figure, creating a new career track for them (Cohen and Florida, 1996).

13. For an analysis of the introduction of quasi-markets into the delivery of public services see, for example, Broadbent and Laughlin (1997), Glennerster (1991), Hughes, Griffiths and McHale (1997) and Le Grand (1991).

14. The British university system is the one with the clearest market orientation.

15. To develop an economic approach to university behaviour requires the implicit hypothesis that a well-defined institution called university exists. This issue is dealt with in the next chapter which develops a systematic basis for the 'European University' as a unit of analysis in this book.

16. Of the 160 institutions recognised in Palombara (1991) as universities in the USA, one third are private.

17. For a critical analysis of the representative agent model see Kirman (1992).

18. For an introduction to statistical mechanics approaches applied at the analysis of the growth of firms see Steindl (1965). For a critical survey of the literature see Sutton (1997).

19. A promising approach would appear to be the one that sought to integrate the following two streams of literature. On the one hand, behavioural theories of the firm can be fruitfully applied to model the individual organisational behaviour as boundedly rational (satisficing), in which systematic responses to viability or threatening changes in external constraints are predictable (Cyert and March, 1963; Simon, 1955). On the other hand, the statistical approach to the theory of market demand provides a useful framework to model the aggregate behaviour. This approach makes minimal assumptions, of the sort that require the agent/organisation to operate within a reasonably tight inter-temporal budget constraint; assumes that there is a positive probability that at least one agent/organisation will visit every point in the opportunity set; and replaces the von Neuman–Morgenstern axioms with stochastic dominance axioms on the way the changes in the total resource availability distribution will be related to changes in the distribution of expenditures upon each of the activities in the consumption basket, in the application presently contemplated, the agents'/organisations' 'activity-basket' (Becker, 1962b; Hildenbrand, 1989; Sanderson, 1974).

20. See, among others, Hare and Wyatt (1988) for a criticism of to the use of research incomes as a research performance indicator.

21. Particularly during the 1980s and early 1990s, a considerable number of studies on the research output of university departments have been produced in the field of bibliometric studies. Among others see Carpenter et al. (1988), Moed et al. (1985) and Nederhof and Noyons (1992).

22. For an early work on the difficulties involved in constructing research performance indicators see Martin and Irvine (1983). For references and further discussion see, for example, Cave et al. (1997, Chapter 4), and van Raan (1988).

23. See Appendix 1: Resource Performance Indicators in Chapter 4 for the analysis of the difficulties and drawbacks in using these indicators.

24. A number of studies analysing university research productivity have recently appeared; see, among others, Johnes (1988, 1992) and Johnes and Johnes (1993). Of particular interest is the work of Adams and Griliches (1996). Using data on 40 American universities for the period 1981–89, they study the relationship between research output and university R&D expenditures.

25. Especially in the UK, but also in other European countries, the general research grant from the government is also awarded via competitive criteria. The Research Assessment Exercise allows the distribution of government funds depending on the past performance of the institution. See Chapter 5 for the analysis of the funding structure of the British university system.

26. In some countries, such as the UK, the government pays the large majority of tuition fees to universities. Currently, a debate on the opportunity for increasing the contribution of students and their families is taking place in all the EU countries. To the extent that this book emphasises mainly university research, this issue will not be dealt with here. For a clarifying analysis of the introduction of income-contingent charges for higher education in Australia

see Chapman (1997). For the current debate in the UK see National Committee of Inquiry into Higher Education (1997).

27. See, among others, Commission Jacques Attali (1998) and National Committee of Inquiry into Higher Education (1997).

28. For example, the report of the French 'Commission Attali' puts particular emphasis on the fact that the university has to act directly as a producer of innovation: 'les universités devront contribuer à la création d'entreprises et à leur développement. Pour cela, elles devront valoriser leur recherche, prendre des brevets, organiser des entreprises en leur sein' (p. 23).

29. For a criticism of this view on the contribution of university to the welfare of society see Vavakova (1998).

30. This view of a changing process of scientific discovery is highly controversial; the analysis of the debate is, however, beyond the scope of this book (for a brief discussion see Section 3.3). For an analysis supporting this view see, among others, Gibbons et al. (1994); for a criticism of the approach see, for example, David, Foray and Steinmueller (1998) and Pestre (1997).

31. See Section 3.2 for a description of the evolution of the university in the early nineteenth century.

32. In addition, it creates the potential for quasi-rents accruing to the new 'gatekeepers' or intermediaries brokering this knowledge.

33. A series of administrative measures has had to be created to enable the evaluation of performance.

34. See Section 4.1 for the analysis of the changes in Higher Education Expenditures in R&D during the 1980s and 1990s. The budget cuts in the UK system were so important that the 1996 forecast of the Higher Education Funding Council for England reports that 77 (or nearly 55 per cent) of English HEIs were expected to be in deficit by the end of 1999/2000 (quoted from The National Committee of Inquiry into Higher Education, 1997, p. 263).

35. See the report of the Commission Jacques Attali for France and Guerzoni (1997) for Italy.

36. See Chapter 6 for the analysis of university participation in Community Framework Programmes.

37. For a criticism of this approach see Getz, Siegfried and Zhang (1991).

38. Arora and Gambardella (1997) show that due to an information externality problem, firms have lower incentives than public agencies to fund scientists and institutions of uncertain scientific capabilities. However, especially for small firms, the fact that universities are located nearby can become a factor as important as their scientific capabilities.

39. An interview with the manager of the transfer office of the Université Louis Pasteur of Strasbourg confirmed that, although the university has a long history of university–industry relationships, a large number of professors still have problems in correctly accounting for their opportunity costs.

40. For the analysis of the process of scientific innovation see Kuhn (1970) and Lakatos (1970).

41. For the building blocks of this new theoretical approach to the organisation of scientific production, see Dasgupta and David (1987, 1994) and David (1994).

42. For the original definition of path-dependence see Arthur (1988) and David (1985).

43. Although it is possible to imagine some form of co-ordination that would reduce the negative unintended consequences of a diversified funding sources structure, co-ordination failures are likely at both national and European levels.

44. For the analysis of the changing relationships between the allocation of funds and scientific research output in the British university system see Chapter 5.

45. For the analysis of EU funding of university research see Part III, Chapters 6 and 7.

3. An evolutionary account of European universities

In the previous chapter it was illustrated that an increasing number of scholars of economics and policy-oriented studies have recently carried out research on the different aspects of university behaviour. In most of these studies the university is treated as a single type of organisational entity despite significant differences in the institutions labelled as universities. On the one hand, this is a general problem with economic thought that tends to treat heterogeneous institutions as homogeneous organisations – for example, the use of the term firm to describe all profit-seeking business organisations. On the other hand, this is an acute problem in the definition of university as noted by Rothblatt and Wittrock (1993, p. 1):

> the problem of defining university has long preoccupied politicians, planners, reformers, academics, theologians, philosophers, historians, and litterateurs. They have often found the task impossible. So much has this been the case, especially since the eighteenth century, that universities are now subsumed under a broader if less romantic category called 'higher education'.

Still, to understand the ongoing changes in the structure, role and goals of the university, a better definition of the contemporary European university is needed.

Referring to the university as a group of institutions, a sub-group of the class 'higher education institutions', does not add much clarity to the debate. Rothblatt and Wittrock (1993, pp. 3–4), among others, consider the higher education institution an ambiguous definition:

> Higher education . . . is very likely a neologism of the last century. It was, and remains, imprecise. Nations do not define 'higher' in the same way, just as they do not define 'lower' education in the same way. Academic work deemed appropriate for a school in one country is inappropriate in another, and courses of study pursued at college or university in one nation are located in an 'upper secondary' or 'post-compulsory sector' in another.

The term 'higher education institutions' is not suitable for identifying a particular kind of organisation. This term encompasses groups of institutions that differ by country of origin and period of time considered. Therefore, the university cannot usefully be described merely as a sub-group of 'something' that cannot be defined. It would be better simply to describe the attributes of the subclass itself.

After the Second World War the university went through a process of rapid growth and diversification. The number of students, number of researchers and the level of financing have more than quadrupled in the 30 years between the early 1950s and the late 1970s. The elite pre-war institution has become a mass institution, mostly, but not only, concerned with research and teaching. New universities and new kinds of higher education institutions, with different structures, roles and goals, have been established. This process of increasing diversification makes the task of precisely defining the university problematic if not impossible.

In 1992 the total number of Higher Education Institutions[1] (HEIs) in the EU[2] countries was approximately 1429 (International Association of Universities (IAU) 1991, 1993). Looking at the official national classifications, it is possible to subdivide them into 379 universities and 1050 Post Secondary Institutions (PSIs).[3] Nonetheless, when one considers the International Standard Classification for Education (ISCED), the difference between universities and PSIs becomes less clear (see Table 3.1 for students' subdivision). ISCED level 5 – that is, education at the tertiary level, first stage, of the type that leads to an award not equivalent to a first university degree – is usually offered by PSIs, but sometimes also by universities. ISCED level 6 – that is, education at the tertiary level, first stage, of the type that leads to a first university degree or equivalent – is usually supplied by both universities and PSIs. Finally, ISCED level 7 – that is, education at the tertiary level, second stage, of the type that leads to a postgraduate university degree or equivalent – is usually the domain of universities, but sometimes PSIs also offer Masters degrees and PhD degrees. Thus, degrees granting specialisation do not seem relevant for justifying a division between universities and PSIs.

When knowledge creation and transmission aspects – that is, norms, incentives and organisational structure of the 'open science'[4] kind of research – are put at the core of the analysis, a subdivision is still possible. Nevertheless, as highlighted at the end of Section 3.3, the most crucial differences in research orientation, independence in the pursuit of new knowledge and availability of funds, are between a restricted group of elite research-intensive universities and a cluster of universities and PSIs, and not between universities and PSIs. The official distinction between universities and PSIs is, in general, a precarious one and therefore not useful.

The institutional stability, or inertia, of the university historically has led to a slow process of incremental institutional innovation. This process of institutional change can be depicted as a continuous series of adjustments to a changing environment. Unless a profound and disruptive change impelled by shifts in the external socio-political environment of the organisation takes place, the roles played, rules followed, and aims to be accomplished can be traced back to the historical development of the institution. Highly diversified modern universities are the result of this process of evolution. The historical and sociological analysis of university development has highlighted a few main features – for example, the independence from external powers of the medieval university, the pursuit of knowledge for its own sake of the nineteenth-century university – that have characterised the university throughout its history. Some of these attributes are still present, with different degrees of importance, in contemporary universities.

Table 3.1   Students by ISCED level of programme

	Tertiary level Non-university equivalent	Tertiary level university or equivalent	Tertiary level postgraduate degree	All levels
B – 1990	123 970	136 664	15 614	276 248
D – 1990	22 843	120 125	+	142 968
F – 1990	454 055	1 065 600	179 283	1 698 938
G – 1990	220 802	1 578 592	+	1 799 394
Gr – 1989	77 159	117 260	–	194 419
I – 1991	10 378	1 474 719	48 105	1 533 202
Ir – 1990	n.a.	n.a.	n.a.	90 296
Nl – 1990 #	252 346	181 795	8 653	442 784
P – 1990	–	182 032	3 730	185 762
S – 1989	366	1 143 080	25 695	1 169 141
UK – 1990	383 026	706 089	169 073	1 258 188
Total	1 544 950	6 705 962	450 160	8 791 340

Notes:
+: The figure is included in the figure of Level 6; –: Magnitude is either negligible or zero; #: Excludes the students of distant learning institutions.
B = Belgium, D = Denmark, F = France, G = Germany, Gr = Greece, I = Italy, Ir = Ireland, Nl = The Netherlands, P = Portugal, S = Spain, UK = United Kingdom.

Source: UNESCO Statistical Yearbook (1993).

Contemporary European universities are the product of about 800 years of evolution.[5] Their current standing is the result of a series of historical events. Hence an historical approach is required to fully understand the characteristics of this peculiar institution. Focusing on university contribution to social purpose and on the governance and organisation of the institution, this chapter will try to highlight the path of evolution of the institution, delineating the presence of continuity within change. On the basis of the evidence put forward by the historical analysis of university development it will be maintained that the roles played, rules followed, and aims to be accomplished of contemporary universities find their roots in the medieval traditions, in the approach to scientific discovery developed by the scientific societies of the late eighteenth century, in the nineteenth-century German model and in the postwar 'endless frontier' ideal.[6]

Broadly speaking, one can subdivide the historical development of the university into four phases. First, *the birth of the university*: the period of time between the late twelfth and the early sixteenth century that witnessed the birth and development of a unique institution that would have assumed the name of *Universitas Magistrorum et Scholarium* or *Studium Generale*. Second, *the decline period* that runs from the second half of the sixteenth century up to the end of the eighteenth century. Third, *the recovery and German transformation*, from the early nineteenth century up to the Second World War.[7] Fourth, the *expansion and diversification*, from the end of the Second World War up to the end of the 1970s. Probably, we are now entering a fifth phase that can be called the *institutional reconfiguration* of the university. This chapter provides an analysis of first, third and fourth phases.

3.1   THE BIRTH OF THE UNIVERSITY

The university is essentially a European creation. During the Middle Ages, between the twelfth and thirteenth centuries, in some European towns (mostly in Italy and France) a peculiar institution of higher education developed to a level of organisational and educational complexity and could be considered the ancestor of the modern university. For more than 3000 years the development of various civilisations has included the flourishing of higher learning. Nonetheless, only the medieval higher education institution, known as *studium generale*, 'employing regular teaching staff, offering specific courses of higher studies . . . and granting certificates of accomplishment in the form of generally recognised diplomas or degrees' (Rudy, 1984, pp. 14), showed a continuity through time that enables one to consider it as the predecessor of the modern university. In particular, Paris and Bologna are often considered as the homes of the oldest universities.[8]

The origins of the university of Paris[9] are to be found in the ecclesiastical and private schools that flourished in the twelfth century. The former were schools of theology, the most important being the school of Notre-Dame with its chancellor who operated under the authority of the bishop. The latter were schools of arts which, although private, were under the direct control and exaction of the chancellor of Notre Dame. Due to the rapid growth in the number of students and masters, a proliferation of new schools and a disciplinary confusion occurred. The danger of losing control over the subjects being taught convinced the bishop and the chancellor to accept the formation of an autonomous guild of masters. This 'university' was responsible for the organisation of curricula, examinations, and faculties' distinction in a way that respected the 'classification and hierarchies upon which Christian knowledge had traditionally been based'. Nonetheless, the compromise between the bishop and the autonomous guild of masters was fragile. In subsequent times, the direct intervention of the Pope or of the King[10] was required to settle such disputes. The confrontation reached the point of the *cessatio* (moving the institution out of the town) in 1228, when the members of the arts faculties withdrew from Paris. Three years later, Pope Gregory IX issued a bull granting full chartered rights to the university, and the whole institution was reassembled. Due to the importance of art and theology, the students were mainly *clerici* and/or young students, thus the only members of the university to enjoy all of the rights and prerogatives were the teachers and the masters.[11]

Bologna had a long tradition in the teaching of law. At the start of the twelfth century the law schools developed into a 'university' (guild) and acquired international prestige. After some years other subjects developed to the level of complexity that allowed the creation of other 'university' organisations that were then associated with the one of law. Among the professional courses, it was medicine and not theology that flourished. Especially in the case of law and medicine, the students were generally adults from high social class. Coming from different European regions, they went to Bologna to specialise in a professional career. Consequently, the university of Bologna was organised as a corporation of different mono-disciplinary 'universities'. In each 'university', depending on the locality of their origin, the students were grouped into 'nations'. The students were the only members of the institution to enjoy university rights,[12] while the teachers were simply hired through annual contracts.

The so-called students' universities that sprang up mostly in the south of Europe during the fourteenth century, adapted the model (the statutes) of Bologna to local circumstances. As in the case of Bologna, these universities generally had an important faculty of law and a few other, less developed, faculties. In the fifteenth century, after the Great Schism (1378), the northern and central part of Europe also witnessed a rapid rise in the number of new universities. These new institutions, generally created *ex-novo* by the emperor, kings or dukes, structured their organisation following the Parisian model – that is, the masters' university.[13] Usually all four faculties of art, theology, law and medicine were present in the new institutions.[14]

Two names were most commonly used to define the university. They were: *Universitas Magistrorum et Scholarium*[15] and *Studium Generale*. In the early period the 'commonest term in texts . . . would seem to be *universitas* and not *studium generale*' (Verger, 1992a, p. 37). More precisely, as the term *universitas* – that is, the totality or the whole – was applied to corporate bodies (guilds) of the most different sorts, 'one had to specify the object to which one was referring' (ibid.). Thus the name *universitas magistrorum et scholarium or universitas studii* were used to signify the guild of the masters and student or the guild devoted to the study. The term *studium generale* became the legal definition of the university only after the second half of the thirteenth century. During the first half of the century, *studium generale* was used with descriptive intent, 'the *studium* part indicating a school . . . and *generale* referring . . . to the ability of the school to attract students from beyond the local region' (Cobban, 1975, p. 23). Only towards the end of the century did the concept of *studium generale* acquire a legal connotation.[16]

Three particular rights were connected to the status of *studium generale*. First, the higher education institution recognised as a *studium generale* was entitled to award masters or doctoral degrees, which were acknowledged throughout Christendom. The holder of such a degree had the right 'to teach in any other university without undergoing further examination' (ibid., pp. 27), the *jus ubique docendi*.[17] Second, the institution was secured from the action of the local, religious and lay authority; it was under papal or imperial protection. Third, clergy (both residents and non-residents) studying at a *studium generale* were entitled 'to receive the fruit of their benefices'. As described in the case of Paris, the achievement of a certain degree of independence was the result of conflicts with both the local authority and the universal authorities – that is, the Pope and the Emperor. The confrontation with the former was related to the claim of self-governance. The university opposed the direct control and exaction of the local authority. Although located in a specific town, it refused to submit itself to the local jurisdiction, calling for special rights of universal character. To obtain them, two connected strategies were employed. On the one hand, due to the fact that the presence of the university increased the wealth and importance of the town, the threat and use of the *cessatio*[18] put pressure on the town's authorities. On the other hand, the university looked to the support of the Pope or of the Emperor, applying to universal entities to have universal rights. The protection of the Pope or the Emperor depended upon the adherence to their rules. Yet, the fact that *Imperium* and *Sacerdotium* were two conflicting powers enabled the university to retain sufficient bargaining power with both of them.

In most of the cases, the title of *studium generale* was granted by papal bull[19] to new institutions or to pre-existing ones that requested the official recognition.[20] Up to the end of the fifteenth and early sixteenth centuries the use of the term *studium generale*, and the connected papal bull, was the norm throughout Europe.[21] Then, due to religious and political changes, both the terminology and the requested papal charter disappeared, although there were a few exceptions in the Catholic countries. Since the eighteenth century, and more evidently since the nineteenth century, the term *universitas litterarum*, translated into national languages, has become the official definition of the university. Furthermore, the papal bull has been substituted with an imperial, royal or government charter.

As the name *universitas* testifies, the medieval university was a peculiar kind of guild. Peculiar, in so far as a community of *magistres* and *scholares* – that is, masters and students – were involved in the elaboration and transmission of a peculiar good: knowledge. As with other types of guild, it was composed of members that decided to join it freely. It was a community with internal cohesion, articulated organisation and a corporate personality. It was a moral and legal entity enjoying a degree of independence from external powers – that is, Pope, emperor, princes, towns' rulers and so on – and capable of continuity through time. The primary objective of this community of practitioners was the transmission of knowledge from masters to students. The medieval university was a teaching institution responsible for the preparation for education, ecclesiastical, government and professional careers. The common curriculum of the seven liberal arts, subdivided into apprentice – that is, grammar, logic and rhetoric – and bachelor – that is, arithmetic, geometry, astronomy and music – was followed by the three advanced professional courses, then postgraduate faculties, of theology, law and medicine. All of them were often 'taught side by side in the same institution', the university (Perkin, 1984). The differences between the university, the *studium generale*, and other professional training schools were: (a) its organisational guild-like status; (b) its special right to award master or doctoral degrees[22] recognised throughout Christendom, the *jus ubique docendi*; (c) its ability to attract students and masters from regions (countries) other than the one of its geographical location; and (d) its multidisciplinary features. The other professional schools (sometimes subsumed under the name of *studium particolare*), ranging from elementary to higher education schools, were under the control of the local authority (religious or lay), and served the need of a town or a limited region. They only offered courses in a few of the liberal arts and did not offer advanced professional courses.

To better understand the late medieval development of the university, some remarks concerning financial issues are appropriate here.[23] Although the independent medieval universities were characterised by a heterogeneous organisational structure, a similar pattern of finance can be found. University incomes can be subdivided into internal and external sources. The former were: (a) fees for matriculation and graduation; (b) dispensations from the statutory conditions for degree and other dispensations; (c) *collectae* – that is, money collected from the students once or twice a year; and (d) fines for violation of university statutes and discipline. The latter were: (a) ecclesiastical benefices; (b) salaries paid by the church, king, duke, or town; (c) gift and legacies; and (d) grants and endowments given for the permanent support of the university.

In the early periods, university expenses were modest, but then, due to the development and the consequent increase in capital investment (houses, buildings and libraries), they grew rapidly. The expenses were: (a) salaries to teachers; (b) administration costs; (c) salaries to officials; (d) law suits; (e) cost of academic solemnities and religious feasts; and (f) acquisition and maintenance of houses, buildings and libraries.

Of particular interest is the way in which teachers' costs were covered. During the thirteenth century the masters that were clergy endowed with benefices did not charge fees, while fees for private teachers and clergy without (or with extremely low) benefices were paid directly by the pupils. However, this system was against the belief of the church – that is, knowledge is a gift of God, thus students do not have to pay for it. Therefore, clergy without benefits started to receive a salary covered by part of the *collectae* and examination fees. With a growing number of teachers and the inclusion of all the masters in the scheme, the need for external support rose rapidly. Thereafter, salaries of all teachers[24] were increasingly paid by the Church (Spain), the Commune and the Duke (Italy), and the town (Germany). In France the salary system did not develop until the end of the medieval period. Due to their expansion, the independent universities[25] of the late Middle Ages could no longer be self-supporting. Teachers' salaries and costs of acquisition and maintenance of academic buildings were too high to be covered by the universities' resources. Kings, dukes, and towns, in return for their support, became more and more involved in the control and management of university finances.

Counter to the politically fragmented nature of medieval society, the university developed as a cosmopolitan, 'super-national' institution. A common language (Latin), a common course of education and a common organisation enabled the creation of an international community of masters and scholars that travelled from one institution to another enjoying the same privileges and duties regardless of location. The various medieval universities were not only a peculiar kind of teaching institution, but they were all members of a 'super-national' intellectual unity devoted to the cultivation of knowledge, enjoying a certain degree of independence from the papacy, the empire and the municipal authority.

In the late medieval period, due to political and religious changes, and to increased financial needs, the university started to lose both the 'super-national' feature and its independence on external powers. It became more local in character and dependent on the support of local powers. Connected to these changes, the first symptoms of an intellectual sclerosis emerged in the conservatism of the curriculum. Humanist thought, with the revival of classical literature and philosophy – for example Cicero and Plato – was considered a danger to religion, and was thus opposed by the religious establishment. The university aligned itself to the church and tended to resist the new learning; it was only in the sixteenth century that universities accepted Humanism. The conservatism of the university in the late fifteenth and sixteenth centuries favoured the development of new institutions, the learned society and academies.[26] These, and other institutions alternative to the university, were the centre of the development of new knowledge. In the late fifteenth and the sixteenth centuries they were mainly concerned with literary issues, then, with the development of the Scientific Revolution and the acceptance of Humanism by the university, they became the locus where scientific research was presented and they formed the channels through which the new knowledge was disseminated.

To avoid giving a misleading description a few observations, relevant for university development in general, are required here. Medieval universities were heterogeneous institutions sharing some common characteristics. Thus, university conservatism, as in the above paragraph for the late medieval universities, meant that a majority of universities resisted change. Nonetheless, in some universities the new ideas developed extremely fast. Furthermore, some of the scholars meeting in institutions outside the university were often also teachers at the university.[27] They were thus aware of the new ideas, and they were bringing them inside the university challenging the traditional knowledge organisation of the institution. Therefore, on the one hand, the university system tended towards conservatism, but, on the other hand, the seeds of change were germinating inside it.

3.2   THE RECOVERY AND GERMAN TRANSFORMATION

Over the seventeenth and eighteenth centuries universities did not play a crucial role in the advance of knowledge. On the contrary, universities were not responsive to new ideas (in particular science) brought by the Scientific Revolution and the Enlightenment, and they resisted the change. According to Rudy (1984, p. 87): 'They [universities] still retained narrow and antiquated curriculum and methodologies, made few contributions to thought, and opposed the ideologies spawned by the Enlightenment.' The institutions where scientific research was carried out and diffused were scientific societies and academies. At the end of the sixteenth and the early seventeenth centuries, on the model of the literary academy, private non-professional institutions for the study of science sprang up. The Accademia Secretorum Naturae founded in Naples in 1589 is considered the first scientific academy (Ferrone, 1992). However, it was only in the seventeenth century that the Accademia dei Lincei in Rome (1603–30) and the Accademia del Cimento in Florence (1657–67) developed to a level of institutional organisation (with well-defined membership, hierarchical control and an international scientific community of reference) that made them the prototypes of the late seventeenth- and eighteenth-century societies. Among other reasons, the strong limitations imposed by the counter-reformation[28] have been particularly important in hindering the development of the Italian academies.

Scientific societies and academies flourished outside the Italian peninsula. The private and official[29] institutions that developed in Europe essentially had two organisational models, the one of the Royal Society, founded in London in 1662, and the other of the Académie Royale des Sciences, founded in Paris in 1666. The former was the model for fellows' societies. The society was controlled and directed by its members, neither state finance nor state interference was present. The institution was mainly a site for confrontation and verification of scientific findings, it never became a real site of scientific research. With more than 300 scientific and non-scientific fellows from around the world and the publication of the journal of Philosophical Transactions the institution provided the foundations for the development of an international scientific community.

The French academy was the model for the state academies that followed. It was a state institution for the co-ordination, control and development of scientific research in the kingdom. The institution was not only a site for scientific confrontation and verification, but also a place where scientific research was developed. State finance enabled the creation of laboratories and libraries and, for the first time, scientists were paid to carry out scientific research. At the beginning of the eighteenth century, with about 200 national and foreign scientists, belonging to the academy in various ways, the Académie Royale des Sciences was the dominant model of scientific organisation (Ferrone, 1992; McClellan, 1985).

In the interim between 1660 and the French Revolution, in Europe and in America, private and official scientific societies and academies showed an impressive increase, with over 100 institutions active during this period (McClellan, 1985). An international scientific community, as we understand it nowadays, began to develop. A common set of norms and incentives for the pursuit of scientific knowledge – that is, the institution of 'open science'[30] – was emerging. The professionalisation and the development of new fields of scientific inquiry induced the development of specialised societies and academies. The resulting institutions, however, proved unable to cope with the specialisation of science (McClellan, 1985). Their failure paved the way to the rise of scientific research within the university.

After approximately two centuries of atrophy, the nineteenth century saw the university's recovery. In the new political, religious and scientific environment the university evolved into a new kind of institution, preserving some of the features of its medieval ancestor, and incorporating and developing methodologies and social organisation of the scientific research carried out in the eighteenth century societies and academies. In the late eighteenth century the pursuit of modern scientific and technological knowledge was not carried out within the university. The late medieval, early modern universities had not been able to cope with the changes and were relegated to a marginal role.[31]

In the early nineteenth century, due to the pressing needs of society, new universities were founded and the old ones underwent a process of complete renewal. In particular, in Germany, England and France new models of teaching and research institutions were developed. Although different, the German, English and French models had a few main common characteristics: (a) some of the features of the old medieval university; (b) the methodologies and social organisation of the scientific research carried out in the eighteenth-century societies and academies; and (c) the new and the crucial subdivision of knowledge into disciplines. The teachers were no longer masters able to teach all required subjects, but specialised, single-discipline professors focused on the advancement and transmission of a specific, well-defined portion of knowledge.

Although the German model is traditionally considered the source of this 'division of labour' approach, subject specialisation originally was developed in eighteenth-century Scotland. During the Scottish Enlightenment the development of the subdivision in disciplines enabled various prominent scholars to advance the knowledge frontier of their specific subject within the structure of the university (Wood, 1994) and not outside it, as was the case in the other European countries. One century later, due to the Scottish influence, the same process took place in the English universities and autonomously in the new German universities.

Following these two models – that is, the English and the German – the structuring of knowledge into disciplines spread to all other European countries. Thus, the second half of the nineteenth century witnessed the emergence of a modern research-oriented university in the whole of Europe. Although national differences existed, which will be discussed below, it is possible to describe the new university as an institution committed to: (a) the production of knowledge for its own sake; (b) the preparation for professional careers; (c) being structured in well-defined disciplines and (d) being characterised by an articulate organisation and a legal status. Moreover, the university became a national institution[32] allowed to pursue the unconstrained development of knowledge but to the advantage of the nation-state.[33]

The university model developed in Germany during the nineteenth century has had the greatest influence on the rise of the modern research-oriented university. Following the defeat and French occupation of Prussia, a diffused perception of the need of innovations and reforms to regain the lost power was present. In this environment, a group of reformers succeeded in overcoming the opposition of conservative circles, and received the royal approval for the foundation of a new university in Berlin. In 1809, Wilhelm von Humboldt (1767–1835)[34] and a small group of civil servants of the Ministry of the

Interior[35] defined the aims, structure and organisation of what would become a new model of the university. As accurately summarised by Spinner (1993, p. 142), this 'ideal university would be an institution for the cultivation of excellence, which is free in the internal realm of research, privileged by the State and the Law, discharged (*entlastet*) in relation to the normal state affairs in the broader society'. At the basis of this model there is the combination of teaching and research and the idea that teachers and students are 'devoted to science as such for its own sake, within the proper domain of an autonomous realm of knowledge organised according to the principles of free-self-formation' (ibid.). A new 'social organisation' of science and a new classification of science developed. The concept of 'pure science', carried out within the university, and conversely 'non-pure science', performed outside the university, are the results of the cognitive changes originated by the development of and resistance to the new university (Spinner, 1993; Wittrock, 1993).

Founded in 1810, the university of Berlin was the most genuine, and probably the only, example of the Humboldtian model of university. On the basis of this model – that is, the union of teaching and research, and the research for its own sake – the evolution of the German university followed other paths. '[D]espite rather than because of the Humboldtian ideal, the German university became the embodiment of the specialised research-oriented ideal and the model for the progressive system of higher education in the other advanced societies' (Perkin, 1984, pp. 34–5). The crucial feature of what is considered as the paradigmatic German model is, indeed, the subdivision into specialised disciplines,[36] that is incompatible with the 'holistic thinking and broad historical cultural categories' that were inspiring the Humboldtian university. Nevertheless, the Humboldtian reform enabled 'the creation of an autonomous institutional setting for intellectual activities' (Wittrock, 1993, p. 320) that during the nineteenth century evolved into what is considered the institutional paradigm of collective disciplinary specialisation and research-orientation in the approach to acquiring and transmitting knowledge. Thus, the development of the German university during the nineteenth century can be seen as the result of the interaction between a new social organisation of science, the Humboldtian model, and a new structure of science – that is, the spontaneous trend towards the subdivision of knowledge into scientific fields.

The state played a crucial role in the development of the German university. The Prussian state, and from 1871 the imperial state, through the ministry of education and culture, carried on an organised series of actions, in modern terms science policy actions, to develop, support and improve the university system.[37] In particular, the state became the principal founder and financier of the university. The German state saw the university not only as the source of knowledge and of future welfare, but also as the way to strengthen national and cultural identity. As stressed by Wittrock (1993, p. 321): 'the rise of the [German] research-oriented university was largely coterminous with the formation of a modern nation-state. Universities came to be the key institutions both for knowledge production and for strengthening a sense of national and cultural identity.'

As pointed out above, the nineteenth century witnessed the renewal and restructuring of the university system in the whole of Europe. Some countries imitated the German model to a large degree, while others borrowed only some of its aspects, developing their higher education and research system on the basis of national specificity. Of particular relevance are the English and French cases.

At the end of the eighteenth and the early nineteenth centuries English universities were still characterised as training places for Anglican clergy, and gathering places for rich students. Oxford and Cambridge were still the only two recognised institutions.[38] Oxford is considered the first English university. Although it was never formally recognised as a *studium generale*, at the end of the twelfth century it was regarded as a *studium generale ex consuetudine*. The origin of university at Cambridge is usually connected with the *cessatio* of the Oxford university in 1209–1214/15. After the closure of the Oxford *studium* a considerable number of students and masters migrated to Cambridge giving birth to the new university. The organisation of both universities adapted the masters' model of Paris to the local context. Due to the low power of local bishops the universities developed higher independence, and the chancellors were nominated from the assembly of the masters (*congregazio/convocazio*). At the end of the thirteenth century, despite the fact that Oxford was internationally known for the study of mathematics and natural sciences, and Cambridge attained an international reputation in the humanities in the early sixteenth century, the members, both masters and students, of the two universities were mostly from the British Isles. During the early thirteenth century, together with other institutions of higher education, Oxford and Cambridge were supported by the crown. However, at the end of the thirteenth and the early fourteenth centuries the crown favoured the two institutions giving them the monopoly of English higher education.

Under the influence of secularism and the success of German scientific and technological research, in 1828 the first purely secular institution of higher education in British history, University College London, was founded. Following this model new institutions sprang up throughout the country. In particular, the second half of the nineteenth century witnessed the development of what would then be called 'civic universities', or 'redbrick' universities: Birmingham, Leeds, Liverpool, Manchester, and so on. Contrary to Oxford and Cambridge these new institutions were more responsive to the technological and scientific needs of the country (Rudy, 1984; Wittrock, 1993), and their mission encompassed not only liberal education, but also professional education and research. New comprehensive curricula with utilitarian subjects such as engineering, architecture, agriculture were offered in the new institutions. Although less promptly, and keeping an elitist approach, Oxford and Cambridge also developed their scientific and technological capabilities along the line of the German research model (Perkin, 1984). Nonetheless, it was under the influence of the Scottish system, more than the German model, that English universities and colleges developed the professorial system (ibid.). Contrary to the German model, the professor was not a civil servant appointed by the state, but an employee of the independent university. Moreover, he was a member of a department, *primus inter pares* and not an autonomous chair holder with his 'research institute' (Perkin, 1984). As in Germany, research found its place in the university, but the core of the system was the idea of a 'liberal education free from narrow consideration of utility and vocational interest' (Rothblatt, 1976; Wittrock, 1993). Together with the research function and the emphasis on liberal education the university was also serving the goal of preparing students for a professional career. In some universities there was the confluence of the different aims, while others tended to be specialised in only one. Converse to the homogeneous and state-driven German system, the English system was characterised by a high degree of institutional heterogeneity and institutional independence.

To trace the peculiarity of the French system one has to go back to the end of the eighteenth century. As previously highlighted during the eighteenth-century Enlightenment, under the Old Regime, the French universities were playing a minor role in the process of knowledge creation and they tended to be conservative if not reactionary in their teaching. In 1793, the revolutionary authorities abolished the 22 French universities (Rudy, 1984; Verger, 1986). Two new types of institutions with a clear mono-disciplinary orientation were established. On the one hand, independent faculties pursued the study of the liberal arts;[39] on the other, new schools, *les grandes écoles*[40] – for example, École Polytechnique (1794), École Normale Supérieure (1795), focused their research and teaching on utilitarian subjects. During the Napoleonic period a highly centralised state organisation emerged. The main aim of this higher education system was 'to train for state service [military or bureaucratic] citizens loyal to their prince, fatherland, and family' (Rudy, 1984; p. 102). The complete control of the university was in the hands of the Ministry of Education, and in 1808 the whole public instruction was set under the Imperial University of France. This structure lasted up to 1896 when faculties were reunited in 17 provincial universities. Still, the centralised state organisation did not disappear, but persisted well into the twentieth century (Karady, 1986). During the nineteenth century, the dominant role in research was played by *les grande écoles*. These institutions, utilitarian in character, were devoted to the production of scientific and technological knowledge and they provided highly trained students for bureaucratic and managerial careers. Only after the re-founding of the provincial universities, with the development of better research facilities, were some research activities carried out in the university. At the end of the nineteenth and the early twentieth centuries the French system came to be characterised on the one side, by a clear-cut subdivision between *grandes écoles* and universities and, on the other, by a bureaucratic state control. The institutional independence typical of the English system, or the autonomy of the chair holder of the German system, was impossible in the French system. Higher education in general was considered essentially utilitarian and at the service of national interests.

3.3   THE EXPANSION AND DIVERSIFICATION

Over the period stretching from the end of the Second World War to the end of the 1970s the university went through a process of rapid growth. The four main driving forces behind this large expansion were the following. First, due to internal logic – that is, the mechanism of subdivision and reconfiguration of fields of research into new sub-disciplines and the increased reliance on instrumentation – the process of scientific inquiry has required an enlarged number of practitioners and wider financial involvement. Second, the successful use of scientific discoveries made during the Second World War[41] set in a definitive way the 'belief' in the direct applicability of scientific findings. Governments, first in the US and then in the European countries, regarded scientific research as a source of future welfare, thus directing a large amount of financial resources towards university research. Third, in particular during the 1960s, the shift in demand for the level and range of skills by industry and government together with social pressures for democratisation of the university system[42] transformed the perception of the educational role of the university. The university was no longer considered an elite institution open only to a minority of students from the higher classes. It became an institution open to all persons qualified by ability to attend it. The opening of new institutions, and the creation of student support schemes tried to implement this new educational role of the university. Fourth, due to the strong economic growth of the post war period, and to the demographic boom, during the 1950s and early 1960s, the number of students attending secondary school increased at an extraordinary pace. Consequently, the potential demand for higher education – that is, the number of students finishing secondary school – expanded dramatically.

The expansion of higher education, from approximately one million students in 1960 to approximately nine million students in 1990 in the 11 EU countries considered, brought together a process of institutional diversification (see Table 3.1 for levels, and Table 3.2 for the gross enrolment ratio for tertiary education – that is, total enrolment, regardless of age, divided by the population of the age group 20–24). Mainly under the influence of the respective governments,[43] the enormous increase was absorbed by the enlargement of existing universities, the creation of new universities and the foundation of new types of higher education institutions.

Table 3.2   Gross enrolment ratio (%)

	B	D	F	G	Gr	I	Ir	NI	P	S	UK
1960	9.1	11.4	7.4	6.1	3.8	6.6	8.1	16.7*	3.5	3.9	9.0
1970	17.5	18.4	19.5	13.4	13.5	16.7	13.6	19.5	8.0	8.9	14.1
1980	26.3	28.6	25.5	26.2	17.4	27.6	20.3	30.0	11.2	24.2	20.1
1990	38.2	35.6	39.7	36.1	25.0	29.8	33.8	37.6	22.7	35.5	27.8

Notes:
* 1965 value
B = Belgium, D = Denmark, F = France, G = Germany, Gr = Greece, I = Italy, Ir = Ireland, NI = The Netherlands, P = Portugal, S = Spain, UK = United Kingdom.

Source: UNESCO Statistical Yearbook (1975, 1983, 1993).

Throughout the 1960s and 1970s the EU higher education system witnessed an impressive growth in the number of students and researchers, and in the financial commitment. Although in some of the less wealthy countries such as Greece, Ireland and Portugal the increase started only in the 1970s, the whole EU higher education system had grown five-fold by the end of the period (see Table 3.A1 in Appendix 3.1). This transformation from elite to mass higher education has put the university under strain. Part of the expansion has been absorbed by new universities and new institutions, but also the pre-war universities have seen a large increase in their size. The university structure, defined in the nineteenth century on the basis of the medieval guild-like model, was shaped for an elitist system and not for a mass system. In the attempt to satisfy the new demand, the old universities tried to accommodate the growing numbers. Due to the urgent need for teachers, less qualified lecturers found first temporary, and then tenure, positions in the university (Trow, 1984; Simone, 1993). The number of students attending a class increased dramatically, with a consequent decrease in the quality of instruction. Training-oriented courses for new and emerging professions were added to the traditional curricula, creating tensions in the old faculty subdivision. The loss of intellectual pre-eminence of faculties and departments together with the increased organisational complexity (due to growth and to the diversification of goals) opened the way to the bureaucratisation of the university. The university was no longer a community of peers engaged in the production and transmission of knowledge, but a bureaucratic organisation run by officials where scholars were involved in teaching and research together or only in one of the two. The budget constraints and the increased demand for accountability of the 1980s have further weakened the independence and status of universities.

Following the three-fold classification made by Martin A. Trow in 1984, the different kind of higher education institutions can be categorised as: (1) the pre-war universities, (2) the new postwar universities, and (3) the non-university institutions of higher education or, in our words, the post-secondary institutions of higher education. Although sometimes the second and third kind of institutions are under the same institutional hat, as in the case of the German *Gesamthochschulen* and the comprehensive universities in Sweden,[44] the diversity among the three classes becomes evident when one considers the differences in: (a) research orientation, (b) funding patterns, (c) degree-granting power, (d) organisational forms, (e) teaching and training orientation and (f) autonomy. In particular, focusing on the degree-granting power and on the research orientation, it is possible to distinguish the universities (pre-war and postwar together) from the PSIs. Except for the French *grande écoles* and a few other PSIs, the university has retained the right to award the PhD degree. The university still has a monopoly position in the highest level of education. Although PhD students represent only a small fraction of the total number of students (see Table 3.1) they are a crucial input both for the education system, as lecturers and researchers in the higher education institutions, and for the knowledge-oriented production system, as researchers in public and private research centres. Due to political choice, the university, and not the PSI, became the site where the government directed a large amount of financial resources for the development of scientific research.[45] Politics directed the new institutions founded by the national governments primarily to satisfy the educational demand and so, originally, they did not have any research orientation. History mattered, too, in that the pre-war universities were already the places where research was carried out, and thus, due to the accumulated capabilities, they were the most suitable places to develop scientific research.

Having said this, it is nonetheless important to acknowledge that, during the 1980s and early 1990s, the distinction between universities and PSIs has become less clear. Relevant for the understanding of this new trend is what the higher education literature has called the academic drift phenomenon. Since their foundation PSIs have tended to emulate universities. The most important reason for this behaviour was that their teaching staff, mainly trained in the university, aimed to gain the rights and privileges of their peers working in the university. This tendency gained strength after the budget constraints of the late 1970s. A process of increased competition for the best professors and teachers, for the most promising students and for scarce research funds took place. This process found a fertile ground in the diffuse perception of the existence of relevant status differences. The lower status institutions (PSIs) developed policies aimed at catching up with institutions of higher status (universities) that had higher funding. The consequence has been a polarisation of the system into three main groups. At the top are almost exclusively the pre-war universities. They have a higher status, more rights and privileges, and wider sources of funds. These high status universities are the sites where much of the top scientific research is carried out. A second group is composed of the majority of the new universities and some of the PSIs. They are characterised by a lower status and lower funds, but they have rights and privileges similar to the pre-war university. They are involved in mainly technical research usually applied and oriented to regional needs. Finally, at the lowest level are the group of vocational PSIs that exclusively undertake teaching responsibilities.[46]

National governments resisted the academic drift because it was undercutting the policy objective of a diversified higher education system containing a large component of vocational and technical education. Nonetheless, as highlighted above, the combination of budget constraints and the push towards a more market-oriented approach reinforced the process of academic drift. The response of the government has been to try to level the system downward instead of opposing the trend of levelling upward, allowing only for a few centres of excellence.[47] Policies of higher control and less autonomy have been developed. The higher education *in toto* has been made more accountable to specific aims of national policy.

An illuminating example of the trends described above is the higher education policy developed in the UK during the 1980s and early 1990s. Throughout the 1980s university, polytechnic and college budgets were restructured in ways that put new pressures (and incentives) on the institutions. The actions were undertaken on the one hand, to stimulate a process of financial restructuring aimed at reducing costs and, on the other hand, to provide incentives, through mechanisms such as the Research Assessment Exercise and the Technology Foresight,[48] by which it was hoped that better direction of research effort would result. In 1988, with the Education Reform Act, the role of universities, polytechnics and colleges was suddenly transformed from that of public institutions subsidised by the state into that of private suppliers of specific services. Finally, in 1993, 39 polytechnics and colleges were granted university status. The old and new universities now share a common identity. Thus they are all competing for the same research funds and are exposed to a process of selectivity on the basis of assessment of research quality (David, Geuna and Steinmueller, 1995).[49]

The trends and forces described in the previous paragraphs have originated a process of change in the structure of knowledge production within the university. First, although most of the prestigious universities of the pre-war period have retained a position of pre-eminence, their position tends to be limited to particular research fields rather than spanning the knowledge spectrum. Second, the loss of intellectual pre-eminence of faculties and departments has been followed by the rise of the research centre as the intellectual unit of research.[50] This fragmentation has been supported not only by the internal logic of subdivision and re-configuration of research fields, but also by a higher degree of autonomy[51] and lower constraints[52] granted to the centre. Increasingly the university owes its prestige to the research centre, usually associated with a graduate school, and not to particular departments or to undergraduate teaching. Finally, on the one hand, the process of fragmentation seems to point to a more specialised type of knowledge, while on the other hand, the knowledge production process at the frontiers of science and technology tends to be more trans-disciplinary in character (Gibbons et al., 1994).

The reconciliation of the process of fragmentation with the trend towards more trans-disciplinary knowledge production is possible when one looks at the development of the research network.[53] Due to the increased complexity of the scientific research and to the development of cross-field research, such as in the case of information technologies and molecular biology, scholars sitting in different centres and concerned with fields of research that were traditionally considered separate, interact in the production of new trans-disciplinary knowledge.[54] The rise in cross-country and cross-discipline scientific collaboration is connected to the development of large international scientific institutions, such as CERN, to the rising importance of international co-operative R&D programmes of the Commission of the European Communities, and to the increased mobility of researchers. In particular, the mobility of researchers can be realised both in physical terms – for example, through visiting professor schemes, and by the use of electronic media – for example, through the development of telecommunication services[55] such as the Internet that enable intimate interaction among geographically distant researchers.

3.4   CONCLUSIONS

Until recently, the university has played a unique and essential role in the process of knowledge creation and transmission. As clearly stressed by Perkin (1984, pp. 45–6) 'A knowledge-based society depends on both the constant advancement of knowledge and the reproduction of knowledgeable people as much as industrial society depends on the constant investment of capital and the reproduction of skilled managers and workers.'

According to Geiger (1985, p. 53):

> The development of science in the modern era has taken place in a variety of institutional settings. However, since the widespread recognition of German scientific leadership in the last third of the nineteenth century, and continuing through the

ascendancy of American science in the mid-twentieth, the university has served as the predominant home of science. Although this nexus between universities and research has been considered virtually axiomatic for a century, it can no longer be regarded as so today. The vast proliferation of modern science has long-since overflowed the confines of the university, while the parallel expansion of higher education has necessitated departures from the university model.[56]

Due to its success both in research and in teaching, the university has grown in number of students, number of researchers and financing. In particular, after the Second World War its rapid growth was also connected with a rise in society's expectations for economic returns. These two phenomena, the growth and the rise of expectations, put the university under strain. A range of topics such as compatibility between the demands of elite and mass higher education, free research enterprise versus targeted research, private versus public financing, free advancement of the knowledge frontier versus dependence from the needs of the society, competition from teaching-oriented and research-oriented institutions, have led to counteracting pressures on the institutional organisation and roles played by the university.

The historical development of the university testifies to 'its protean capacity to change its shape and function to suit its temporal and socio-political environment while retaining enough continuity to deserve its unchanging name' (Perkin, 1984, p. 18). Although a large part of the literature concerned with university development has highlighted the present crisis of the university,[57] when we look at its historical capacity for adaptation and at its 'special sort of cultural inheritance with idealistic, spiritual, and high-minded aspirations derived from important philosophical and theological traditions' (Rothblatt and Wittrock, 1993, p. 1), hope again rises. The recognition of the adaptive ability of the university enables a better evaluation of its current situation. Instead of being in a phase of loss of importance, the university is going through a period of institutional change. A complex institution like the university tends to resist re-configuration of its structure and institutional organisation, thus the result of change is only observable after a long period of time.

One of the possible outcomes of the ongoing changes is a clear cut division between a small group of dynamic research-oriented universities and a large group of mainly teaching-oriented institutions. The national university developed in the nineteenth century, composed of a community of mainly national peers, covering a broad spectrum of disciplines and focused on both teaching and research, will tend to disappear. A new kind of institution, in its international character and in its disciplinary specialisation more similar to the old medieval university, will start to develop. The research universities, usually elite pre-war institutions and a handful of new postwar universities, will be the privileged actors in this development. These institutions, internationally well-known for their competencies in specific fields of knowledge, interconnected by international

(European) research networks, will tend to increase their international focus. The action of these universities will be influenced not only by local government policy, but also by the initiative of the Commission of the European Communities and other international organisations, and by the opportunities offered by industry at the international and multinational level.

The next two chapters, focusing on university research, describe the contemporary university situation both at the European and at the British level. One of the aims of the two chapters is to provide statistical support to the view presented above of the stratification (polarisation) of the university system. Particularly in the analysis of the British case, some tentative evaluation of the ongoing changes and of the policies steering them is put forward.

NOTES

1. Higher education institutions are institutions that offer education programmes at the tertiary level – that is, programmes classified as either ISCED (International Standard Classification for Education) level 5, 6 or 7. For the definition of tertiary education and ISCED classification see the Glossary of OECD (1995, pp. 366–9).
2. This count does not include Austria, Finland, Luxembourg and Sweden.
3. To calculate the number of PSIs an estimate of the PSIs in the UK was used. For the selection criteria of the 379 institutions classified under the class universities see Chapter 4, Section 4.1.1.
4. For an analytical history of the emergence of the institutions of 'open science' see David (1997a); for the role played by norms, incentives and organisational structure in the creation of knowledge see Dasgupta and David (1987, 1994).
5. Together with the Roman Catholic Church the university is the oldest institution with a continuous history in the Western world.
6. The 'endless frontier' ideal is associated with the report to President Roosevelt titled 'Science The Endless Frontier' by Vannevar Bush (1945).
7. A more detailed division is offered by Björn Wittrock (1993) who subdivides the recovery and German transformation into two sub-phases: the resurrection of the university (1800–1850) and the rise of the research-oriented university (1850–1939).
8. Bologna claims to be the first, dating its foundation to 1088. However, different investigations into the history of medieval universities have failed to produce any evidence in support of this claim (Ruegg, 1992; Rashdall, 1936).
9. The following description of the universities of Paris and Bologna draws particularly heavily upon Verger (1992a), but see also Rashdall (1936) and Cobban (1975).
10. The Empire and the Papacy were struggling to assume the jurisdiction over the new education institution, thus they were available to support the 'university' one against the other.
11. The term master referred to a scholar that held a master's degree in art, that is to say, that succeeded in the first two tiers of the curriculum – that is, apprentice and bachelor. Often he was a student of the advanced courses in theology, law and medicine, and, in the meantime, he taught undergraduate courses.
12. In particular, only the foreign students were full members of the university. The local students did not need to be members of the university as they were citizens of Bologna, and thus they enjoyed municipal rights.
13. In the thirteenth century, Oxford and Cambridge developed following the masters model too.
14. An idea of the historical university development can be found in Verger (1992a). He maintains that: 'The twenty-eight (or thirty-one) universities operative in 1378 became thirty-one (or thirty-four) in 1400 and sixty-three (or sixty-six) in 1500' (Verger, 1992a, pp. 57).

15. It is possible to find both the term *Universitas Magistrorum* and the term *Universitas Scholarium*, in relation to the type of organisational structure utilised. Sometimes the term *Universitas Studii* is also used as a more general way to define the new institution.

16. Considerable scholarly work has been dedicated to the discussion of the meaning of the terms *universitas* and *studium generale*. See, for example, Chapter 1 of Rashdall (1936) and Chapter 2 of Cobban (1975).

17. Although always associated with the status of *studium generale*, in the reality the *jus ubique docendi* has not been always acknowledged. With the increase in the number of *studia generalia*, the long-established universities, in the attempt to defend their monopoly position, tended to refuse the *jus ubique docendi*, requiring a re-examination for the candidates coming from other universities (Cobban, 1975; Brizzi and Verger, 1990).

18. The *cessatio* was a serious threat because the early universities were constituted only of masters, students and a few books. Capital investments – for example, buildings and a library – started only at the end of the thirteenth century. The frequent use of the *cessatio* is confirmed by the origins of different universities. For example, the foundations of Vicenza (1204), Arezzo (1215), Padua (1222), Siena (*c*. 1246) and Pisa (1343) were linked with the migration of students and masters from Bologna.

19. In most of the cases the university status was granted by the Pope, only in a few cases was the privilege granted by the Emperor. It is interesting to note that Naples, in 1224, was the first university established by Imperial Decree. It was founded to rival the pro-Papacy university of Bologna that, although considered with Paris as the most pre-eminent university of the period, was invested with the same privilege by papal bull only in 1291 (Rudy, 1984; Rashdall, 1936).

20. Oxford, one of the initial universities, never received such a recognition.

21. Where the political power was sufficiently strong, as in the cases of the Kings of Poland, Portugal and Spain, the *studium generale* status was granted by the King and then confirmed by papal bull.

22. Every faculty had its own master degree, in the case of the advanced professional courses the degree was called *doctores* or *professores*.

23. The following analysis of the university financing draws particularly heavily upon Gieysztor (1992) and Verger (1992b).

24. There were strong discrepancies between the income of the masters of the higher faculties and the teachers of arts. The income diversity was due to differences in salary, benefices, fees, and examination fees. Furthermore, the masters of the professional training schools had also non-university sources of income due to their professional activity.

25. The universities controlled by the crown were not financially independent since their foundation.

26. The phenomenon of the academies had its birthplace in Italy. In the period between 1442 and 1462, the first three important *accademie lettararie* were founded. In 1442, in Naples the Accademia Pontaniana was established, followed in 1460 by the Accademia Romana in Rome, and finally in 1462 the famous Ficino's Accademia Platonica was founded in Florence. Throughout the sixteenth century, the Italian model of *accademia letteraria* spread all over Europe (Mantovani, 1991).

27. Copernicus, Descartes, Huygens, Kepler, and Tycho Brahe, among others, accomplished their major works independently of the university, nonetheless they collaborated with scholars that were teaching at the university.

28. See for example Galileo's trial in 1633.

29. The official institutions had a corporate status, they were legally chartered by some civil authority: emperor, king, prince, town, and so on (McClellan, 1985).

30. For an analytical history of the emergence of the institutions of 'open science' see David (1997a); for the role played by norms, incentives and organisational structure in the creation of knowledge see Dasgupta and David (1987, 1994).

31. Nonetheless, especially in Scotland, The Netherlands and Germany, there were a few exceptions. For example, the universities of Edinburgh, Göttingen, Halle and Leiden were important centres of research and training during the Enlightenment (Rudy, 1984).

32. This is more true for the continental countries where the university was seen as a tool for the cultural, economic and social development of the nation.
33. The university should, in the words of Humboldt, be 'the summit where everything that happens directly in the interest of the moral culture of the nation comes together' (Wittrock, 1993, p. 317).
34. It is interesting to notice that Wilhelm von Humboldt started his university studies in the Prussian University of Frankfurt an der Oder, then, dissatisfied with the conservative and pedantic kind of studies offered by the university, he moved to the Hannoverian University of Göttingen. As previously pointed out, in the eighteenth century Göttingen was one of the few European universities in which scientific research and the new organisation of scientific inquiry flourished.
35. More exactly in the part of the ministry devoted to culture and education, that would have become the ministry for education and culture in 1817 (Spinner, 1993).
36. The structure of the university was built around the autonomous, state supported, chair holder (*Ordinarius*). He was the director of a centre of research in which a number of assistants (*Dozent*) were working without a fixed state salary. He enjoyed a large degree of independence both in the setting up of the research priorities and in the management of the centre.
37. A critical role in the development of German science policy at the end of the nineteenth century has been played by Friedrich Althoff(1837–1908). In a period of 25 years (1882–1907) he developed a complex set of policy actions that has been named the 'Althoff system'. Among others, the foundation of technical universities and the structuring of research institutions, the Kaiser-Wilhelm-Gesellschaft, that was to become the Max-Planck Institut after the Second World War, have been extremely important for the development of the German research and education system. For a detailed analysis of the Althoff system see Backhaus (1993) and Brocke (1991).
38. The following brief description of the universities of Oxford and Cambridge draws heavily upon Evans (1990) and Cobban (1975).
39. 'With the exception of medicine, the faculties remained examining bodies, providing some public lectures, but they were not meant to organise formal curricula' (Frijhoff, 1992 p. 1254).
40. Some special institutions, focused on research and on training for high managerial positions, already existed before the revolution, for example, École des Ponts et Chaussées (1747), and École des Mines (1783).
41. See especially the Manhattan Project and the Radiation Laboratory at MIT. For a clear analysis of government expectations from scientific research, generated by the war experience, see Geiger (1993, Chapters 1 and 2). For the rationale used to justify the public support of science see Bush (1945).
42. For the UK case see the report on Higher Education of the Robbins Committee (1963). For an analysis of the Robbins achievement see Scott (1984, Chapter 5).
43. It is only recently that Europe has developed a number of private higher education institutions. Historically, only a few private religious institutions were active.
44. In France in some cases the Instituts Universitaires de Technologie (IUT) are part of pre-existent universities, while in other cases they are independent institutions.
45. This observation is clearly referring only to the higher education system. After the Second World War the development of scientific and technological research took place not only within the university but also in other public and private sites.
46. As one of the main forces of this process is the competition for funds, the consequent polarisation is more clear in those countries such as the United Kingdom, where the higher education system is more exposed to market forces.
47. Again, this observation is more true for countries such as the UK where mission-oriented policies (selective policies) are applied, while it is less relevant for countries like Italy where proportional allocation policies (*finanziamento a pioggia*) are the norm. Still, as the UK system is becoming a potential attraction pole for the other European systems, its current implications are of general relevance.
48. While the Research Assessment Exercise is run by the Funding Council with the aim of a better allocation of research funds to universities, the Technology Foresight, run by the Office of Science and Technology, tries to pull scientific research more towards the 'need of the nation'. Research Assessments Exercises, formerly termed research selectivity exercises,

were conducted in 1986, 1989, 1992 and 1996; for an official evaluation of the impact of the 1992 exercise see HEFCE (1997).

49. See Chapter 5 for the analysis of the changes that occurred in the UK higher education system during the 1980s and early 1990s.
50. For an analysis of the importance of research centres in the US research intensive universities see Stahler and Tash (1994).
51. The research centre enjoys a higher degree of independence in the setting up of research priorities. Furthermore, due to its flexibility it can better exploit the external sources of financing, an extremely important advantage in a period of budget cuts.
52. Usually the researchers of the centre are less involved in undergraduate teaching.
53. For a broad approach to the development of the scientific network see Callon (1991).
54. For the development of international scientific collaboration see Luukkonen, Persson and Sivertsen (1992) and Leydesdorff (1992). For the development of trans-disciplinary and public-private collaboration see Hicks (1995).
55. The development of the information and communication technologies and the forecast fall of the telecommunication costs, down to the level of the simple access cost, can have a crucial impact on the changes that are going on in the higher education system. For example, it is possible to think in terms of interactive video-conferencing at zero variable costs.
56. A similar view is presented in Gibbons et al. (1994).
57. See, for example, Gibbons et al. (1994), Hague (1991) and Scott (1984).

APPENDIX 3.1: TABLE

Table 3.A1   Students, teachers and growth indices of real public expenditure by countries

	Years	Students	Teachers	Expenditure*
Belgium	1960	52 002	n.a.	n.a.
	1970	124 857	n.a.	100 (1975)
	1980	196 153	27 796 (1988)	117
	1990	276 248	28 058	118 (1988)
Denmark	1960	28 289	4 408 (1965) +	n.a.
	1970	76 024	4 498 (1973) +	n.a.
	1980	106 241	6 702 (1978) +	n.a.
	1990	142 968	n.a.	n.a.
France	1960	272 037	10 824 +	n.a.
	1970	801 156	35 679 +	100 (1974)
	1980	1 076 717	44 678 (1984) +	97
	1991	1 840 307	50 331 +	123 (1988)
Germany	1960	265 366	21 635 ~	n.a.
	1970	503 819	81 993 (1972)	100
	1980	1 223 221	171 708	142
	1990	1 799 394	208 881	135 (1987)
Greece	1960	29 339	926	n.a.
	1970	85 766	3 162 +	100
	1980	121 116	10 542	204
	1989	194 419	13 451	358 (1988)
Ireland	1960	12 438	884 +	n.a.
	1970	28 510	4 088 (1975)	100
	1985	70 301	6 002	218
	1990	90 296	5 598	268 (1987)
Italy	1960	191 790	17 171	n.a.
	1970	687 242	44 171	100 (1971)
	1985	1 185 304	51 539	110
	1990	1 452 286	55 766	224 (1986)
Netherlands	1960	105 995	n.a.	n.a.
	1970	231 167	11 500 +	100
	1980	360 033	n.a.	119
	1991	493 563	41 348	142 (1987)

Table 3.A1   (continued)

	Years	Students	Teachers	Expenditure*
Portugal	1960	24 236	1 617	n.a.
	1970	50 095	2 869	100 (1973)
	1980	92 152	10 694	240
.	1990	185 762	14 432	503 (1988)
Spain	1960	87 388	3 928	n.a.
	1970	224 904	29 701 (1975)	n.a.
	1980	697 789	42 831	n.a.
	1989	1 169 141	59 310	n.a.
United Kingdom	1960	168 759	17 863	n.a.
	1970	601 300	50 489 ~	100
	1985	1 032 491	79 621	102
	1990	1 258 188	86 200	90 (1987)

Notes:
*: National currencies deflated with education PPPs.
+: Only universities and equivalent institutions, other third level institutions are not included.
~: Incomplete figures.

Source: UNESCO Statistical Yearbook (1975, 1983, 1993); OECD (1992).

PART II

Allocation of Funds and University Research

4. Contemporary European universities: relationships among age, size and research output

The final part of the previous chapter presents a brief description of the ongoing changes in the higher education system in Europe. After the rapid growth of the 1960s and 1970s, the 1980s have been a period of stall or decline in budgets accompanied by policy changes. Contemporary universities are undergoing a phase of transition and redefinition. Among other forces, national and EU policy actions have an important impact on the ongoing changes. To better understand the implications for the university of policy actions stemming from the competitive approach to university research behaviour and funding, a clearer description of the contemporary population of European universities is needed.

This chapter will mainly focus on the university as a producer of knowledge. The research aspect of the university is put at the centre of the analysis. A methodology for describing the university system in terms of its main characteristics is employed to group universities into clusters with small within-cluster variation for discriminating variables – that is, the institutions in a specific cluster have similar characteristics – and high between-cluster variation – that is, the universities in the various clusters have different features. This type of analysis is not definitive. There are no clear *a priori* grounds for the selection of discriminating variables, nor are there clear *a priori* reasons for selecting the number of clusters (other than purely numerical relationships). Nonetheless, this methodology allows the identification of groups of universities with similar characteristics. The study of the characteristics of the universities included in the different groups enables one to underscore a few main features of the European university system.

The analysis addresses two main problematiques. On the one hand, the study of the different characteristics of the institutions included in the various clusters gives some indication of the policy impact. As will be discussed in the following sections, the clusters are formed on the basis of size and output indicators, thus the existence of different clusters indicates that groups of universities tend to have similar research output 'strategies'. Among other factors, university policies strongly influence the different behaviours. On the other hand, the existence of different groups of institutions with high between cluster variation points to the fact that, due to the heterogeneity of the university system, the consequences of policies are different in the various clusters. Therefore, it highlights the need for national and European policies shaped in relation to the various sub-groups of institutions.

The chapter is organised as follows. Section 4.1 introduces a set of statistical indicators of the European higher education system for the period 1981–95, followed by a statistical analysis of the total population of European universities (Section 4.1.1). Section 4.2 presents the methodology used and its implementation in the case of the total European population. Finally, in the conclusions some policy implications will be put forward.

4.1   THE EUROPEAN HIGHER EDUCATION SYSTEM

The aim of this section is to draw an accurate picture of the European university system. The section is divided into two main parts. First, the higher education R&D statistics and the main publication indicators for the period 1981–95 will be analysed. Second, a statistical analysis of the total population of European universities in 1992 will be put forward.

In the Frascati manual, the basis for measuring R&D in OECD countries, the higher education sector is defined as:

> All universities, colleges of technology and other institutions of post-secondary education, whatever their source of finance or legal status. It also includes all research institutes, experimental stations and clinics operating under the direct control of, or administered by, or associated with higher education establishments.

This definition has been interpreted in different ways by the OECD member countries. Important differences are present in the way government-funded research institutions are classified. For example, while the Centre National de la Recherche Scientifique (CNRS) in France is classified in the higher education sector, the Consiglio Nazionale delle Ricerche (CNR) in Italy, which has broadly the same functions of the CNRS, is accounted for in the government sector (OECD, 1981). Keeping in mind these limitations, the R&D performed in the higher education sector can be used to analyse the development of the research effort in the European higher education system.

Table 4.1 illustrates the higher education expenditure on R&D (HERD) – values and intensities – for the four main EU countries and for the EU countries together[1] in the period 1981–95. The four main EU countries account for about four-fifths of the total R&D expenditure on higher education in the EU countries. In the period considered, Germany, France and UK showed a compound annual growth rate of about 3.5 per cent while, in part due to the lower starting level, the growth rate for Italy was 5.6 per cent. The share of HERD in the gross domestic expenditure on R&D (GERD) allows an evaluation of the changes in the higher education expenditure on R&D compared to the total R&D expenditure. On the one hand, the 1980s are characterised by a group of countries (Denmark, Finland, France, Germany, The Netherlands, Spain and Sweden) with a reducing HERD intensity, and a group (Greece, Ireland, Italy and the UK)[2] with increasing HERD intensity. The early 1990s witnessed an increased importance of higher education expenditure in all the countries except for Denmark and Sweden. Finally, the mid 1990s seem to be characterised by a general stagnation or reduction of HERD intensity. The rise of HERD share in the early 1990s is due more to a reduction in the GERD growth rate, as pointed out by the reduction from 1.97 per cent in 1989 to 1.92 per cent in 1993 of the ratio GERD/GDP for the EU countries together, than to a relevant increase in the HERD share. This view is confirmed by the small increase of the ratio HERD/GDP; of the four main EU countries only Italy showed major improvements. In particular, after a period of increasing intensity, decreasing or constant HERD intensity characterised all EU countries in the mid 1990s.

Table 4.1   Higher education expenditure on R&D

		1981	1985	1989	1993	1995	CAGR 81–95
	Germany	3515	3600	4551	5757	5753	3.6%
	France	2586	2869	3333	3852	4041	3.2%
HERD	UK	2231	2566	2995	3351	3744	3.8%
	Italy	1161	1711	2212	2623	2501	5.6%
	EU10	11859	13688	16773	20416	21064	4.2%
	Germany	15.6%	13.5%	14.4%	18.1%	18.1%	1.1%
	France	16.4%	15.0%	14.9%	15.8%	16.7%	0.1%
HERD/GERD	UK	13.6%	14.7%	15.3%	17.1%	19.0%	2.4%
	Italy	17.9%	19.2%	19.8%	25.0%	25.5%	2.6%
	EU	17.4%	16.6%	17.4%	20.4%	20.8%	1.3%
	Germany	0.38%	0.37%	0.41%	0.44%	0.42%	0.7%
	France	0.32%	0.34%	0.35%	0.39%	0.39%	1.4%
HERD/GDP	UK	0.32%	0.33%	0.33%	0.37%	0.38%	1.2%
	Italy	0.16%	0.22%	0.24%	0.28%	0.26%	3.5%
	EU	0.30%	0.31%	0.34%	0.39%	0.38%	1.7%

Note: Millions of US$ PPP; Price index 1990.

Source: Elaboration OECD data.

Overall, the EU higher education expenditure on R&D has experienced a moderate growth all along the considered period. There are, however, important differences among countries. While the R&D-intensive countries have shown constant or slightly increasing R&D expenditure, both at the gross domestic level and in the higher education system, the countries that started with lower expenditure levels realised higher increases.

The R&D performed in the higher education system can be analysed in relation to the different financial source. The higher education sector usually draws from four national sources of funds and from a generic 'abroad'. They are:

- *Government*, subdivided into *direct government funds* (DGF) – for example, contracts and earmarked funds – and *general university funds* (GUF);
- *Business enterprises* – for example, R&D contracts;
- *Abroad* (including foreign companies' research contracting and EU research funds);
- *Private non-profit organisations* (NPO);
- *Higher education* (HE), own funds – for example, income from endowments.

Table 4.2   HERD source of funds for and aggregate of seven EU countries (%)

	Total Gov.	GUF	DGF	Business	Abroad	NPO	HE
1983	94.0	68.3	25.7	2.9	0.6	1.5	1.1
1985	92.7	65.2	27.5	3.7	0.7	1.7	1.3
1989	89.9	60.2	29.7	5.4	1.4	2.1	1.2
1991	89.4	61.7	27.7	5.5	1.6	2.3	1.2
1993	87.7	60.1	27.6	5.8	2.5	2.7	1.4
1995	85.6	57.2	28.4	5.7	3.2	3.7	1.8

Notes:
The seven countries are: Denmark, France, Germany, Italy, Ireland, The Netherlands and the UK. Belgium, Greece and Spain have been excluded due to missing or not comparable data.

Source: Elaboration of OECD data. The breakdown in GUF and DGF has been estimated for Italy.

Table 4.2 presents the evolution of the relative share of the HERD funding sources for an aggregate of seven EU countries between 1983 and 1995 (see Table 4.A1 in Appendix 4.2 for a ten countries breakdown[3]). These seven countries are responsible for about 80 per cent of total HERD performed in the EU countries throughout the period.

In six of the ten countries considered government funds account for more than four-fifths of total expenditures. Only Greece, Ireland and the UK have lower shares of about 70 per cent in 1995.[4] All countries, without exception, witnessed a decrease in the importance of government funds. For example, in France the share of government funds decreased from 98 to 91 per cent while in the UK it fell from 82 to 68 per cent. Greece, the UK and Ireland show the largest reduction and have the lowest share of government funds at the end of the period. On the other hand, Germany, France and Italy suffered only a small reduction in government funding and had the highest shares at the end of the period. These changes mask differences by the type of government funding. While general university funds tend to be allocated on the basis of incremental funding or some form of formula funding, direct government funds are principally funnelled through contractual funding – for example research funds from the Research Councils or Ministries. In all the countries, the share of general university funds has substantially declined, while the share of direct government funds has increased, although not sufficiently to offset the decrease in the other component of government funding.

Among the other possible reasons for these changes, the following two are particularly important. First, the budget constraints suffered by the various national governments during the 1980s and early 1990s, have caused an overall reduction in the funds to the higher education sector. Second, governments have developed policies aimed at a more purpose-directed allocation of the research effort, and at the creation of quasi-market incentive structures to increase the contribution of the higher education system to specific objectives.[5] Thus, the decrease of GUF and rise of direct government funds can be interpreted as the result of the implementation of selective policies.

The declining importance of government funding has been compensated for by a rise in the share of the other sources of funds. Where the figures are available, abroad, private non-profit organisations, business, and higher education sources of funds show positive trends.

The growth in finance from abroad is particularly important. In the period under consideration funding from a country different from that of the institution experienced a compound annual growth rate of 23 per cent for the aggregate of the seven countries. Funding from abroad became extremely important for the higher education systems of the small less-advantaged countries such as Greece, Ireland and Portugal.[6] Particularly for these countries, but also for the other EU countries, an important part of the funds received from abroad can be ascribed to the European Commission (Commission of the European Communities, 1994a, 1997a).[7] Generally, the growth in foreign funding for R&D performed in the higher education sector is an indication of the increased internationalisation (Europeanisation) of university research.

A continuous increase throughout the period under consideration has been witnessed in the funds from private non-profit organisations (usually private foundations). In the European context, different from the US, private foundations started to play a significant role in the funding of university research only at the end of the 1980s. Although at the aggregate level NPO funds account for only 3.7 per cent of total higher education expenditures on R&D, in countries such as the UK, The Netherlands and Denmark private non-profit organisations have become the second most important source of funding at the end of the period.

The share of HERD financed by business showed positive growth rates in all EU countries during the 1980s. The increase has been particularly important for the nations that started from a low share, while countries such as Germany and Ireland, which already had relatively high values, witnessed only a moderate rise. The case of Belgium is peculiar. Although Belgium had the highest share of HERD financed by business enterprises in 1983, Belgium showed a relevant growth rate, maintaining the highest share throughout the considered period (industrial funding was responsible for about 10 per cent of HERD performed in Belgian institutions in 1995). From 1989 onwards, at the aggregate level (seven countries together) the share of business enterprise funding remained almost constant. However, at the country level different tendencies can be highlighted. The countries with high levels of industrial funding of university research witnessed constant or decreasing shares of business funds (for certain countries there has been a reduction in real amounts of funding), while most of the nations that started from a low share showed positive growth rates.

In the 13 years considered the share of HERD financed by government decreased by about eight percentage points. Two periods can be identified. In the first, up to *circa* 1989, the increasing industrial funding accounted for most of the difference. In the second period, during the 1990s, other sources of funds, such as private foundations and the European Commission, contributed significantly to the funding of higher education expenditures on R&D, while business funding stagnated or, in certain cases, even decreased.

The analysis developed above is concerned with a limited number of input indicators of the R&D process carried out in the higher education sector in the EU countries. In the following a few aggregate research output indicators will be briefly examined. The three methods most commonly used to evaluate research performance are publications counts, citations analysis and peer review. They are usually calculated from the database Science Citation Index of the ISI. As discussed in Appendix 4.1, these indicators have some relevant limitations such as the fact that depending on the selected type of publications (journal articles, book articles, reviews, notes, letters, books, and so on) the output indicator may vary considerably. Moreover, the publicly available data used in the following analysis refer to the aggregate country production without allowing a separate identification of the higher education sector output. For example, in the period 1981–91, in the UK the higher education sector accounted for about 60 per cent of the total number of publications, hospitals, academic and non-academic, between 19 and 23 per cent, research council laboratories 11 per cent and industry 8 per cent (Katz *et al.*, 1995).

Table 4.3　Scientific publications, world and EU shares, and impact factor

	World weight			EU weight			Impact factor
	1995	Growth 83–91	Growth 90–95	1995	Growth 83–91	Growth 90–95	1995
EU	32.6	103	108	100.0	100	100	0.9
Austria	0.6	106	110	1.8	n.a.	102	0.8
Belgium	0.9	100	110	2.7	96	102	1.0
Denmark	0.8	89	103	2.4	86	96	1.0
Finland	0.7	99	118	2.1	n.a.	110	0.9
France	5.1	110	108	15.6	107	100	0.9
Germany	6.3	95	101	19.5	92	94	1.0
Greece	0.4	140	127	1.2	135	118	0.4
Ireland	0.2	102	85	0.7	98	78	0.7
Italy	3.1	123	119	9.7	119	110	0.8
The Netherlands	2.1	118	109	6.4	114	101	1.1
Portugal	0.2	209	148	0.5	202	137	0.6
Spain	2.1	206	153	6.4	199	142	0.6
Sweden	1.6	99	98	4.8	n.a.	91	1.0
UK	8.5	91	103	26.2	88	95	1.0

Notes:
Values in 1991 = mean value 1989–91; value in 1983 = mean value 1981–83.
Values in 1995 = mean value 1993–95; value in 1990 = mean value 1988–90.
For the growth index 1983 = 100 and 1990 =100.

Source:　OST (1994, 1998).

Table 4.3 illustrates the world and EU publication share, and the impact factor[8] for the EU countries in 1995, and their evolution in the period 1983–91 and 1990–95. The EU countries together account for 32.6 per cent of world publications, showing a constant increase over the period. This rise is mainly due to the growth in the publication output of the southern European countries, probably also due to the increasing propensity of these countries to publish in English. The European situation is characterised by a similar pattern. The UK with 26.2 per cent of European publications is the country with the largest share; together with Germany and France they account for about 65 per cent of EU publications. The citations counts put the EU slightly under the world mean. Only The Netherlands succeeded in having an impact factor higher than 1. The indicator of growth points to a slight reduction in the impact of EU publications throughout the period under consideration. Only a few countries, and especially Spain, have witnessed an increase in the relevance of their publications as measured by the impact factor.

To better understand the implication of the ongoing changes in the higher education system, an analysis at a more detailed level is needed. The following study aims to develop a better understanding of the characteristics of the European universities in the early 1990s.

4.1.1   Contemporary European Universities

In 1992, the total HEI population in the EU countries considered[9] was approximately 1429 institutions. Of these, 379 were universities and 1050 PSIs.[10] An institution is classified in the category university following the official national classification. However, in Europe there is no standardisation on the definition of PSI and university. In the different countries these terms carry varying connotations. Nonetheless, in all the EU countries, the institutions (the new postwar universities) that have been granted university status went through a national selection process that can be considered more stringent than that for the granting of PSI status. Therefore the category including universities can be considered more homogeneous at the European level. In addition to the national classification systems two other main sources of information have been used: (1) the *International Handbook of Universities* (1991, 1993), and (2) the *World of Learning* (1995). Where discrepancies between the sources were found, an institution has been classified in the category university if that institution was entitled to grant a doctoral (PhD) degree. In a few cases, mainly in Spain and Portugal, the most recent and not yet developed universities were not taken into account. When clearly distinguishable Art, Physical Education and Education schools were excluded.[11] The three institutions Universitair Centrum Antwerpen, Universitaire Faculteiten Sint-Ignatius te Antwerpen and Universitaire Instelling Antwerpen have been subsumed under the hat of the University of Antwerp. Finally, to calculate the number of UK universities the data from the Universities' Statistical Record (1994) was used. The resulting value of 71 is due to the fact that the University of London is subdivided into 22 colleges; both the University of Cambridge and the University of Oxford are included as single institutions (the different colleges forming them have not been considered); the three institutions Manchester Business School, Manchester University and UMIST have been subsumed in the University of Manchester.[12]

Table 4.4   Count and share of HEIs and universities in 1992, by country

	B	D	F	G	Gr	I	Ir	Nl	P	S	UK	Tot
HEIs	76	41	535	270	17	69	34	32	57	48	250*	1429
Percentage	5.3	2.9	37.4	18.9	1.2	2.4	4.8	2.2	4.0	3.4	17.5	100
No. Univ.	15	7	73	75	15	47	7	13	17	39	71	379
Percentage	4.0	1.8	19.3	19.8	4.0	12.4	1.8	3.4	4.5	10.3	18.7	100

Notes: B = Belgium, D = Denmark, F = France, G = Germany, Gr = Greece, I = Italy, Ir = Ireland, Nl = The Netherlands, P = Portugal, S = Spain, UK = United Kingdom.

Table 4.4 shows the count and share of universities and HEIs broken down by EU country. France (73), Germany (75) and the United Kingdom (71) together have about three-fifths of all European universities. About one-fifth is shared between Italy (47) and Spain (39). Finally, the universities of the six small countries, Belgium, Denmark, Greece, Ireland, The Netherlands and Portugal, account for the last fifth of the population.

For each university, on top of the geographical information, the following data have been gathered:[13]

NEWOLD: — the institution founding year. This has been turned into a categorical variable (with four values) to classify the institutions in relation to their historical age.

No. researchers: — the number of researchers in 1992[14]

No. students: — the number of full-time students in 1992.

EU participation: — the number of times the institution has been involved in an EU R&D project. Refers only to shared-cost actions funded by the DG XII under the First, Second and Third Framework Programmes[15]

Publications: — the number of papers published within a specific institution in 1993.

From these row data, two other variables have been constructed. They are:

Researchers per student: — the ratio between the number of researchers and the number of students. It is used as a proxy for the research orientation of the university.

Publications per researcher: the ratio between the number of publications and the number of researchers. It is used as a proxy for the scientific research productivity of the university.

To avoid giving a misleading description, a few remarks concerning the kind of data gathered are required here. First, the figure for the number of researchers refers to both teachers and researchers. Due to different ways of classifying university personnel in the various EU countries – that is, in Germany and The Netherlands the teachers' group accounts also for short-term lecturers and student assistants – the Germanic countries tend to have a positive bias in the number of researchers.

Second, the variable *Publications* has been built only on the basis of the Science Citation Index. *Publications* is, thus, relevant for medical, natural and engineering sciences and not for the other fields of knowledge present in universities. Three main approaches are usually applied to the count of publications. They are: (1) a fractional count, where the paper is divided up between the contributing authors; (2) an all-author count, in which the paper is credited to each of the participating authors; and (3) a first author count, in which the paper is attributed to the first author only. All three methods have advantages and drawbacks. For the purposes of this book, the all-author count approach has been applied.[16] This method has been chosen for the following reasons. First, it is a rather simple and straightforward method especially in the case of a large number of institutions. Second, the fact that the indicator is calculated for similar institutions, with similar publication profiles, reduces some of the impact of differing publication practices. On the other hand, due to the variance in the disciplinary composition of universities systematic differences may still exist in the propensities to co-author in various scientific fields. This can introduce a positive bias in favour of those disciplines, such as medicine[17] or physics, where it is more common to have publications with a large number of co-authors.[18] Finally, co-authorship requires common competencies and common work, making it difficult to assign a fraction of the credit to the contribution of each author. Therefore, the variable *Publications*, due to the way in which it has been built, can be considered only as a partial proxy of the scientific research output of each university.

Third, the variables *NEWOLD*, *Publications* and *EU participation* are arguably poor measures for the French university system. In 1970 a large number of French universities were subdivided into two or more different institutions. It was difficult to assign an exact founding year to these institutions. In listings all of them report the founding date of the predecessor, although at the same time new institutions were established. Still, the old founding year has been used, pushing up in an artificial way the share of old universities.[19] In the process of gathering the publication data, due to the fact that for a number of French authors the faculty affiliation was before the university name, an amount of publications larger than in other countries has not been classified under a specific institution. The variable *Publications* is, thus, biased downward for some of the French institutions. Besides, due to the fact that a large share of scientific research is realised outside the university system,[20] the participation of French universities in EU-funded R&D co-operative projects was underestimated (Geuna, 1996).[21] Finally, the variable *EU participation* refers only to scientific R&D projects, thus, institutions with a clear focus on humanities and social sciences are badly represented in all the countries.

In short, due to the bias present in the variables *Publications* and *EU participation*, the observations concerning research output and scientific research productivity of the universities presented in the following analysis will not be relevant for institutions with an important involvement in humanities and social sciences. The conclusions developed in this chapter, based on research output and scientific research productivity measurements, are only pertinent for natural, medical and engineering sciences.

Table 4.5   Distribution of universities by historical classes

Historical class	No. of Universities	Percentage
Post-1945	144	38.0
1900–1945	32	8.4
1800–1899	77	20.3
Before 1800	126	33.2
Total	379	100

Looking at the historical development of European universities four broad phases can be found.[22] In relation to the founding year of the university, the total university population has been subdivided into four historical classes. They are: (1) the new postwar universities (post-1945); (2) the early twentieth-century universities, that were founded over the period stretching from the starting of the twentieth century to the end of the Second World War (1900–1945); (3) the nineteenth-century universities, that were founded in the period of the so-called German transformation after the founding of the university of Berlin in 1809 by Wilhelm von Humboldt (1800–1899); and (4) the old universities, that were founded before the French revolution (before 1800). Table 4.5 illustrates the count and share of universities broken down by historical classes. The largest class, with 38 per cent of the universities, is the one of the new postwar institutions.

Approximately two-fifths of the active universities were founded in the last 50 years.

Table 4.6   Descriptive statistics for the main variables

Variable	Cases*	Mean	Std dev.	Min.	Max.
No. researchers	371	887	946	15	7 330
No. students	371	15 376	17 628	100	166 301
EU participation	371	49	65	0	420
Publications	371	415	520	5**	3 185
Researchers per student	371	0.078	0.074	0.010	0.652
Publications per researcher	371	0.568	0.971	0.005	12.340

Notes:
* Eight cases have been excluded due to missing data.
** Estimated value.

Table 4.6 presents the descriptive statistics for the six other variables. All the variables show a high kurtosis and a positive skewness (in particular in the case of *Researchers per student* and *Publications per researcher*) that indicate concentration in the values.[23] Taking into account also the high standard deviations and the large differences between Min. and Max., the population of universities can be described as being composed of a large number of small–medium-sized institutions and some very large institutions. Moreover, as the variable *Researchers per student* can be interpreted as the propensity of the institution to carry out research – that is, scientific research orientation – its high skewness points to the fact that a large number of universities have a low scientific research orientation. Finally, as the variable *Publications per researcher* can be used as a proxy for the research productivity of the institution,[24] the population of universities is characterised by a large group of institutions with a low scientific research productivity, and a small group of institutions of high research productivity.

4.2   CLUSTERS OF EUROPEAN UNIVERSITY

On the basis of these observations cluster analysis is used to group the total university population in clusters of institutions with small within-cluster variation for discriminating variables and high between-cluster variation – that is, the institutions in a specific cluster tend to have similar characteristics, while the universities in the various groups have different features. Due to the peculiarities of the French data the analysis has also been carried out with a database that did not include the French universities. As comparable results were found the following discussion will focus on the results for the case of the total university population while the results of the case where the French universities are excluded will be presented only when particularly interesting.

Table 4.7   Latent roots and per cent of total variance

Variable	Prin. comp.	Latent root	% of variable	Cum. %
No. researchers	1	2.54883	42.5	42.5
No. students	2	1.32907	22.2	64.6
Publications	3	1.04758	17.5	82.1
Publications per researcher	4	0.63088	10.5	92.6
Researchers per students	5	0.25512	4.3	96.9
EU participation	6	0.18853	3.1	100.0

The six variables used for the analysis (*NEWOLD* is excluded at this stage of the analysis), due to the high correlation, are firstly combined under principal component – that is, in this way uncorrelated linear combinations of the observed variables are formed.[25] Table 4.7 illustrates the latent roots (variances) and the percentage of total variance explained by each principal component. The first three principal components are selected, all of them have a latent root higher than 1, and 82.1 per cent of the total variance is attributable to them. To construct the three new variables on which the cluster analysis is run, the latent vectors associated with the latent roots after a Varimax rotation[26] are used as weights of the linear combinations

Table 4.8 illustrates the rotated loading matrix for the three principal components. When one looks at the loading (the correlation of the original variables with the principal components) of the first principal component, *No. researchers* and *No. students* have the higher loading (correlation), also *Publications* and *EU participation* have important loading, thus, the new variable represents the combined dimensions of the institution. It is a proxy for the size of the institution. The second principal component has high correlation with *Publications*, *EU participation* and *Publications per researchers*, thus it can be interpreted as an index of the science research output. Finally, the only important correlation of the third principal component is with *Researchers per student*. Therefore, the new variable depicts the research orientation of the institution.

In order to analyse any possible grouping of the institutions according to their salient characteristics a hierarchical cluster analysis[27] on the three new variables – that is, the uncorrelated linear combinations of the six original variables: PRINCOM1, PRINCOM2, PRINCOM3 – was performed. Ward's minimum variance method, that combines clusters with the smallest increase in the overall sum of the squared within-cluster distances, has been chosen due to its propensity for joining clusters with a small number of observations. One characteristic of the hierarchical cluster analysis is that the number of clusters is not fixed. To determine the number of clusters to be analysed, a Scheffé test has been performed with a significance level of 0.05. For each variable used, the test makes a comparison of the means of the various clusters. The best solution by these criteria is given by the grouping into four clusters. The clusters are well separated into the variables PRINCOM1 and PRINCOM2, and less clearly in the variable PRINCOM3. The four cluster solution has also been tested with a non-parametric Kruskal–Wallis Test; the hypothesis that the four clusters come from populations having the same distribution is rejected.

Table 4.8   Rotated loading matrix

Variable	First principal component	Second principal component	Third principal component
No. researchers	0.90903	–0.00894	0.24568
No. students	0.85033	–0.00832	–0.27436
Publications	0.66416	0.64028	–0.01062
Publications per researcher	–0.21552	0.85673	0.11344
Researchers per student	–0.00766	0.05094	0.98412
EU participation	0.48950	0.61628	–0.07248

Grouping the universities according to their salient characteristics – that is, number of researchers, number of students, participation in EU R&D projects, publications, researchers per student and publications per researcher – four main clusters of institutions are identified. Cluster I is composed of 192 universities, Clusters II and IV include a smaller number of institutions, respectively 107 and 64, and only eight institutions form Cluster III.

Table 4.9   Cluster composition, count and share of universities

| Clusters | Total university population | | Exclusion of France | |
	Frequency	Per cent	Frequency	Per cent
Cluster I	192	51.8	168	56.2
Cluster II	107	28.8	56	18.7
Cluster III	8	2.2	7	2.3
Cluster IV	64	17.3	68	22.7
Total	371	100.0	299	100.0

Table 4.9 shows the number and share of universities in each cluster. The exclusion of France causes the movement of eight universities from the second to the fourth cluster and one the other way, while thirty-three universities transferred from the second to the first cluster and one from the third to the first.

What are the characteristics of the cluster? First, the historical composition of the clusters is studied. Tables 4.A2a and 4.A2b in Appendix 4.2 illustrate the frequency chart for the four historical classes defined above for the case of the total university population and for the case of the exclusion of France. Most of the institutions included in Cluster I were founded after the Second World War; more than 73 per cent of the new postwar universities are included in this cluster. Cluster IV is composed of a majority of medieval universities and only 7.8 per cent of the institutions of this cluster are new postwar institutions. Clusters II and III do not show a relevant concentration of institutions in any of the four historical classes. If one thinks in terms of pre-war versus postwar universities Cluster IV can be defined as the cluster of the pre-war universities, while for Cluster I it is possible to speak only of stronger polarisation towards the new postwar universities. When the French universities are excluded from the analysis the share of the new postwar universities included in Cluster I increases. This is consistent with the bias in the historical classification of French universities, and thus Cluster I can be defined as the cluster of the new postwar universities.

Second, size, scientific research quality and research orientation of the universities in the three clusters with a relevant population are analysed (see Table 4.10). Cluster I is composed of institutions with a mean of 454 researchers and a mean of 9364 students. They have participated in a mean of 13 EU R&D projects, and they have published a mean of 81 publications. The research orientation, expressed in number of researchers per student, has a mean value of 0.066. The mean scientific research productivity of the institution in terms of publications per researcher is 0.198. Comparing these values with those of the total population one can highlight that the 192 universities of Cluster I tend to be of small size, they have a low output in terms of publications and participation in EU R&D projects, and they have a scientific research productivity and research orientation lower than the mean of the population. The 64 members of Cluster IV are large universities (mean number of researchers of 2115 and mean number of students of 38 304), they participated in a large number of EU-funded R&D co-operative projects (mean number of EU participation of 125) and they tend to publish prolifically (mean number of publications of 1174). Their mean scientific research propensity and research orientation tend to be higher than those of the total population, but not in an extremely important way. Cluster II is characterised by institutions with a mean number of researchers and students slightly smaller than the total population (782 and 13 532) and a mean number of participation and publications higher than the total (72 and 560).

The research orientation is a bit lower then the average (0.069), while the mean scientific research productivity of the institutions tends to be higher than that of the total population, and the highest of the four clusters (0.912). Of particular interest, not for the statistics but for the institutions included, is Cluster III. Five of the eight institutions are London University Medical Schools. Due to way the publications are gathered these schools are characterised by an extremely high number of publications, and they have extremely high values in both researchers per student and publications per researcher. The existence of a cluster of this type testifies to the discriminatory power of the statistical methods used.

Table 4.10   Cluster composition, mean values for the 6 variables

	Cluster I (Mean values)	Cluster II (Mean values)	Cluster IV (Mean values)
No. researchers	454	782	2 115
No. students	9 364	13 532	38 304
EU participation	13	72	125
Publications	81	560	1 174
Researchers per student	0.066	0.069	0.091
Publications per researcher	0.198	0.912	0.617
No. of universities	192	107	64

Note: For each variable the non-parametric Kruskal–Wallis Test has been run. The hypothesis that the four clusters come from populations having the same distribution is rejected.

The same kind of analysis has been carried out with the database in which the French universities are excluded. The movement of institutions among the above-mentioned clusters tends to slightly increase the mean values of output, scientific research productivity and research intensity for Cluster I, pushes all the value of Cluster II only a bit above the average of the total population (954, 17 730, 79, 583, 0.061, 0.755) and increases in a significant way the scientific research quality of the institutions of Cluster IV (0.734). A possible interpretation of these results is that the exclusion of the French universities[28] induces the attraction in Cluster I of the institutions on the left side of the distribution of Cluster II. Consequently some of the institutions on the right side of the distribution of Cluster II are attracted to Cluster IV. In this case the divide between Cluster I and Cluster IV becomes even clearer, while the institutions in Cluster II tend to have characteristics, including the scientific research productivity, that position them somewhere between the two extreme configurations of Cluster I and Cluster IV.

A frequency analysis has also been carried out. The variables *No. researchers*, *EU participation*, *Publications*, *Researchers per student* and *Publications per researcher* have been transformed into categorical variables at the quartile. In this way five indexes, one of size, two of research output, one of research intensity and one of scientific research productivity have been built. The association of these indexes with the clusters formed enables us to confirm the previous observations.

The analysis of the European university population in the early 1990s points to the existence of two clearly distinct clusters of institutions. The first (Cluster I) is mainly composed of new postwar universities characterised by: (1) small size, (2) low research output in terms of scientific publications and participation in EU R&D projects, and (c) low research orientation and low scientific research productivity. The second (Cluster IV) comprises almost exclusively pre-war universities (in particular medieval institutions) characterised by: (1) large size, (2) high research output, and (3) high scientific research productivity. These two models of university – on the one hand new postwar, small, teaching-oriented universities, and on the other hand old, very large, research active institutions – are the extremes of a continuum of possible configurations. A third group of universities (Cluster II) characterised by a less clear-cut configuration has been identified too.

4.3   CONCLUSIONS

The picture of the European university population drawn in the previous sections tends to confirm the view that after a period of rapid growth and a period of budget cuts and policy changes, some of the prestigious pre-war universities have managed to retain a position of pre-eminence, whereas the large majority of the new postwar universities did not succeed in increasing their status. Although some of them tried to upgrade their status, perhaps due to the impact of cumulative and self-reinforcement phenomena, they usually did not succeed.

One of the main reasons for the polarisation of the university system can be found in the increased competitive character of university research funding, aimed at the concentration of research resources, that exacerbates the consequences of the Matthew effect. A good researcher is usually attracted by centres or universities of excellence where she can find the human and physical capital that will enable her to develop high level research. Thereby she will improve her quality and the overall quality of the institution, with the consequence of attracting new research funds and new high value researchers. This situation is characterised by two interrelated virtuous circles. First, a centre of excellence attracts high quality researchers that have a high probability of doing valuable research, thus increasing the quality of the centre and therefore attracting new talented researchers. Second, a high level of human and physical capital implies a higher chance of achieving important research results, hence as a consequence of the high quality research there is an increased probability of having new research funds and therefore a possibility of expansion in the investment in human and physical capital.

The changes in the knowledge production emphasised at the end of Chapter 3, Section 3.3 – that is, (1) the old universities are no longer spanning the knowledge spectrum, (2) the rise of the research centre as the intellectual unit of research, and (3) the development of the research network – are more likely in the pre-war institutions highly involved in scientific research. These research-intensive universities, usually elite pre-war institutions and a handful of new institutions, probably will go through a process of institutional change adapting to the changing environment, while retaining a few of the features, such as their autonomy, that characterised universities in their historical evolution. The institutions in the lower scientific research productivity cluster, either involved in technological research or purely teaching institutions, will tend to be marginalised by the ongoing changes. These institutions, pushed by government policy to satisfy the current needs of the society in terms of mass higher education and industrially-oriented research, will tend to increase their national or local focus and will be only partially influenced by the changes in the international production of knowledge. Less clear is the position of the universities in the intermediate cluster. For them, the changes in the knowledge production process probably will be a strong challenge to move towards the cluster with higher scientific research productivity.

The results of the econometric analysis suggest that the changes that occurred in the university research funding structure (decrease of general university funds, less than proportional increase of direct government funds, increase of the other sources of funds based on competitive allocation mechanisms) during the 1980s have already produced an extremely high level of concentration of university research. A further increase in the use of competitive mechanisms for the allocation of public funds may result in a drift of those institutions that were classified in an intermediary position towards the low research-intensive configuration.

Although this situation is more evident in a country such as the UK where budget cuts and market push have been more relevant, it can be considered a general trend. The other EU countries are following, with different delays, the British path. For example, currently in The Netherlands and in some German Länder, research assessment exercises after the model of the first UK Research Assessment Exercise have been developed. Systems of linking government research contract funds with industry receipts – that is, if this year the research centre raises £50 000 from research contracts funded by industry, next year the government will offer contracts for the same amount – are becoming common in all university systems. Selective reductions of state financing of university research, in the expectation of a substitution of industrial research funding, are part of the changes going on in the university systems of all EU countries.

During the last ten years the Commission of the European Communities financed a series of programmes targeted at developing university–university and university–industry research cooperations at the European level. Programmes such as Human Capital and Mobility, for the mobility of graduate and postgraduate students, and the other research actions of the Framework Programmes supported the development of international relationships. As will be shown in Chapter 6, due to the selection criteria used by the Commission of the European Communities, the elite research-intensive universities tend to be the higher education institutions with the highest level of participation in these international research networks. An example is the situation in the UK. In the period 1990–1993 the universities that had large receipts from the Research Council also obtained a large amount of funds from the EU (David, Geuna and Steinmueller, 1995). Thus, national policies aiming at the concentration of university research may be further reinforced by the action of the Commission of the European Communities.[29]

To better understand the possible consequences of current changes an analysis at a more detailed level is needed. In the following chapter a specific group of British universities is studied to assess how they are adapting to recent modifications to funding allocation procedures. Next, in Part III, the implications for European universities of participation in EU-funded R&D co-operative projects will be directly examined.

NOTES

1. Luxembourg is never included. HERD values for Austria, Belgium, Greece and Portugal are not available for all the points in time considered, hence they have not been included.
2. The positive trend of the UK is mainly due to a very low growth rate of total R&D expenditure.
3. See Kyvik (1997) for the analysis of university research funding in the four Nordic countries in the period 1981–93.
4. Also Belgium and Spain had a low share of government funds in 1995, however the figures for the last year are a break in the series and therefore are not discussed here.
5. See Section 2.2 for the analysis of the competitive approach to university research behaviour and funding. See Chapter 5 for the analysis of the changes that occurred in the UK higher education system during the 1980s and early 1990s.
6. The share of HERD financed by 'abroad' in Portugal was 16.8 per cent of the total in 1992.
7. See Chapter 6 for the analysis of the participation of European universities into the EU Framework Programmes.
8. The impact factor is the mean number of citations received in the two years following publication compared to a world average of 1.
9. Austria, Finland, Luxembourg, and Sweden are not included.
10. The 1050 also included 39 new British universities. These were polytechnics and colleges that had been granted university status in 1992–93; as they were mainly teaching institutions, it

is important to differentiate them from the 'old' British universities. Moreover, many of the PSIs, especially in France, also fall within the framework of one of the universities.

11. In most of the countries these schools are not included in the university category. In the few cases in which they have university status, they were not counted.

12. Both in the case of the University of Antwerp and the University of Manchester the different institutions have been subsumed due to the impossibility of identifying a more detailed institutional association of the scholars in the publications counts.

13. Data sources are given in Annex A.

14. The number of researchers includes the totality of full-time academic staff plus, when present, 50 per cent of part-time academic staff.

15. See Chapter 6 Section 6.3 for a detailed description of the data source.

16. A similar approach is also applied by Katz et al. (1995) in the bibliometric analysis of British science.

17. Special mention must be made of the peculiar role played by hospitals. Their weight in the presence count is not just overestimated because of the effect of co-authorship, it is also often unclear whether they are linked to the university or not. Hence in some cases the publication is counted as university and in others as hospital. This varies among the European countries due to institutional variety (Commission of the European Communities, 1994a).

18. To limit the importance of this problem in the regression analysis carried out in Chapter 6, control variables for the disciplinary composition of the university have been included.

19. With this attribution of the founding year, 66 per cent of French universities were established before the French revolution. This is the highest figure for the European countries.

20. The CNRS is the principal site where publicly funded scientific research is carried out. Although a part of it is overlapping with the university system, the participation in EU-funded R&D co-operative projects is attributed to the CNRS. Moreover, engineering sciences are primarily studied at the *grande écoles*, that are institutions not included in the class 'university'.

21. See Chapter 6 for the analysis of university participation in EU R&D projects.

22. More detailed sub-divisions, considering also the history of non-European universities, can be found in the historical literature. See, for example, Perkin (1984) and Wittrock (1993).

23. Moreover, the variables are correlated as noted below.

24. The sociology of science and, more recently, empirical studies in the new economics of science have made use of bibliometric analysis. In particular, the idea behind publications or citations counts is that they can be used as an indicator of the underlying productivity of the researcher. Consequently it is possible to depict the scientific research productivity of the university as the ratio between the publications realised in one year and the number of researchers attached to that institution.

25. For a clear description of principal component analysis see Dunteman (1989).

26. The Varimax method attempts to minimise the number of variables that have high loading on a factor. This orthogonal rotation does not affect the goodness of fit of a factor solution, the total variance explained does not change.

27. For a clear description of cluster analysis see Aldenderfer and Blashfield (1984).

28. Due to data gathering problems the French universities tend to be large, but with low output, low scientific research productivity and low research intensity. Thus, the high number of French universities in Cluster I biases the mean values of the cluster.

29. The implications of the overlapping of national and EU university research funding will be analysed in Chapter 7.

APPENDIX 4.1: RESEARCH PERFORMANCE INDICATORS

The main difficulties and drawbacks in using publications counts, citations analysis and peer review are briefly considered here.

Publications counts allow the evaluation of the research output of individuals, research groups, departments or institutions. The per capita publications counts are used as a proxy for the research productivity. Among the most commonly cited shortcomings in the use of publications counts are:

1. Depending on the selected type of publication output (journal articles, books, review articles, and so on), and on the weighting scheme applied, the output indicator may vary considerably (see, for example, Johnes, 1990).
2. The mobility of staff may alter the output of a department in a significant way, consequently different ways of ascribing the output of a researcher to a department – for example, to the one where he was based or to the current one – may have an important impact on the output indicator (see, for example, Nederhof and van Raan, 1993).
3. The determination of the number of staff in a department depends on who is classed as a research member of the department; different counts for research students, PhD students, visiting staff, and so on result in an important variation in the per capita figures (see, for example, Hare and Wyatt, 1988).
4. Particularly in medicine and natural sciences it is common practice to have a large number of co-authors. The publication can be credited to each of the participating authors (all-author count), divided up between the contributing authors (fractional count), or attributed to the first author only (first author count). These different counting methods may give rise to different output indicators.
5. Biases favouring publications of established authors may exist in the publishing process, distorting the significance of the indicator.

The use of publications analysis to measure research performance is constrained by the fact that it represents only a measure of quantity and it does not capture the impact, quality and utility of the research.[1] Citations analysis (the count of the citations obtained by a scientist or a department) is used to assess the impact (quality) of the research output. The database most commonly used is the Science Citation Index (SCI) of the ISI. Some of the shortcomings referred to above are also relevant for citations counts; particularly important for the latter are the following:[2]

1. The SCI tends to have a bias in favour of publications in the English language and especially towards North American sources.
2. The SCI reports only the first author; moreover is not uncommon to find programming errors both in the authors' name and in the journal citation (see, for example, Moed et al., 1985; Cave et al., 1997).
3. Citations are not only to works considered of high quality, but also negative or derogatory works; however, citations counts cannot distinguish between the two.
4. Different citation windows (how many years are considered after their publication) may give rise to variations in the indicator measurement.
5. Self-citations, citations to co-authored papers and citations to different journals all require the development of weighting schemes that at present cannot be done in an objective way.
6. Seminal or radical works may be difficult to understand or, after their acceptance, they become common knowledge, hence they may not receive the number of citations that they deserve (see, for example, Cole and Cole, 1972).
7. Citations counts can be distorted by the inappropriate use of the citation such as in the case of citations circle (researchers unduly citing each other) or citations for reconnaissance (junior staff citing senior researchers).

The difficulties and drawbacks of citations analysis and its costly and time-consuming character indicate that, at the current level of methodological development and with the available technology, this technique is not optimal for a comparative evaluation of the research performance of universities.

The last research performance indicator briefly considered here is peer review. A large body of literature has been devoted to the analysis of the peer review system in science.[3] As a performance indicator peer review is most commonly understood as the evaluation (ranking) of the research output of a department by peers. It allows a quantitative judgement of the research including the analysis of cognitive aspects such as contribution to basic knowledge and contribution to methodology. The three most important shortcomings of peer review as a performance indicator are:

1. Peer judgement tends to be subjective and not sufficiently systematic.
2. Large departments are usually better known and they contain active researchers in a large set of sub-disciplines, hence they tend to be favoured in peer reviews not supported by quantitative data.
3. The reputation of the whole institution may exercise a positive bias (the halo effect) on the peer review of the department (Fairweather, 1988).

NOTES

1. A certain level of quality correction can be introduced in the publications counts if the publications are weighted by the impact factor of the journal. For an application of this methodology see, for example, Arora, Gambardella and David (1998).
2. For the analysis of the drawbacks of citations analysis see, among others, Cozzens (1989).
3. For a recent study see Wood (1997).

Allocation of funds and university research

APPENDIX 4.2: TABLES

Table 4.A1   HERD funding sources by countries

		B*	D	F	G*	Gr	I**	Ir	Nl	S	UK*
Direct Govern. %	1981	39.4	10.9	45.1	18.7	10.5	0	14.9	5.7	13.0	20.5
	1985	43.4	12.2	47.0	19.8	n.a.	0	11.5	7.1	24.1	25.0
	1989	25.5	20.6	48.1	22.4	12.0	0	19.0	7.8	27.7	27.6
	1993	25.3	20.9	46.2	21.0	15.7	0	23.0	5.2	20.4	27.4
	1995	38.0	22.6	46.0	n.a.	13.3	0	20.0	6.3	30.1	29.9
GUF %	1981	46.8	85.6	52.6	75.6	89.5	96.2	67.6	91.1	87.0	64.8
	1985	43.4	80.7	49.4	74.3	n.a.	98.0	66.0	88.1	74.7	57.2
	1989	52.2	70.5	45.5	70.6	71.6	96.4	46.7	87.6	62.0	47.3
	1993	50.4	66.5	46.1	69.9	43.4	93.4	41.1	90.7	69.6	41.9
	1995	34.9	66.8	44.6	n.a.	59.1	92.0	42.0	79.3	40.3	37.8
HE %	1981	2.9	0	0.9	0	0	0	0.4	0.3	0	3.8
	1985	2.7	0	1.4	0	n.a.	0	2.3	0.2	0	4.2
	1989	5.6	0	1.0	0	0.3	0	4.2	0.1	0	4.8
	1993	3.4	0	2.3	0	5.9	0	4.4	0.1	0	4.3
	1995	6.8	0	4.0	0	4.1	0	4.5	0.3	13.7	4.2
Business %	1981	9.3	0.7	1.3	5.7	0	2.7	7.1	0.3	0	3.1
	1985	8.7	1.0	1.9	5.9	n.a.	1.5	6.9	1.0	1.1	5.2
	1989	12.6	1.5	4.6	7.0	6.2	2.6	9.2	1.1	9.2	7.7
	1993	14.6	1.8	3.3	8.1	3.8	4.8	7.1	1.5	5.9	7.6
	1995	10.6	1.8	3.3	7.9	5.6	5.6	6.9	4.0	8.3	6.2
NPO %	1981	0	1.6	0.1	0	0	0	2.6	2.3	0	5.6
	1985	0	4.3	0.1	0	0	0	1.9	3.1	0	6.4
	1989	0	4.4	0.1	0	0	0	1.8	2.9	0.5	8.4
	1993	0	5.0	0.2	0	0	0	2.1	2.2	0.6	12.2
	1995	1.0	4.5	0.5	0	1.0	0	2.5	6.5	0.5	14.1
Abroad %	1981	1.6	1.3	0	0	0	1.1	7.3	0.3	0	2.2
	1985	1.8	1.8	0.1	0	n.a.	0.6	11.4	0.4	0.1	2.1
	1989	4.1	3.0	0.7	0	10	1.0	19.1	0.5	0.7	4.1
	1993	6.2	5.8	1.9	0.9	31.1	1.8	22.3	0.3	3.5	6.5
	1995	8.7	4.2	1.6	1.2	17.0	2.4	24.0	3.5	7.0	7.8

Notes:

* 1983–95.

** Italy does not supply a breakdown between direct government and GUF, the value refers to total government.

B = Belgium, D = Denmark, F = France, G = Germany, Gr = Greece, I = Italy, Ir = Ireland, Nl = The Netherlands, S = Spain, UK = United Kingdom.

Due to the different ways of classifying the various funds, a zero value either refers to zero funds or the inclusion of the funding type in a different class. With the exclusion of Denmark, France, Italy, Ireland and the UK, in all the other countries there are breaks in the series for a few sources of funds.

Source: Elaboration of OECD data.

Table 4.A2a   Cluster composition, by historical classes (total university population)

Historical Cl.	Cluster I			Cluster II			Cluster III			Cluster IV		
	Count	Row %	Col %	Count	Row %	Col %	Count	Row %	Col %	Count	Row %	Col %
Post-1945	100	73.5	52.1	30	22.1	28.0	1	0.7	12.5	5	3.7	7.8
1990–1945	13	40.6	6.8	9	28.1	8.4	2	6.3	25.0	8	25.0	12.5
1800–1899	28	36.4	14.6	37	48.1	34.6	2	2.6	25.0	10	13.0	15.6
Before 1800	51	40.5	26.6	31	24.6	29.0	3	2.4	37.5	41	32.5	64.1

Table 4.A2b   Cluster composition, by historical classes (excluding French universities)

Historical Cl.	Cluster I			Cluster II			Cluster III			Cluster IV		
	Count	Row %	Col %	Count	Row %	Col %	Count	Row %	Col %	Count	Row %	Col %
Post-1945	99	83.9	58.9	13	11.0	23.2	0	0	0	5	4.3	7.4
1990–1945	16	50.0	9.5	7	21.9	12.5	2	6.3	28.6	7	21.9	10.3
1800–1899	33	45.8	19.6	21	29.2	27.5	2	2.8	28.6	16	22.2	23.5
Before 1800	20	25.6	11.9	15	19.2	26.8	3	3.8	42.9	40	51.3	58.8

5. Allocation of funds and research output: the case of British universities

As the previous two chapters have shown, universities, especially in the UK but also in other European countries, are undergoing profound modifications due to budget constraints and changes in policy regarding their purpose in society. These changes are straining the university structure developed after the Second World War. The role of universities is changing from that of public institutions subsidised by the state into that of suppliers of specific services. Research services offered by the universities are bought by research councils, government departments, charitable foundations, commercial firms and (increasingly) international organisations such as the Commission of the European Communities. On the one hand, the developing market system for university research services has beneficial influences such as reducing financial inefficiency. Nonetheless, on the other hand, given the peculiar features of knowledge production and distribution processes, the market for university research is far from a perfect market, so that the development of a more 'competitive' market does not necessarily imply the production of desirable results from an economic and social point of view (Ziman, 1994).

In this context, and in order to understand the possible results of current changes, it is useful to assess how a specific group of institutions – the multi-disciplinary old British universities – are adapting to recent modifications in funding allocation procedures. The British case has been chosen due to its unique characteristics. The UK is the country of the EU with the most market-oriented university system, and consequently with a clearer propensity, or push, towards a more utilitarian, applied, type of research (a summary of the philosophy behind it is the famous statement 'value for money'). The UK system, with its mission-oriented policies (selective policies), can be considered an 'attraction pole' or model for emulation that other European countries may follow in the restructuring of their university funding systems. Therefore, the understanding of the possible consequences of the ongoing changes in the UK universities can provide insights which can be used to better direct the evolution of the other European university systems.

Current developments in the university research system suggest changing relationships between resource allocation and research output. Using the methodology developed in the previous chapter the 'old' UK universities are clustered in groups of institutions with similar characteristics. The study of the different groups at two points of time and, in particular, of the movement of institutions among groups indicates the existence of relationships between funding and research output.

The chapter is organised as follows. The first section gives a description of the evolution of the funding structure of UK universities. The changes in the different sources of funds in the period 1989–93 are analysed paying particular attention to the evolution of the receipts from specific services (Section 5.1.1). In Section 5.2 the methodology to explore the relationships between allocation of funds and research output is developed. A cluster analysis for the two periods 1989–90 and 1992–93 and the preliminary analysis of the results are presented in Section 5.2.1. The study of the changes in cluster membership and some interpretations are offered in Section 5.2.2. Finally Section 5.3 presents the conclusions and policy implications.

5.1 THE EVOLUTION OF THE FUNDING STRUCTURE OF BRITISH UNIVERSITIES

In recent years the UK higher education funding structure has gone through some marked changes. These transformations were the result of government policies that began, in 1980, with the decision to charge fees to foreign students to cover the full costs of their courses. Then, throughout the 1980s, university, polytechnic and college budgets were restructured in ways that put new pressures (and incentives) on these institutions. A major instrument of reform was a reduction in block grants to HEIs which then were offset, less than proportionately, by increases in funds from other government sources. The actions were undertaken, on the one hand, to stimulate a process of financial restructuring aimed at reducing costs and, on the other hand, to provide incentives (through mechanisms such as the Research Assessment Exercise and the Technology Foresight)[1] by which it was hoped that a better direction of HEIs' research effort would result.

The turning point in the process of change of the funding system was, however, the Education Reform Act of 1988. This Act created two new funding agencies, the Universities Funding Council (UFC) and the Polytechnics and Colleges Funding Council (PCFC), but most importantly it modified the 'logic' of higher education funding. The two agencies were created to act as buyers of academic services. The role of universities, polytechnics and colleges was suddenly transformed, from one of public institutions subsidised by the state into that of private suppliers of specific services – that is, teaching and research. This change implied the creation of a new market for HEIs' services. HEIs had to learn the new rules of the game, such as bidding for students and interacting with other potential buyers of their services such as industry, or the Commission of the European Communities. Furthermore, they had to adapt their management structure and allocation of funds to the new external situation.[2]

The latest step of this revolution has been the merging of UFC and PCFC into a single Higher Education Funding Council (HEFC) with separate agencies for England, Scotland and Wales in 1993. In addition, 39 polytechnics have been granted university status. This new situation is also the result of the White Paper of May 1991 *Higher Education. A New Framework*. The report drew the outline for the new structure of the higher education sector in the UK. Of particular relevance for the funding system are the following. First, it has favoured competition for research funds among all the 'old' universities and polytechnics, which now share a common identity as universities. Second, it endorsed and reinforced the dual support approach. Universities should receive public funds for research from both the national HEFC, and from the Research Councils[3] for specific projects. Third, together with *competition* among institutions and the *dual* system, *selectivity* on the basis of assessment of research quality and the *subdivision* of the block grant in teaching and research are the principles that inform the new structure for public funding.

Finally, in May 1993, as a demonstration of the Government's concern for the science and technology situation, a new White Paper (the 'Waldegrave Report') on science and technology, *Realising our Potential – A Strategy for Science, Engineering and Technology*, was published.[4] Rather than just being another proposal for further changes, it offered an evaluation of what had happened in the preceding years, and a re-thinking of the system of science, engineering and technology in general. Central to the Waldegrave Report is an examination of the research councils' operations. The report proposed to modify two of the existing five research councils. From 1994 there are six active research councils, namely the Natural Environment Research Council (NERC), the Medical Research Council (MRC), the Economic and Social Research Council (ESRC), the new Engineering and Physical Science Research Council (EPSRC) and Particle Physics and Astronomy Research Council (PPARC), and the renamed Biotechnology and Biological Sciences Research Council (BBSRC). The Office of Science and Technology has responsibility for all the research councils and for the LINK programme, 'a cross-Government initiative that aims to bridge the gap between the science and engineering base and industry for the benefit of the United Kingdom economy' (HMSO, 1993, pp. 35).

5.1.1   The Aggregate Situation

Due to the relevance of the Education Reform Act, and the fact that data after 1992–93 are not consistent with those of the previous years, this analysis will focus on the period between 1989–90 and 1992–93. Furthermore, the 'old' universities are the only institutions included due to their distinct research orientation. Indeed, polytechnics and colleges receive much less research funding; in 1989–90 the levels were £1620 million for the 'old' universities and £70 million for polytechnics and colleges (HMSO, 1991, p. 16).[5]

For the four years considered, the Universities' Statistical Record provides an annual report on university funding. All the 'old' universities are covered in this survey. The university funding (income) is broken down in detail by income source. At the most aggregate level the breakdown is between general incomes and specific incomes. The former represent the incomes attributed to teaching and to the part of research not covered by specific sources. The main part of it is due to the HEFC grant (exchequer grants) and to tuition fees (fees). Specific incomes consist of the funds gathered by academic departments or academic services for the supply of specific services to outside parties. Among these services, research grants and contracts are the most important items and the following are the largest buyers of university research: research councils, government bodies, UK-based charitable bodies, UK industry and the Commission of the European Communities.

Table 5.1 shows the evolution of the relative share of the main sources of funds. The most striking trend is the decrease of more than 15 points of the exchequer grants' share in university funding (from 48.4 to 33.3 per cent of the total). This is the result of both the policy of funding a higher share of university research directly through specified projects, and the decision to link part of teaching money to the number of students, via the increase in fees.[6] In addition, the share of fees grew by 11.5 points, raising the share of this funding component to 25.3 per cent. There are two main reasons for this increase. First, the government sought an incentive for increasing the number of students admitted to the university. Thus, to spur on universities to accept more students they increased the money given to the institution for each admitted student. Second, this policy was successful in the sense that the number of students admitted to higher education markedly increased during the period, raising the total funds paid through this source.

Table 5.1   Relative share of university incomes (%)

Year	Excheq. grant	Fees	Total specific	Research councils	Govern. bodies	UK industry	EU
1989–90	48.4	13.8	23.1	6.5	3.0	2.6	1.1
1990–91	39.8	20.7	24.2	6.4	3.3	2.6	1.3
1991–92	35.5	25.0	23.9	6.0	3.1	2.5	1.6
1992–93	33.3	25.3	25.1	7.1	3.1	2.3	1.9

Source: Elaboration of Universities' Statistical Record data.

The share of total specific incomes grew by only 2 points. Consequently, part of the university research that previously was covered by the exchequer grants did not find direct support through specific projects. In particular, the research councils' share of funds, after a slight decrease over two years, increased in the last year. This is mainly due to the new regulation that states that from 1992–93 the research council 'will become responsible for meeting all the costs of the projects, except for academic salaries and premises, which will continue to be met from institutions' general funds' (HMSO, 1991, p. 17).[7] The result is that part of the costs associated with the conduct of research facilities, like libraries, were then paid for by the research councils. The share of funds from UK industry, contrary to the expectations of the government, decreased over the period. This may also be due to the recession period. Nonetheless it points to the fact that, at least in the period analysed, industry funds did not counterbalance decreasing government support at the aggregate level. Finally, the EU funding share, although very low, consistently increased, almost doubling its value over the period. Taking into account that the EU source is part of specific incomes, not only does its relevance increase, but about 50 per cent of the growth of the specific component is the result of the increase of EU funding.

Table 5.2   Annual growth rate of university incomes, constant price 1986, by source (%)

Year	Total	Excheq. grant	Fees	Total specific	Research councils	Govern. bodies	UK industry	EU
89/90–90/91	0.0	–17.7	49.7	4.7	–1.6	11.0	0.4	19.1
90/91–91/92	2.9	–8.4	24.2	1.8	–4.8	–4.6	–1.5	21.6
91/92–92/93	5.9	–0.6	7.2	11.2	26.4	6.1	–4.2	26.4

Source: Elaboration of Universities' Statistical Record data.

Table 5.2 presents the annual growth rate of the various sources of funds expressed in constant 1986 prices.[8] First, the decrease in the real value of exchequer grants, which started during the 1980s, is moderating. Indeed, in 1992–93 there was a nominal (without taking into account inflation) increase. Second, the research council component after two years of decline realised an increase of 26.5 per cent. However, when the real value of the flow of money from the Funding Council (see note 7) is computed, the research council component decreased by 2.3 points. Therefore, it appears that even over the recent past the two most important sources of government funding have shown negative trends. Only in the last year, after the policy decision of increasing the overheads for the contracts funded by the research councils, does it seem possible to identify the impact of the government strategy oriented towards an increase of specific incomes[9] rather than simply cutting both general and specific incomes. Third, UK industry funding receipts, after a negligible rise in real terms during 1989–90/1990–91, show increasingly negative growth rates. Fourth, EU funding receipts have risen throughout the period, whereas the positive growth of university income from fees has been slowing down. Fifth, and finally, after approximately no changes in real terms during 1989–90/1990–91, total recurrent income has shown a positive growth rate during the two following periods.

In summary, these changes have led to offsetting impacts. On the one hand, taking into account the differences in the relative share of funds for exchequer grant and fees,[10] and the fact that student enrolment has grown in the three periods by 5.0, 9.1 and 8.6 per cent respectively, the increase in receipts in real terms from tuition fees has balanced the decrease in the income from the exchequer grant for the teaching side.[11] On the other hand, the growth of specific incomes has not been sufficient to cover the diminishing of general funds for research.

To study the impact on university research output of the changes described above, a more disaggregated approach has to be used. In the next section the relationships among scientific research output, size and funding structure will be analysed at the institutional level.[12]

5.2   ALLOCATION OF FUNDS AND RESEARCH OUTPUT

In order to investigate the relationships among scientific research output, size and funding structure only 'scientific' faculties (natural sciences, engineering sciences, medical sciences and agricultural sciences) have been considered. Social sciences and humanities are not included in the analysed sample of universities. In the period considered there were 72 'old' universities in the UK,[13] of these five did not have scientific faculties. Twenty universities granted a PhD degree in only one or two scientific fields. To reduce the variance in the sample and in order to compare similar institutions, only the institutions that granted a PhD degree in at least three scientific fields have been included in the analysis. For each of the 47 universities considered, the following data have been gathered:[14]

NEWOLD: The founding year of the institution.
NSCIRES: The number of academic staff in the 'scientific' faculties: 1989–90, 1992–93.[15]
SPRUPUBS: Number of papers published by a scholar associated to a specific institution: 1990, 1993.[16]
SCIPRO: The ratio between the number of publications and the number of researchers (*SPRUPUBS/NSCIRES*).

RETOT: The share of research grant and contract receipts in total recurrent income: 1989–90, 1992–93.

INDRE: The share of UK industry receipts in the total amount of funds from research grants and contracts: 1989–90, 1992–93.

The first variable describes the institution in terms of historical development. The variable number of researchers is a measure of input to research; while the number of publications is an indicator of the scientific output dimension. The ratio between the number of publications and the number of researchers is used as a proxy for the scientific research productivity of the university. The share of research grant and contract receipts to the university's total recurrent income is used as a proxy for the research orientation of the institution. Finally, the share of UK industry receipts in the total amount of funds from research grants and contracts can be interpreted as a proxy for the propensity to carry out research of a more applied nature.

The representation of the data according to the analysed characteristics of the universities allows us to highlight the existence of relationships among scientific research output, size and funding structure. Moreover, indications of the impact of the changes occurring in the UK university system during the period 1989–90/1992–93 may be extracted by comparing the data at the start and at the end of the period considered.

5.2.1   Cluster Analysis

In order to analyse any possible grouping of the institutions according to their characteristics a cluster analysis is implemented. More exactly, first principal components are extracted from the original four variables (*NSCIRES, SCIPRO, INDRE, RETOT*), then a hierarchical cluster analysis is performed on the principal components.[17] To define clusters that have small within-variation and high between-variation the same methodology is used for the 47 universities both in 1989–90 and in 1992–93. For simplicity, only the figures that refer to the period 1989–90 are presented in the following description of the methodology.

Table 5.3   Rotated loading matrix

Variables	First principal component	Second principal component	Third principal component
INDRE90	–0.10525	0.98633	–0.06006
SCIPRO90	0.21735	–0.06591	0.97099
RETOT90	0.87844	0.03923	0.25805
NSCIRES90	0.88620	–0.22842	0.09530

The first step consists of extracting the principal components from the original data. Given that 94 per cent of the total variance is explained by the first three principal components (the first two account for only 74 per cent) the four original variables can be reduced to three. The loading (correlation) of the four variables with the three principal components are presented in Table 5.3.[18] The first principal component combines the number of academic staff in the scientific faculties and the share of research grant and contracts receipts in the total recurrent income; it can be defined as a proxy for the scientific research size of the university. The second principal component has a high loading only for the share of UK industry receipts, thus it can be interpreted as an index of the propensity to carry out research of a more applied nature. Finally, the only important loading of the third principal component is related to the ratio between the number of publications and the number of scientific researchers; it can be defined as a proxy for the scientific research productivity of the institution.

To investigate the possible clusters within the three new variables a hierarchical cluster analysis (Ward method) is used. As in the previous chapter, the Scheffé test with a significance level of 0.05 has been used to determine the number of clusters that should be analysed. The best representation of the data is given by the grouping into three clusters. This solution has also been verified with a non-parametric Kruskal–Wallis Test. The hypothesis that the three clusters come from populations having the same distribution is rejected.

Grouping in 1989–90

In the first period three main clusters are identified.[19] Cluster II is composed of the largest number of institutions (42.6 per cent), Clusters I and III include a smaller number of universities (31.9 per cent and 25.5 per cent respectively). What are the characteristics of these clusters?

The first cluster is composed of institutions with a mean of 346 researchers who have published a mean of 173 publications; the mean scientific research productivity of the institution in terms of publication per researcher is 0.51. The average research orientation is 0. 13, and the mean propensity to carry out applied research is 0.20. The institutions that are members of the second cluster are generally of larger size (mean number of researchers of 479) and tend to publish more (mean number of publications of 350). Their mean scientific research productivity is higher than the previous cluster (mean publications per researcher of 0.75). While the research orientation is higher, the average share of industrial funds tends to be lower. Finally, Cluster III is composed of large universities (with a mean number of 1206 researchers) with high publication output (mean number of publications of 1001) and high scientific research productivity (mean publications per researcher of 0.82). As in Cluster II, while the research orientation increases (mean research grant and contract funding share of 0.23)

Allocation of funds and university research

the applied research propensity tends to be lower (mean industry funding of 0.11) (see Table 5.4).

The variable *NEWOLD* is used to study the historical composition of the clusters. Half of the postwar universities are in Cluster I; 60 per cent of the institutions in the cluster were founded in this century. The second cluster is polarised towards old institutions; 60 per cent of the universities in this cluster were created before the twentieth century. In the third cluster the share of institutions founded before the end of the nineteenth century rises to 83.3 per cent; none of the postwar universities are in this cluster.

Table 5.4   Cluster composition in 1989–90, mean values for the 5 variables

Variables*	Cluster I	Cluster II	Cluster III
No. of researchers 90	346	479	1 206
Publications 90	173	350	1 001
Publications per researcher 90	0.51	0.75	0.82
Research funding share 90	0.13	0.16	0.23
Industry funding share 90	0.20	0.15	0.11
No. of universities	15	20	12

Note: * For each variable the non-parametric Kruskal–Wallis Test has been run. The hypothesis that the three clusters come from populations having the same distribution is rejected.

The analysis of the data according to the considered characteristics enables us to define three groups of institutions with small within-cluster variation for discriminating variables – that is, the institutions in a specific cluster have similar characteristics – and high between-cluster variation – that is, the universities in the various clusters have different features. Cluster I is composed mainly of twentieth-century universities with small science faculties that tend to have low scientific research productivity and have the highest propensity to carry out applied research. The institutions in Cluster II are mostly nineteenth-century universities, they tend to have science faculties of bigger size with larger scientific research output and higher research orientation. However, while their mean scientific research productivity is high, their propensity to develop research in collaboration with industry is lower than in the previous cluster. Finally, Cluster III is almost entirely composed of medieval and nineteenth-century universities of very large size that have high scientific research productivity and a low applied research propensity.

In 1989–90 the 47 multidisciplinary UK universities were characterised by a positive relationship among size, research orientation and scientific research output, and a negative relationship between these three variables and applied research propensity (share of contract research and grant financed by UK industry). On the one hand, the institutions of small scientific size with low scientific research productivity of Cluster I, on average, received only 13 per cent of their total recurrent incomes from grants and research contracts, but 20 per cent of these funds were receipts from UK industry. On the other hand, the very large high scientific research productivity universities of Cluster III had 23 per cent of their total recurrent incomes originating in research grants and contracts, but only 11 per cent of these were funded by UK industry. Moreover, the institutions in Cluster I were those with the largest share of UK industry receipts in total recurrent income.

The above analysis seems to point to the existence of a divide between a group of universities of smaller scientific size, with lower scientific research productivity, that tend to have relatively higher relationships with industry, and a group of large institutions with high scientific research productivity that, despite having a significant research orientation, tend to have less important interactions with UK industry. Between these extremes a large group of institutions tend to have average values for the variables considered.

Grouping in 1992–93
In 1992–93 the three-cluster solution also gives the best representation of the data.[20] The first two clusters encompass a similar number of institutions, while the third includes only the universities of Cambridge and Oxford. What are the characteristics of these clusters?

The institutions in the first cluster tend to be of small size (both in the case of the science faculties only and in the case of the complete university),[21] with low scientific research productivity. While their research orientation is low the share of UK industry funds tends to be high. The second cluster is composed of universities of larger size with larger scientific research output and higher scientific research productivity. Even if they have higher research orientation, they tend to have a lower share of research financed by UK industry. Finally, Cambridge and Oxford, due to their peculiar characteristics (the highest scientific research productivity, extremely high research orientation, low share of UK industry funds, and large size and scientific research output) form Cluster III (see Table 5.5). Contrary to the 1989–90 case the analysis of the historical composition of the clusters does not allow us to highlight any historical polarisation either in Cluster I or in Cluster II.[22]

In 1992–93 the 47 UK universities considered tended to be characterised by relationships among size, research orientation and scientific research output similar to the ones of four years before. Also, the negative relation between these three variables and the applied research propensity (share of contract research and grant financed by UK industry) is confirmed. On the one hand the universities of Cluster I received, on average, 14 per cent of their total recurrent incomes from grants and research contracts, and 16 per cent of these funds were receipts from UK industry. On the other hand, the institutions of Cluster II had 20 per cent of their total recurrent incomes originating in research grants and contracts, but only 9 per cent were financed by UK industry.

Table 5.5   Cluster composition in 1992–93, mean values for the 5 variables

Variables*	Cluster I	Cluster II	Cluster III
No. of researchers 93	478	836	1 698
Publications 93	293	667	2 266
Publications per researcher 93	0.60	0.84	1.33
Research funding share 93	0.14	0.20	0.33
Industry funding share 93	0.16	0.09	0.08
No. of universities	24	21	2

*Note: * For each variable the non-parametric Kruskal–Wallis Test has been run. The hypothesis that the three clusters come from populations having the same distribution is rejected.*

Going from 1989–90 to 1992–93 some institutions moved between the clusters. The intermediate Cluster II of 1989–90 disappears. Nine universities have moved to the lower scientific research productivity cluster, while eleven institutions have been attracted by the cluster at the other extreme. What are the characteristics of these institutions? Did their funding structure change in the time interval considered?

5.2.2   An Analysis of the Changing Membership of Clusters

The representation of the data according to the analysed characteristics has underscored the existence of particular relationships among scientific research output, size and funding structure. Given the fact that two different cluster structures are present at the start and at the end of the period considered, it is possible to study whether this modification – the movement of institutions among groups – is related to changes in the funding structure.[23]

In the following section the analysis will focus on the 20 universities that were members of Cluster II in 1989–90.[24] Four years later nine institutions were attracted by the first cluster and eleven by the third cluster.[25] For convenience the first nine are defined as 'downgrading' and the other eleven as 'upgrading', meaning that the former were attracted by Cluster I and the latter by Cluster III. Did the characteristics of these universities change over the time interval under study? In the first period the downgrading institutions were of larger size, with lower scientific research productivity, but they had a research orientation and a propensity to carry out research of a more applied nature (share of contract research and grant financed by UK industry) similar to those of the upgrading universities. Compared to four years before, in 1992–93 the eleven upgrading institutions were characterised by an extremely high scientific research productivity, while their applied research propensity was much lower. The nine universities attracted by Cluster I witnessed only minor changes; nonetheless, given the fact that all the other institutions, on average, saw an important decrease in the share of UK industry receipts (in real terms), their roughly unchanged share of UK industry funds indicates a change in their propensity towards research of a more applied nature.[26]

Going from 1989–90 to 1992–93, on the one hand the eleven upgrading universities increased their scientific research productivity and decreased their applied research propensity, while on the other hand, the nine downgrading universities had a nearly unchanged scientific research productivity retaining a high propensity to conduct research of a more applied nature – that is, financed by UK industry.

Table 5.6   Fractional changes in the real value of university receipts; mean values for institutional receipts from selected funding sources

	9 Downgrading universities	11 Upgrading universities
Exchequer grant	−0.28	−0.23
Research council	0.16	0.34
UK industry	0.15	−0.25
Industry funding share	−0.03	−0.39

Note: For each variable the non-parametric Kruskal–Wallis Test has been run. The hypothesis that the two groups come from populations having the same distribution is rejected.

Table 5.6 shows the mean real changes in the receipts from exchequer grant, research council, UK industry and in the industry funding share[27] for the two groups of institutions. Both groups of universities suffered important cuts in the exchequer grant receipts, and witnessed an increase of the funds from the research council. However, while the reduction in the exchequer grant has been more relevant for the downgrading institutions, the rise of research council receipts has been more important for the upgrading universities. The funds from UK industry followed opposite trends for the two groups. On the one hand the downgrading institutions succeeded in attracting a larger amount of funds from UK industry, and the share of these receipts in their total amount of funds from research grants and contracts stayed approximately constant. On the other hand, both the total amount and the share of UK industry fell dramatically for the upgrading universities.

In the period considered the nine downgrading universities suffered extremely large cuts to their general state support, consequently they tried to increase their income from specific sources, and in particular they succeeded in attracting an increasing number of contracts from UK industry. The eleven upgrading institutions saw their exchequer grant receipts decreasing, although less than in the case of the other group. They too had to rely more on specific sources of funds, but instead of orientating their research effort more towards the needs of UK industry, like the downgrading universities, they managed to obtain a larger amount of funds from research contracts and grants from the research councils.

Are the characteristics of the universities which are members of the two groups related to the changes in their funding structure? A clear answer to this questions is not possible with the current level of analysis. Nonetheless, it is important to notice how the negative relationship between the applied research propensity (share of contract research and grant financed by UK industry) and the scientific research productivity highlighted in the two-period analysis is confirmed also when the changes are studied. The downgrading universities that suffered extremely large cuts in their exchequer grant receipts, and partially substituted these funds with industry money, are also the ones that tend to have a decreasing scientific research productivity.[28] The upgrading institutions that partially counterbalanced the cuts in the exchequer grant with an increase of receipts from the research councils, reducing at the same time their interactions with UK industries, are the ones that showed a significant rise in their scientific research productivity.

The findings both at the static level and dynamic level form a consistent picture. At each point in time the universities with smaller science faculties and with lower average scientific research publications per researcher tend to depend more heavily on industrially funded research.[29] Where the cuts in the general public support not offset by an increase of public specific funds were greatest, the universities involved were pushed to rely more heavily on industry funding, and this was accompanied by further lowering of the average scientific publication rate.[30] The evidence offered suggests the possibility that two mechanisms were at work in the adaptation to change in state funding: (1) the removal of research support from Cluster I and from the nine downgrading institutions,[31] pushed these universities to accept industry funding for work that did not lead to high publication output; (2) changed research orientation led to the departure of researchers with stronger academic research records and aspirations; this was reflected in a reduced publication output in the downgrading institutions, and a rise in the upgrading universities to which the researchers went.

The subdivision in two groups of the UK universities, one of lower scientific research productivity more involved in applied research oriented to the commercialisation of research, and the other of higher scientific research productivity with relatively lower interactions with industry may seem, at least to some observers, a desirable outcome. Nonetheless, if the budget cuts and the push towards higher university funding from industry will continue[32] what is now true for the lower scientific research productivity group may become true for the majority of the universities. Moreover, as pointed out in Faulkner and Senker (1995) and confirmed by the aggregate real decrease of UK industry receipts shown in Chapters 4 and 5, Section 2, there are indications that industrialists are beginning to think that contracting to universities may cause a diminution of the available stock of basic knowledge that is most useful to their innovation processes.

In this situation further cuts in government support will put universities in a funding crisis causing a decrease in the bargaining power with industry that may lead the way to the destruction of the norms, incentives and organisational structure of the 'open science'[33] kind of research typical of the university. In a context of reducing state support the increase in commercialisable research in universities, possibly to foster state economic development, may result in a shift away from basic research (to the extent that this is measured by publications per researcher) that will cause a lower rate of technological innovation in the long term (Feller, 1990).[34] This shift is more relevant for those universities with tighter budgets more dependent on the general funds that, in a period of reducing state support, are constrained to involve a large amount of their scarce resources for research in contracts with industries.

5.3   CONCLUSIONS

Government and industry decisions are influencing the evolution of the university system. The modifications involved in this process will affect, for better or for worse, the production and distribution of scientific and technological knowledge. The science and technology policy frameworks of today, that originated in a period of continuously expanding state financing, are of little use in the current context of budget restrictions. Contemporary policy initiatives, to increase the amount of commercialisable research carried out in universities with the aim of possibly fostering state economic development, are being taken more on the basis of the *laissez-faire* philosophy in fashion than on the basis of a sound theoretical analysis. In the most influential policy circles it is thought that what has been beneficial for the industrial sector (deregulation and privatisation) will also be good for publicly funded scientific research. This neglects the peculiarities of knowledge production and distribution processes. With a lack of theoretical guidance, the medium- to long-term results of government and industry decisions may be far from desirable from an economic and social point of view, creating a variety of unintended consequences.

This exploratory work is an attempt to develop an empirical approach for analysing the relationships between funding and research output. In particular, it focuses on how the changes in the funding structure of multidisciplinary 'old' British universities have affected their propensity to carry out research of a more applied nature. First, the evolution of the funding structure of UK universities in the period 1989–93 is studied. Then, in order to assess the influence of the funding structure on the research output, the characteristics of 47 multidisciplinary universities are examined at the start and at the end of the period considered.

The competitive approach to university research behaviour and funding pursued by the British government, that originated from a *laissez-faire* or perfect competition model of how institutions should be made to operate, favours, directly and indirectly, the receipt of incomes from specific services rather than general funds which have been systematically cut. The aggregate analysis of university funding has shown that in the four years considered the real growth of specific incomes has not been sufficient to cover the reductions in general funds. Moreover, of particular importance, and contrary to the alleged increase of university–industry co-operation, is the decrease of UK industry funding receipts. Despite British government programmes to facilitate research collaborations between university and industry, at the aggregate level the share of funds from UK industry declined over the period.[35]

The methodology used to represent the data according to the analysed characteristics of the 47 universities has allowed us to highlight the existence of specific relationships among scientific research output, size and funding structure. The analysis at the static level (at the start and at the end of the period) offers some evidence that universities with smaller science faculties and with lower scientific research productivity tended to depend more heavily on industrially funded research. Although they had a lower share of receipts from grants and research contracts, the share of these receipts received by the universities from UK industry tended to be high. At the dynamic level (changes between the two periods) some indications have been found that where the cuts in the general public support not offset by an increase of public specific funds were greatest, the universities involved were pushed to rely more heavily on industry funding, and this was accompanied by further lowering of the average scientific publication rate.

On the one hand, the leading research-intensive UK universities are the most important recipients of industry support; on the other hand, when industry funds are considered relative to the total amount of R&D funds – that is, the share of UK industry receipts in the total amount of funds from research grants and contracts – the leading research-intensive universities tend to be among those less dependent on industrially-funded research.

The analysis offers some evidence to support the hypothesis that policies oriented towards decreasing state financing of university research in the expectation of a substitution of industrial research funding, possibly to foster state economic development, may be disappointed in two senses: (1) industrial funding is not likely to be large enough to replace major cuts in public support for R&D, so that the net effect is a contraction of R&D; (2) universities hit hardest by budget cuts are pushed to do routine contract research for industry, which neither leads to high publications (and spillovers), nor does it lay a basis for long-term fundamental innovation. Putting university researchers at less prestigious institutions at the 'service' of industry is a form of 'subsidy' for the kind of research that industry can and has to pay for itself.

Further analysis taking into account better indicators of the scientific research activity, such as publications weighted by their impact factor, publications by scientific field, movement of researchers, is needed to support these conclusions. Nonetheless, the outcomes of this study point to the existence of a series of problematiques that the current policy approach has avoided. A rethinking and reassessment of the science and technology policy frameworks that take into account the benefits and the drawbacks of the market approach on a medium-to long-term horizon are needed. In particular, regarding the university system, the answers to questions such as the following have to become the building blocks for the development of a new policy framework. What are the consequences for research and teaching of a more contract-oriented type of university research? What are the economic and social returns of a larger industry funding of university research? What share of university incomes should be financed by industry? Are the advantages of scientific agglomeration – that is, geographical concentration of scientific capabilities, and the localisation of the large part of research in a few universities – offset by the negative externalities imposed on smaller universities which are excluded or marginalised by this process?

NOTES

1. While the Research Assessment Exercise is run by the Funding Councils with the aim of a better allocation of research funds to universities, the Technology Foresight, run by the Office of Science and Technology, tries to pull scientific research more towards 'the needs of the nation'. Research Assessments Exercises, formerly termed research selectivity exercises, were conducted in 1986, 1989, 1992 and 1996; for an official evaluation of the impact of the 1992 exercise see HEFCE (1997).
2. For an exhaustive analysis of these changes see Williams (1992).
3. Contract overheads have been increased to 40 per cent so that the Research Councils have to meet all the costs of their projects. Academic salaries and premises continue to be met from institutions' general funds.

4. For a critical analysis of the White Paper 1993 see Webster (1994).
5. However, with the new system of funding, ex-polytechnics and colleges are starting to compete more and more for Research Council funding, and they are therefore becoming more involved in research.
6. The share of self-supporting home fees, paid by UK residents or by residents abroad who are entitled by special circumstances to pay home fees (EC students), ranged from 2 to 4 per cent in these four years. In short, fees are principally paid by the UK Government.
7. In particular, research grants and contracts income from the research council increased from £288 million to £382 million due mainly to the transfer of £87 million from the Funding Council to the Science Vote.
8. The university cost deflator has been used as the index.
9. To favour specific incomes is a way to create incentives for the university in the competitive approach to university research behaviour and funding that the government is pursuing.
10. For example in 1989–90 the receipts from the exchequer grant were about 3.5 times larger than those from fees.
11. In the last period the nominal increase of income from fees is sufficient to balance the increase in the number of students.
12. For the analysis of the determinants of university departments' research productivity see, among others, Gilmore and To (1992), Hare and Wyatt (1988) and Ramsden (1994)
13. Due to their peculiar characteristics the Senate Institutes and Central University of London University, and the University Central Registry of the University of Wales are excluded from the analysis. Manchester University and UMIST have been considered as one institution. Finally, London University is not considered as a single institution. Its 22 component colleges are individually counted.
14. Data sources are given in Annex A.
15. The number of researchers includes the total of full-time academic staff plus, when present, 50 per cent of part-time academic staff.
16. For the methodology used in gathering the data see Katz et al. (1995).
17. For a more detailed description of the methodology used see previous chapter.
18. In Table 5.3 the principal component loading after a Varimax rotation is presented.
19. See Appendix 5.1 for the list of the universities.
20. See Appendix 5.1 for the list of the universities.
21. When the entire university is considered the number of researchers and students, and the total recurrent income have low mean values.
22. Obviously Cluster III includes only medieval universities!
23. Hare and Wyatt (1992) studied the changes in resource allocation of the old British universities in the period 1991/2 and 1992/3. They found some evidence to support the view that the funding policy of the UFC had the effect of strengthening the strong universities while the weak ones were increasingly starved of resources.
24. The following analysis is based on the mean values of the two groups of institutions considered. For each variable used in the discussion the non-parametric Kruskal–Wallis Test has been run. The hypothesis that the two groups come from populations having the same distribution is rejected.
25. In 1992–93 the universities originally in Cluster III (excluding Cambridge and Oxford) plus the eleven institutions that moved from Cluster II.
26. In 1992–93 the nine downgrading institutions had a share of contract research and grant financed by UK industry similar to that of the universities originally in Cluster I.
27. Also the changes of other sources of funds have been studied, however only for the four variables discussed in the text did the non-parametric Kruskal–Wallis Test allow us to reject the hypothesis that the two groups come from populations having the same distribution. Nonetheless, the changes in the other considered sources were coherent with the interpretation presented.
28. A basic feature of scientific production is the increase in the number of publications, thus a stationary trend means in practice a decrease in the productivity. See Katz et al. (1995) for a detailed analysis of publishing patterns in the UK.
29. Baldwin (1996) presents a similar picture for the USA. Using 1991 funding figures for US universities, he points out that 'the universities which have become most dependent on

private industry support for their R&D activities are not, in the main, the nation's leading research universities' pp. 636–70.
30. Senker, Senker and Grossman (1997) found a negative correlation between university department involvement in the Teaching Company Scheme (a programme in which academics in universities work with companies to contribute to the implementation of strategies for technical or managerial change) and publications output.
31. All universities suffered cuts in general public support. However, for the institutions in Cluster I and for the nine downgrading the budget cuts were more important.
32. There are proposals to increase the weight given to the collaboration with industry in the Research Assessment Exercise.
33. For an analytical history of the emergence of the institutions of 'open science' see David (1997a); for the role played by norms, incentives and organisational structure in the creation of knowledge see Dasgupta and David (1987, 1994).
34. On the shift from basic to a more applied type of research see also Cohen, Florida and Goe (1992), and Faulkner and Senker (1995). Arora and Gambardella (1997) show that, on top of the above discussed problematique, industry funding of scientific research will also lead to an excessive allocation of resources to scientists with a great past reputation.
35. This may also be due to the fact that UK industry went through a recession in the considered period.

APPENDIX 5.1: LIST OF UNIVERSITIES

Universities	Clusters	
	1989–90	1992–93
Aston University	I	I
Bath University	I	I
Bradford University	I	I
Brunel University	I	I
Heriot-Watt University	I	I
Hull University	I	I
Kent and Canterbury University	I	I
Loughborough University of Technology	I	I
Nottingham University	I	I
Salford University	I	I
Stirling University	I	I
Ulster University	I	I
Wales University, Swansea	I	I
Wales University, Aberystwyth	I	I
Warwick University	I	I
Aberdeen University	II	I
Exeter University	II	I
Leeds University	II	I
Newcastle University	II	I
Reading University	II	I
Strathclyde University	II	I
Surrey University	II	I
Wales University, Cardiff	II	I
York University	II	I
Belfast Queen's University	II	II
Dundee University	II	II
Durham University	II	II
East Anglia University	II	II
Essex University	II	II
Keele University	II	II
Lancaster University	II	II
Leicester University	II	II
London University, Queen Mary and Westfield Colleges	II	II
Sheffield University	II	II
Sussex University	II	II
Birmingham University	III	II
Bristol University	III	II

Edinburgh University	III	II
Glasgow University	III	II
Liverpool University	III	II
London University, Imperial College	III	II
London University, King's College	III	II
London University, University College	III	II
Manchester University	III	II
Southampton University	III	II
Cambridge University	III	III
Oxford University	III	III

PART III

EU Funding of University Research

6. University participation in Community Framework Programmes

In a context of ongoing profound modification in the funding and structure of the European higher education system, an important role is played by the development of international co-operative R&D projects. Since the early 1980s, HEIs, partially independently and partially pushed by national policies, have increasingly participated in international R&D projects. Although this participation is not completely new from an historical point of view, the scale and intensity of current international co-operative R&D projects makes it a new phenomenon.

Focusing the attention on the European situation, HEIs are taking part in at least two kinds of international co-operation. First, there are the direct links between universities and between university and industry. Second, there are the co-operative relationships formed under the aegis of the Commission of the European Communities through Community Framework Programmes. In the period 1984–94, during the three Framework Programmes, this type of co-operation has become even more important due to the growing budget of the Framework Programmes and to the increasing participation of HEIs in each successive framework. In this chapter the latter kind of international relationship is analysed.

Since the First Framework Programme in 1984, the number of organisations receiving EU funding for R&D co-operative projects has increased considerably. In the Third Framework Programme, the type of organisation that participated in EU-funded R&D co-operative projects with the highest frequency was HEIs – that is, almost exclusively universities.

The increasing participation of HEIs in each successive Framework Programme carries important consequences both for the funding structure of universities and for the process of network formation and internationalisation of research. As an example of the former, consider the situation in the UK. A comparison of funding for each university from the European Community sources versus research grants and contracts from the British Research Council in 1992–93 shows that, on average, the European Community funds are 21 per cent of Research Council funds. However for about 10 per cent of the institutions EU funding represents more than 50 per cent of Research Council funds. Besides, as part of the trend towards the internationalisation of network structure,[1] Framework

Programmes represent a useful vehicle to develop or reinforce linkages for a more extensive European research network. Thus, the participation in EU R&D co-operative projects may have important impacts on the future research potentials of the participants.[2]

The purpose of this chapter is to study university participation in EU-funded R&D co-operative projects, paying particular attention to the factors that can influence the participation. Specifically, it will be highlighted how, among other factors, the characteristics and behaviour of the universities, the behaviour of the funding agency, and the unintended consequences of the selection mechanisms for allocating funds are relevant for the understanding of university participation. The unit of analysis can vary from the most disaggregate level of the research group to the entire institution. For the present study, a cross-country analysis at the university level is developed. To avoid biases, the availability of information on the reference population – that is, participant and non-participant – is extremely important. In this study it is possible to consider the totality of recognised universities in the EU countries as the total population without imposing any selection bias.

This chapter is subdivided into two main parts. In the first, after a short introduction to the EU Framework Programmes, the participation of HEIs in R&D co-operative projects is discussed (Section 6.1); then Section 6.2 introduces an interpretative framework explaining university participation. The second part develops, in Section 6.3, a descriptive analysis of the universities participating in EU R&D co-operative projects; then an empirical model, to test for the relevance of different factors on both the probability of joining an EU R&D project and the number of times a university participated in these projects, is formulated and estimated (Section 6.4).

6.1   THE PARTICIPATION OF HIGHER EDUCATION INSTITUTIONS IN COMMUNITY FRAMEWORK PROGRAMMES

Recent efforts of the EU to establish a targeted programme for improving industrial competitiveness through the mechanism of funded research officially began with the First Framework Programme (1984–87). The framework was set up with the goal of strengthening strategic areas of European competitiveness. The mechanisms selected for the framework included: (a) funding the R&D effort of private firms, research institutes, and higher education institutes[3] in the strategic areas, and (b) attempting to allocate funding to stimulate the formation of research networks spanning organisational and national boundaries. With the Second Framework Programme (1987–91) the Community decided to use the framework as 'the basis and instrument of European research and technology policy . . . thus providing a clear structure for long term overall objectives'.[4] A comprehensive political strategy on technology, enjoying equal status with other key Community policy areas, was set. The Third Framework Programme (1990–1994) is characterised by the regrouping of activities around only three strategic areas with 15 separate programmes and by the reinforcement of the aim of convergence among the member states of the EU. Nonetheless, as is clearly stressed in Commission of the European Communities (1992a, p. 11), 'where projects are evenly matched in qualitative terms, preference will be given to projects involving participants from technologically less well developed regions', the Community shows a lexicographic structure of preferences, with convergence subordinated to quality. The Fourth Framework Programme (1994–98) pursues the guidelines of the previous one, putting more emphasis on the consistency between national and Community policy. The Programme is structured in 13 'vertical' programmes and 3 'horizontal' actions. Two new areas of research, transport and socio-economic research, have been added. Lastly, in April 1997 the Commission of the European Communities put forward the proposal for the Fifth Framework Programme (1998–2002). The new Framework Programme is characterised by a 'problem-solving' approach with a focus on generic technologies and user needs and involvement. The aims of the Programme have been broadened giving higher importance to the socio-economic impact of research.

Table 6.1   The Framework Programmes

Programme	Duration	EU contribution
First Framework Programme	1984–1987	3 750 MECUs
Second Framework Programme	1987–1991	5 396 MECUs
Third Framework Programme	1990–1994	6 600 MECUs
Fourth Framework Programme	1994–1998	13 200 MECUs*
Fifth Framework Programme	1998–2002	14 960 MECUs+

Notes:
*: It includes activities that were not encompassed in the other three Frameworks. The original amount of 12 300 MECUs has been increased after the enlargement of the EU.
+: The Commission of the European Communities proposed a budget of 16 300 MECUs in April 1997. On 12 February 1998 the Council of Ministries approved a budget of 14 000 MECUs; finally, after a long debate, the budget of 14 960 MECUs was agreed on 16 November, 1998.

Sources: Commission of the European Communities (1994a, 1997a).

In the course of implementing the succession of Frameworks, the EU's research and technological development policy has expanded in budgetary scope, as is illustrated in Table 6.1, and has developed a few key goals. In particular, the total budget of the Fifth Framework is about four times that of the First Framework Programme in nominal value. However, the budget of the Fifth Framework has not increased compared to the previous one in real terms.

Table 6.2   Distribution of participation and funding, by organisational type: Second, Third and Fourth Framework Programmes

	Second FP Part.	Third FP Part.	Fourth FP Part.*	Second FP Funds	Third FP Funds	Fourth FP Funds
BIG	21.9	21.3	19.3	41.1	34.2	26.8
SMEs	18.1	14.5	17.3	18.7	16.4	16.1
REC	29.5	29.8	25.1	20.8	23.5	23.9
HEIs	29.2	31.5	29.3	18.9	22.5	27.4
Others	1.2	2.9	9.1	0.6	3.4	5.9

Note: * The figures refer to the period January 1994, December 1996.

Source: Elaboration of data in Commission of the European Communities (1994a, 1997a).

The institutions that participate in the Framework Programmes are classified by the European Commission[5] in one of the following five categories: *big companies* (BIG), *small and medium enterprises* (SMEs), *public or private research centres* (REC), *higher education institutions* (HEIs) and *others*. Table 6.2 shows the distribution of the five types of institutions in terms of (a) number of times they participated in an R&D co-operative project, and (b) funding for shared cost action for the Second and Third Framework Programme.

Three main observations emerge from the analysis of Table 6.2. First, big companies have suffered an important decrease between the Second and Fourth Frameworks both in their participation level and in their funding. Part of the 14.3 percentage point cut in big companies' funding was redistributed to public or private research centres and, especially, to higher education institutions and other organisations, with the result that the funding to HEIs approached 28 per cent in the Fourth Framework Programme, up from 19 per cent during the Second Framework. Second, the share of HEIs has increased, accounting for a bit less than one third of the total participation in projects. Universities, almost the totality of HEIs, as will be shown in the following sections, became in the Fourth Framework Programme the largest single type of institution both in terms of the number of times they participated in an EU-funded R&D co-operative project and in terms of funds received. Third, in all the three periods 'research institutions' have a higher share of participation than their share of funds. This means that funds are more thinly spread, on average, across participating units in the research centres and higher education community than among participating businesses. For HEIs, the difference in share of participation and funding shrank significantly between the Second and Fourth Framework Programmes.

Table 6.3   Collaborative links involving HEIs and REC, by Framework (%)

Organisation type	Second Framework		Third Framework*	
	HEIs	REC	HEIs	REC
HEIs	25.6	36.0	29.8	42.4
REC	36.7	28.6	40.6	28.5
BIG	19.6	18.5	14.8	14.1
SMEs	16.6	15.4	12.1	11.8
Other	1.5	1.5	2.7	3.1
Total	100	100	100	100

Note: * The figure for the Third Framework Programme refers to approximately 85 per cent of the contracts.

Source: David, Geuna and Steinmueller (1995).

HEIs play an important role in the EU's research and technological development policy. On the one hand, they are supplying generic knowledge needed by business enterprises and, on the other hand, they are benefiting from gaining access to complementary expertise and instrumentation in big companies' R&D laboratories. Moreover, for HEIs, participation in a Framework project means not only access to EU funding, but also the opportunity to interact with industry and other research organisations in the formation of potentially new, high quality research networks. This is extremely important, especially for those countries with lower scientific and technological resources, because it enables such countries to overcome the constraints imposed by the small size of their research community.

Table 6.3 describes the evolution of collaborative links[6] by organisation type for HEIs and RECs. In moving from the Second to the Third Framework Programmes, both the number of HEIs' links with other HEIs and with research centres increased, nonetheless 29 per cent of their links are still with industrial partners. The number of links is affected by the increasing numbers of HEIs and REC participating in the framework. Despite this increase, university–industry collaborations remain important in the Third Framework.

When one considers the total number of collaborative links between the same and different types of participants (see Table 6.4), it is possible to identify three relevant groups. First, the *industrial* group – that is, collaborative links

BIG–BIG, SME–SME and BIG–SME – with about 30 per cent and 19 per cent of the links in the Second and Third Frameworks respectively. Second, the *research* group – that is, collaborative links HEI–HEI, REC–REC and HEI–REC – which have not only the largest but also an increasing share of links, approximately 39 per cent and 50 per cent. Third, the *hybrid* group – that is, collaborative links across the institutions of the two previous groups – with about 30 per cent and 27 per cent of the links respectively. The co-operation between 'research institutions' and industry, characteristic of the hybrid group, although decreasing is nonetheless a significant part of the picture.

Table 6.4   Total collaborative links, by Framework

	BIG		SMEs		REC		HEIs		Others		Total	
	2nd FP	3rd FP	2nd FP	3rd FP	2nd FP	3rd FP	2nd FP	3rd FP	2nd FP	3rd FP	2nd FP	3rd FP
BIG	6 609	3 703	4 753	3 954	3 770	3 569	3 898	3 914	81	558	19 111	15 698
SMEs	4 753	3 954	2 643	2 227	3 135	2 986	3 305	3 194	73	630	13 909	12 991
REC	3 770	3 569	3 135	2 986	5 813	7 204	7 320	10 706	305	789	20 343	25 254
HEIs	3 898	3 914	3 305	3 194	7 320	10 760	5 091	7 876	307	700	19 921	26 390
Others	81	558	73	630	305	789	307	700	25	311	791	2 988

Note: * The figure for the Third Framework Programme refers to approximately 85 per cent of the contracts.

Source: Elaboration of CEC data.

Finally, the EU contractual funding across different programmes managed by DGXII (Directorate-General Science, Research and Development) of the Commission of the European Communities is analysed. On the one hand, when one considers the share distribution for each programme by type of participant, it is possible to identify a group of programmes in which HEIs have about 50 per cent of the funds. They are Step/Epoch, Bridge and Science and Technology for Development,[7] in the Second Framework, and Environment, Marine Science and Technology, Biotechnology and Life Sciences and Technologies for Developing Countries, in the Third Framework.[8] On the other hand, when the share distribution for each type of participant by programme is considered the previous group of university-oriented programmes loses importance. The two industrially-oriented programmes, ESPRIT and BRITE-EURAM, and their continuations under the Third Framework Programme, are always the most important sources of HEI funding.[9]

In the Fourth Framework Programme HEIs became the largest single type of institution both in terms of the number of times they participated in an EU-funded R&D co-operative project and in terms of funds received. They have developed collaborative links especially with other research institutions, but are also taking part in a significant number of projects with industrial partners. Finally, although they are the dominant player in a few Framework Programmes particularly oriented towards HEIs, they also participate in a respectable number of projects in the industrially-oriented programmes.

Four main observations can be drawn from the above analysis. First, if the financial trend of the first part of the Fourth Framework Programme is sustained through to its end,[10] the distribution of funds by type of participant will tend to become more homogeneous across the groups. Second, the increasing share of HEIs, within a Framework Programme characterised by a growing budget, implies growing impact over time of EU funds on the higher education finance system. In particular, in a period of budget cuts, restructuring and internationalisation of the European higher education system, the availability of a new competitive source of funds can have extremely important consequences.[11] Third, the growing budget of the Framework Programme represents a vital opportunity for institutions in countries with few resources to overcome the constraints imposed by the small size of their national research community. Fourth, in the course of the four Framework Programmes HEIs have developed various ways to draw upon the EU funds. They have joined co-operative projects that range from grant to university consortia for basic research to university/industry co-operation in market-oriented research.

With these issues in mind, it becomes crucial to understand why some universities and other post secondary education institutions are taking part with different frequency in co-operative projects within the EU Framework Programme.

6.2   AN INTERPRETATIVE FRAMEWORK

Two main phenomena that, in different but interrelated ways, have a strong influence on HEIs' participation in Framework Programmes will be considered here. First, both at the level of building up of research networks and of the funding selection process, the lack of information and the consequent presence of informational asymmetry among different research institutions on the one hand, and between funding agency and research institution on the other hand, point to the extremely important role played by information signalling.[12] Second, the distinctively competitive character of the EU funding[13] system, together with an increased mobility of researchers, have raised the impact of cumulative and self-reinforcement phenomena. In particular, the Matthew effect – that is, research groups that are successful in finding external funding for their research have a higher probability of producing publishable research, which improves their probability of getting funds in the future – that has less relevance in some of the less competitive national systems[14] becomes crucial to understand the EU funding system.

HEIs' participation in Framework Programmes is conceptualised as the result of the interaction among n suppliers – that is, the different institutions – and one consumer – that is, the funding agency. This is a quasi-monopsony situation.[15] The exchanged product is, as a first approximation, the result of the research project, and thus a non-homogeneous good. However, in most cases, the real object of the agency is not to buy the research service but to succeed in reaching the policy goals through the tool of the research contract. Then, a variety of institutions, although each offering distinctive heterogeneous products, can satisfy the agency's potential demand. The emerging competition is based on the ability to perform research – that is, the quality and the research productivity – of the institution. In this situation the producers know their quality, whereas the consumer learns it only if it selects the 'producer'.

In implementing its policy the agency is using various research contracts. They range from the tender for a specific research service to the generic grant via the open call for proposal. The former is characterised by a needed service, well or less specified, and a call for suppliers. The price, if not yet fixed, represents a carrier of information and can be used to signal the quality.[16] In all the other cases, the difficulty of defining a product, previously described, limits the role played by price. Other ways should be used to infer the private information.

Although the agency does not know the quality of the applicant, it does have a number of sources of potentially useful information in the form of verifiable statements, observable characteristics, and actions of individual applicants. Action and statements, together with partially or completely controllable individual features are called signalling, while the term index refers to the unalterable characteristics (Spence, 1974). In the specific case studied here, the applicants can signal their quality at two levels. First, the research group level. Signalling will be related to the recorded history of the researchers that are members of the group. Information, like education, research experience, publications, patents, and so on will be transferred from the applicant to the agency. Second, the university level. Being a member of a particular institution exerts positive or negative externalities on a research group. It is possible to assume that the presence of a good research group in a department creates positive externalities, then there is a strong probability that the average quality of the department is high. In general, it is difficult, although possible, to have a good research group in a low quality university. In this case, the possibility of dynamic improvement in the university's quality is not excluded. Indeed, it is possible to suppose that a single good research group is at the start of the process of quality improvement. Nonetheless, the extremely high inertia and sclerosis of the university system tend to curb this kind of dynamic.[17] The history of the university and its reputation are then signals of the potential quality of the applicant.

To 'digest' additional information is costly for the agency. To evaluate in detail the signals received from the various research groups is not only time-consuming, but it also requires specific competencies in the field of science related to the proposals. Usually these competencies are not present internally in the agency, which must then make use of external reviewers.[18] The agency can reduce the costs of the selection process using the information that it is possible to extract from university signalling. Indeed, its general character implies a low cost of evaluation. Clearly, a trade-off exists between the lower quality of the university signalling information and the higher cost of analysing the research groups' signals. The agency has then to go through a decision process focused on which type and how much additional information to digest. In terms of signals, the funding bureau has to decide how many signalled characteristics it wants to analyse. As a first approximation, it can be assumed that the funding agency analyses both types of signalling, complementing the lower-cost university information with the high value research group information.

From the point of view of a study of the EU funding system, the Matthew effect is characterised not only by an increased probability of producing publishable results, but also by the creation of asymmetry between selected and unselected institutions. The first cumulative effect, or virtuous circle, based on increasing productivity and consequently future funding has been discussed in detail in David (1994). Here the focus is on the creation of asymmetries. The participants that have been selected to get funding and have performed well, have a higher probability of being funded again because their display of good performance is an indication of their high quality. As the funding agency is not able to observe the 'real quality' of the applicants it has to base its decision on the signals received from the institutions and other sources of incomplete information. An institution that has been already chosen and has performed well is less risky than choosing an organisation that has never been funded. The latter, although the funding agency with the information collected can classify it as a high quality institution, has not yet been proven to be a good performer. It is, thus, associated with higher uncertainty and higher risk. A new applicant must overcome this 'barrier to entry'. To be selected its signalled quality must be higher than that of the previously selected candidates.

This condition becomes harder to satisfy after each new call for funding. Indeed, in each subsequent turn there will be a lower probability of choosing low performers. The agency may classify an applicant using two sources: the signalled characteristics, in the case of an institution that has not yet been chosen; the signalled characteristics and a performance indicator μ, when the applicant has already taken part in a project. The value of μ is zero at the starting point. For each good performance of the institution μ rises, while it decreases in the opposite case. The probability of being selected for an institution that has already taken part in a project is thus proportional to the value of μ. In this way the agency tends to keep high performers and to reject low performers. Making the assumption that for each low performer rejected there will be a new applicant selected[19] at time $t + 1$ – that is, a new call for tenders – and that the total population of potential applicants – that is, in this case the totality of HEIs in Europe – is fixed, it follows that the probability of choosing good performers is increasing with time. The average 'quality' of the participants is thus increasing. Moreover, also some of the good performers can be replaced by applicants with higher signalled quality, thus increasing further the average 'quality' of the selected institutions. Allowing for the entrance of higher quality applicants means the following two assumptions can be made:

- The candidates enter the competition whenever they prefer, they are not obliged to start at time t.
- There is space for 'quality' or signalling improvements. During time an institution can enhance its signalled quality.

With subsequent calls for tenders the process may arrive at a situation of lock-in in which a 'club' of good performers is repeatedly selected by the funding agency. This situation may not be optimal. The best performers might be in the club, in which case we have an optimum solution, but also they might be excluded from the club.[20] Indeed, it is possible that the process dynamic leads to a lock-in situation in which there are n institutions not selected with a signalled quality $q_i = f(q_i, q_2, ..., q_p)$, where q_p are the 'digested' signalled characteristics of the institution $i = 1,2, ..., n$, higher than the signalled quality $Q_j = f(Q_1, Q_2, ..., Q_p)$, where $j = 1,2, ..., m$, of m organisations within the club. This is due to the fact that the accumulated experience of the institutions within the club has created a barrier to entry B_j that summed to the signalled quality of these institutions, $Q_j + B_j$, does not allow the entrance to the n organisations. A new applicant will succeed in entering the club only if it has a signalled quality $q_i > Q_j + B_j$. Therefore, the lock-in situation can be characterised by one or more institutions with a signalled quality Q lower than the signalled quality q of some organisations that have not been granted the support.

These mechanisms, in general, and the path to the lock-in situation, in particular, can be reinforced or weakened by the following three phenomena. First, the broad policy vision of the funding agency, in this case of the Commission of the European Communities and indirectly of the European Parliament, is shaping the approaches that are driving the distribution of funds. At the one extreme there is the pure quality-oriented approach that, if followed as described previously, creates a lock-in situation that may not be optimal. At the other extreme, the selection process can be based only on principles like inter-country cohesion, technological convergence, and so on that supplement quality and may outweigh a quality-only measure. Each of the possible combinations of these two extremes has a different impact on the degree of diversity present in the output of the selection process. Second, every time that there is a process of selection for funding there is space for different kinds of pressures on the selection committee. Usually this refers to the 'accepted' form of lobbying. A strong impact of lobbying can cause an earlier sclerosis of the system with a lock-in situation at a lower level of quality. Notwithstanding this, if a broad definition of signalling is accepted, lobbying can be considered as a peculiar kind of quality signalling which can be reintegrated with the previous analysis. Third, as clearly stressed by Peacock (1991) in the case of art subsidies, if the officials in charge of the selection process are members of a particular community, and thus they have a specific reference group within the same community, or if they are bureaucrats who 'for understandable reasons wish to develop congenial relations with a few established clients' the selection may be biased toward well-established groups. The risk that funding support only reaches a selected group of 'incumbent' institutions, in our terms the institutions of the club, is then reinforced by bureaucratic inertia. In particular, a decision-making process can be strongly influenced by preference for the '*status quo*' (Lambert and Willinger, 1994; Samuelson and Zeckhauser, 1988). In our case, an official tends to replicate the same choice as before – that is, selecting the same institutions – due to the presence of psychological transition costs and to its natural loss aversion (Tversky and Kahneman, 1991). To switch from the '*status quo*' to a new configuration, the official should perceive the new choice – that is, selection of new participants – as a carrier of additional benefits and advantages that can compensate for the costs and disadvantages connected with choosing an alternative to the '*status quo*.'

If information signalling and cumulative and self-reinforcement mechanisms are relevant phenomena to explain the participation in EU R&D projects one should expect to have a small group of high quality, well known institutions that obtain the largest share of EU R&D contracts. In the next section, after the presentation of the unit of study and the description of the data-set, the analysis focuses on the understanding of the determinants of university participation in EU R&D co-operative projects. Then, in Section 6.4, an econometric model for university participation will be estimated.

6.3 DETERMINANTS OF UNIVERSITY PARTICIPATION IN EU-FUNDED R&D CO-OPERATIVE PROJECTS

In Europe there is no standardisation on the definition of PSIs and universities. In the different countries these terms carry varying connotations. However, in all the EU countries, the institutions that have been granted the university status went through a national selection process that can be considered more stringent than the one for granting the PSI status. Therefore, this category can be considered more homogeneous. Moreover, most PSIs are teaching-oriented institutions only marginally involved in research. Those that are involved in research are generally more oriented towards the regional or national type of networking, and only when their scientific research quality is high will they try to access the EU funding system.[21] For this reason, whereas all universities can be considered candidates for EU research funds, a minority of PSIs would qualify as such. Therefore, the totality of recognised universities in the EU countries is considered to be the reference population.

The ideal unit of analysis to understand university participation in EU R&D projects would be the research group or research centre that applied for EU funds. This information is currently not available at the cross-country level. Although less informative, the analysis of university participation in EU R&D co-operative projects at the aggregate level of the university can offer useful insights. Clearly, this unit of analysis has a size bias. Large universities tend to have more research groups and consequently tend to participate more in EU projects. Nonetheless, controlling for size, other factors such as scientific research productivity, geographic localisation, scientific orientation are useful to explain the participation in EU projects. Besides, the analysis at the institutional level has independent justifications. First, although the literature on R&D co-operation emphasises the centrality of the research group, particularly in this special case of international co-operation, the identity of the institution – that is, Cambridge University versus De Montfort University – plays an important role. In particular, because the funding agency – that is, the Commission of the European Communities – is not perfectly informed, the institutional reputation or 'the name' of the institution becomes a substitute for missing information on specific researchers or research groups. Second, to develop an international co-operation with a well known university means also establishing positive image externalities for the institution involved. The literature recognises, in the augmented image and prestige due to the link, one of the main incentives for co-operation.[22] Then, again, the institution itself comes to the fore. Third, taking the university as the unit of analysis enables us to have information on the total population – that is, both the universities that have joined EU R&D projects and the ones that have not taken part in them – and consequently the analysis at the level of the university will not have any selection bias. Fourth, from a methodological point of view, the macro analysis at the institution level enables us to draw the background picture of this particular area of R&D co-operation. In future research, the micro analysis at the research group level will be carried out on the basis of the results of the current work.

Universities participating in EU R&D projects are a sub-group of all universities that applied for EU funds, while the ones that applied are a sub-set of all universities that tried to initiate a co-operative project. In addition, some universities did not try to initiate a co-operative agreement and others have not made a decision because they did not have information or they were uncertain about what to do. These different groups constitute the total population of universities in Europe (Figure 6.1).

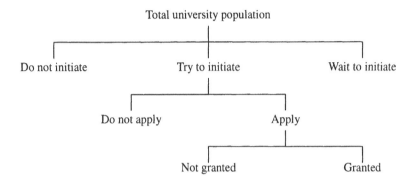

Figure 6.1   Decision tree for the initiation of a co-operative project

At present, the data concerning the universities that have been involved in an EU-funded R&D co-operative project (granted), and the total university population have been gathered. The analysis of this information will enable some of the factors affecting university participation to be highlighted in co-operative projects within the EU Framework Programme.

The data regarding the participation of universities in EU-funded R&D co-operative projects have been provided by DG XII – that is, the Directorate-General Science, Research and Development – of the European Commission. They refer to shared-cost actions funded by DG XII under the First, Second and Third Framework Programmes.[23] However, the data for the First Framework Programme are not complete because the database of DG XII has been created only since the end of the programme, then only part of the data concerning the First Framework Programme has been stored in it. Moreover, the information for the Third Framework Programme is only up to 15/3/1994.

For each university the geographical information and the number of contract partner links were made available. The latter represents the number of times an HEI has been involved in an EU-funded R&D co-operative project. No time or programme information was released. Constructed in this way, the database comprises 330 universities, representing 86 per cent of the total population of universities in the EU countries considered.[24]

The 379 institutions forming the total population of European universities[25] can be subdivided into participants and non-participants. The following variables[26] have been used to study both groups:

EU participation:	The number of times a university has been involved in an EU R&D project (EUPART).
No. researchers:	The number of researchers in 1992 (NRES).
Publications:	The number of papers published within a certain institution in 1993 (PUBS).[27]
Publications per researcher:	The ratio between the number of publications and the number of researchers (RATIO = PUBS/NRES).
Scientific fields:	The scientific fields in which the institution grants a doctoral degree.
NEWOLD:	The institution's founding year.

Table 6.5   Descriptive statistics for the main variables (TP = Total Population, P = Participants, NP = Non-Participants)

	Mean			Std. Dev.			Min.			Max.		
	TP[1]	P[2]	NP[3]	TP[1]	P[2]	NP[3]	TP[1]	P[2]	NP[3]	TP[1]	P[2]	NP[3]
EUPART	49	56	0	65	66	0	0	1	0	420	420	0
NRES	887	922	631	946	896	1232	15	36	15	7330	7000	7330
PUBS	415	461	84	519	530	258	5*	5*	5*	3185	3185	1397
RATIO	0.568	0.636	0.078	0.971	1.016	0.142	0.005	0.005	0.005	12.34	12.34	0.598

Notes:
* Estimated value;
[1] 371 valid cases;
[2] 326 valid cases;
[3] 45 valid cases.
Eight cases have been excluded due to missing data.

Table 6.5 presents the descriptive statistics for the four continuous variables. 326 universities (four cases have been excluded due to missing data) have participated from a minimum of once to a maximum of 420 times in a co-operative project. They have participated on average in 56 projects. The high Kurtosis (5.536) and the positive Skewness (2.130), together with the high standard deviations (66) and large difference between Min. and Max., indicate concentration in the values. Moreover, as the first three quartiles have values of respectively, 10, 32 and 78 one can describe the population of universities participating in EU R&D projects as composed of a large number of institutions with little participation and a small group of institutions involved in a large number of co-operative agreements. Similar observations can be made when the other three variables are analysed. Finally, when the descriptive statistics for the total population are compared to those of participants and non-participants, small positive differences for each of the four variables are present in the participants' distribution, while important negative differences characterise the non-participants' distribution. Thus, the participation or non-participation in co-operative R&D projects financed by the EU appears not to be independent of the size and the scientific research productivity of the institution.

Table 6.6　*Distribution of participating institutions and participation counts, by countries (%)*

	B	D	F	G	Gr	I	Ir	NL	P	S	UK
IC	5.0	2.1	17.6	19.7	4.1	12.6	1.8	3.8	4.1	9.4	19.7
PC	9.8	3.4	7.7	17.5	4.8	10.4	3.5	8.7	3.5	6.2	24.4
TP	4.0	1.8	19.3	19.8	4.0	12.4	1.8	3.4	4.5	10.3	18.7

Notes:
B = Belgium, D = Denmark, F = France, G = Germany, Gr = Greece, I = -Italy, Ir = Ireland, NI = The Netherlands, P = Portugal, S = Spain, UK = United Kingdom.

Table 6.6 illustrates the universities' share in terms of institutions counts (IC), participation counts (PC) and total population (TP) broken down by EU country. The comparison of the institutions counts with the total number of universities present in each country highlights only small differences. When the participation counts – that is, how many times the institution got funding – are considered, important differences appear. On the one hand, France, with 7.7 per cent shows the worst performance, with Germany, Italy, Spain and Portugal also having lower shares. On the other hand, Belgium and The Netherlands more than double their share of participation relative to number of universities. Finally, Denmark and the UK (the country with the largest share of participation, about one quarter of the total) have a PC share significantly higher than their share of institutions.

Table 6.7　*Institutions and participation counts, by size classes (%)*

	Researchers		Weighted researchers	
	IC	PC	IC	PC
Small universities	4.8	0.9	9.7	9.3
Small–medium universities	37.3	20.1	38.2	30.3
Medium–large universities	45.4	53.8	40.3	51
Large universities	12.5	25.1	9.7	9.4

Note:　The share does not sum to 100 due to missing cases.

University participation can be analysed from the point of view of institutional size. To do so, the variable number of researchers has been subdivided into four categories: small university from 0 to 100 researchers, Small–medium university from 100 to 500, medium–large university from 500 to 1800, large university more than 1800. Furthermore, to take into account the fact that some universities are more research-oriented than others, the number of researchers has been divided by the number of students. As for the previous variable, the weighted number of researchers has been transformed into a categorical variable with four size classes. Table 6.7 illustrates institutions and participation counts broken down by size class. In the case of the unweighted researchers' number, the medium–large and large institutions are performing better than the others. It seems thus that the success in raising EU funds is connected with the research size of the university. However, when one looks at the weighted researchers' number variable, a better measure of the research size of the institution, the previous observation is no longer true. Neither small nor large universities show relevant changes, the share of participation and the share of institutions are approximately equal. Only medium–large universities have a higher participation share.

Table 6.8   Institutions and participation counts, by historical class (%)

	Institutions counts	Participation counts
Post-1945	38.8	20.8
1900–1945	8.0	10.5
1800–1899	20.1	31.3
Before–1800	33.1	37.4

University participation in Framework Programmes can be analysed in relation to the age, or period of establishment of the institutions. To do so, the four classes subdivision introduced in Chapter 4 is used. Table 6.8 illustrates institutions and participation counts broken down by historical class. While in institutions counts the new postwar universities have the largest share, in participation counts their share is much smaller. Conversely, the other three classes have higher shares in the second distribution. The distribution of institutions counts is almost equal to the distribution of the total population of universities, while when the participation level is considered the older universities have a larger share.

The widespread institutional variety of the European university system has always constrained the value of international comparisons. For example, the Rheinish-Westphalian Technical University in Aachen, Germany has few things in common with the Eindhoven Technical University in Eindhoven,[28] The

Netherlands. The former has faculties like philosophy and education, while the latter is an engineering school. Nonetheless, starting from the fact that the requirements for the doctoral degree are approximately standardised among the EU countries, the various diversified institutions can be classified according to the scientific fields in which they grant the PhD degree. In particular, taking into account the OECD classification for scientific fields –that is, Agriculture, Medicine, Natural Sciences, Engineering, Social Sciences and Humanities – 28 categories have been created.[29] These are: (a) six for the universities defined mono-discipline, which grant the doctoral degree in only one scientific field. Each of the six classes contains observations. (b) fifteen for the universities defined bi-discipline, which grant the doctoral degree in two scientific fields. Only nine of them include some institutions. (c) seven for the universities defined multi-discipline. In this latter group all the institutions that award doctoral degrees in three or more scientific fields are included. To better classify these universities, the presence of a PhD degree in Engineering, Medicine and Natural Sciences has been used as a discriminatory variable. The multi-discipline group has been thus subdivided into seven categories. All of them contain observations. Table 6.9 shows the shares of institutions and participation counts broken down by the types of institution. First, two types of universities are not present in the Framework Programme. Among the 20 types that have succeeded in entering the system only 13 achieve more than 2 per cent of institutional participation share. Only three (multi-discipline with medicine and natural sciences (MUDMN), multi-discipline with natural sciences and engineering (MUDNE) and multi-discipline with medicine, engineering and natural sciences (MUDMEN)) score more than 10 per cent. These last three categories account for about 56 per cent of the institutions. Second, the system is more concentrated in the participation counts. Nine types of institution have a share higher than 2 per cent. The three multi-discipline categories previously in a dominant position are, in this case, responsible for approximately 73 per cent of the participation. They are performing much better than the others. The prior description points to the fact that although the system includes a large variety of institutions, the largest share of participation is realised by a specific kind of institution. This institution can be characterised as a general university that always includes faculties of medicine and natural sciences and often also engineering.

The number of times an institution participated in EU R&D co-operative projects is a fraction of the number of its applications. Among other factors, the characteristics of the university such as scientific research productivity, reputation, scientific orientation, influence the fraction of accepted applications. In turn, the total number of applications of a university is the sum of the applications of the single centres, thus it depends on the number of the centres – that is, the size of the institution – and on the characteristics of the centres and of the university. In the following section, an econometric model that analyses the importance of a few institutional characteristics to university participation is developed. In particular, the analysis focuses on the relevance of size and scientific research productivity.

Table 6.9   Institutions and participation counts, by university type (%)

	Institutions counts	Participation counts
ModHum	0.6	0.0
ModAgr	0.9	1.9
ModMed	4.1	0.8
ModNat	0.6	0.1
ModEng	4.7	6.5
ModSoc	3.2	0.3
BidNatEng	3.5	2.4
BidNatSoc	3.2	1.2
BidNatHum	2.9	1.1
BidNatMed	2.1	2.8
BidEngSoc	1.2	2.1
BidMedSoc	1.8	0.3
BidSocHum	4.7	0.5
MUDM	0.9	0.3
MUDE	1.8	0.5
MUDN	5.3	3.2
MUDME	2.1	3.3
MUDMN	9.5	23.9
MUDNE	14.2	12.7
MUDMEN	22.7	35.1

6.4   AN ECONOMETRIC TEST OF THE DETERMINANTS OF UNIVERSITY PARTICIPATION

The aim of the regression analysis is to test the relevance of size, scientific research productivity, and other fixed factors on university participation in EU R&D projects. In particular, the analysis of the estimates enables the highlighting of how the behaviour and characteristics of the universities, the behaviour of the Commission of the European Communities and the presence of unintended effects of the selection criteria influence the participation of universities in EU-funded R&D co-operative projects.

As the number of times a university participated in EU-funded R&D co-operative projects (EUPART) takes discrete values between 0 and 420, the OLS regression is not a suitable estimation procedure. Two different approaches can be used. One is a Tobit model with the number of times a university participated in a project as a censored dependent variable. The other is a two-equation model, where the first specification is a Probit model with a binary dependent variable which takes the value 1 when the university has a participation, and 0 when it does not, and the second equation is a truncated regression model for the non-limit observations – that is, for the number of participations greater than zero. The two alternative approaches can be tested against each other.[30] The double specification can also be tested as the unrestricted model against the restricted Tobit model.

The advantage of the two-equation model is that it separates the analysis of the participation or not in a project from the analysis of multi-participation. In this way it is possible to separate the analysis of the probability of joining an EU R&D project from the study on the level of participation in projects. The former reveals the relevance of the considered factors on the selection, while the latter provides information about the level of participation.

In the Tobit model (equation (6.1)) the dependent variable EUPART is regressed on the independent variable number of researchers (NRES), and ratio between number of publications and number of researchers (RATIO). The first independent variable measures the size of the university, while the second is used as a proxy for the scientific research productivity of the institution. A log-linear relation is assumed. Dummy variables (DCOUNTRY) for national fixed effects and control dummy variables (DSCIFIELD) for scientific fields[31] are included. In the Probit model (equation (6.2)) the dependent variable Y is the probability of being involved in a project which takes the value 1 when the university has a participation, and 0 when it does not. The same set of independent variables is used.[32] In the truncated regression model (equation (6.3)) only the universities that have participated in at least one EU R&D project are considered. The dependent variable P is the number of times an institution participated in a project and is recorded only when it is greater than zero. The independent variables are the ones used in the previous two equations. As in the Tobit model a log-linear relation is assumed. The equations (6.1), (6.2) and (6.3) are then formulated as:

$$\ln (1 + \text{EUPART}) = \alpha + \beta_1 \ln \text{NRES} + \beta_2 \ln \text{RATIO} + \Sigma_{i = 1,...,n} \gamma i$$
$$\text{DCOUNTRY}_i + \Sigma_{j = 1,...,m} \delta_j \text{DSCIFIELD}_j + \varepsilon_1 \qquad (6.1)$$

where n = number of countries = 10 and m = scientific fields categories = 8.

$$Y = \theta + \varphi_1 \ln NRES + \varphi_2 \ln RATIO + \Sigma_{i=1,...,n}\chi_i$$
$$DCOUNTRY_i + \Sigma_{j=1,...,m} \psi_j DSCIFIELD_j + \varepsilon_2 \qquad (6.2)$$

where $Y = 1$ if EUPART > 0 and $Y = 0$ if EUPART $= 0$; n = number of countries $= 9$ and m = scientific fields categories $= 7$.

$$\ln(1+P) = .\rho + \eta_1 \ln NRES + \rho_2 \ln RATIO + \Sigma_{i=1,...,n}\lambda_i$$
$$DCOUNTRY_i + \Sigma_{j=1,...,m}\pi_j DSCIFIELD_j + \varepsilon_3 \qquad (6.3)$$

where P is observed only when EUPART > 0; n = number of countries $= 10$ and m = scientific fields categories 8.

Taking equation (6.1) as the restricted model, and equations (6.2) and (6.3) together as the unrestricted model a likelihood ratio test (LLR) has been used to decide the best specification. As the LLR is equal to 136.66, using a Chi-squared test with 21 degrees of freedom, the Tobit model was rejected at 99 per cent probability.

The results of the estimation are shown in Table 6.10. In the Probit equation[33] the scientific research productivity of the institution has a positive and significant effect on the probability of taking part in an EU R&D co-operative project, while the size of the university is not significant. None of the dummy variables for country and scientific field fixed effect have a significant value. These results highlight that the probability of taking part in a co-operative project financed by the EU depends primarily on the scientific research productivity of the university. This is consistent with the results of Arora, David and Gambardella (1998), who showed that, in the case of publicly funded R&D projects, the scientific reputation of the research group, and in particular its weighted number of past publications, is the main factor influencing the probability of being selected. Moreover, these results seem to confirm that the Commission of the European Communities acted consistently with its stated policy objectives of awarding research funds primarily on grounds of scientific and technological excellence.[34]

Important differences in the influence and significance of the explanatory variables are present in the result for the truncated regression model. Both size and scientific research productivity have positive and significant coefficients. Consistent with the analysis in the previous section, the size effect – that is, large universities tend to have more research groups and consequently tend to participate more in EU-funded R&D co-operative projects – has an important positive impact on the number of times a university participated in projects. Nonetheless, given the size, institutions with higher scientific research productivity are involved in more projects. Thus, while the probability of receiving a grant depends primarily on the scientific research productivity of the university, the participation in EU-funded R&D co-operative projects is affected by the size of the institution and, given its size, by its scientific research productivity.

Table 6.10   Estimation results

	Tobit	Probit	Truncated
LL	–495.46	–77.18	–349.95
Constant	–1.312 (.01)**	5.333 (.88)	–1.552 (.00)**
ln NRES	0.847 (.00)**	0.197 (.19)	0.888 (.00)**
ln RATIO	0.560 (.00)**	0.321 (.00)**	0.498 (.00)**
DCOUNTRY			
Belgium	0.769 (.00)**	–3.961 (.94)	0.853 (.00)**
Denmark	0.78E–1 (.84)	–	0.112 (.70)
France	–0.522 (.00)**	–3.958 (.94)	–0.646 (.00)**
Germany	–0.809 (.00)**	–4.604 (.94)	–0.707 (.00)**
Greece	0.706 (.01)**	–2.777 (.96)	0.293 (.20)
Italy	–0.457 (.02)**	–3.654 (.95)	–0.595 (.00)**
Ireland	0.950 (.01)**	–4.280 (.94)	1.139 (.00)**
The Netherlands	–0.18E–1 (.95)	–	–0.283 (.25)
Portugal	0.312 (.29)	–3.997 (.94)	0.346 (.17)
Spain	–0.852 (.00)**	–4.465 (.94)	–0.860 (.00)**
United Kingdom	–	–4.036 (.94)	–
DSCIFIELD			
Eng & Agr	0.804 (.00)**	–3.653 (.95)	0.930 (.00)**
SOC & Hum	–0.844 (.00)**	–5.067 (.93)	0.100 (.68)
Nat & Med	–0.318 (.24)	–	–0.313 (.13)
Mix-scientific	0.46E–1 (.85)	–3.677 (.95)	0.90E–1 (.64)
Mix-technical	0.952 (.00)**	–3.329 (.95)	0.924 (.00)**
Multi-Soc&Hum	–0.124 (.58)	–4.240 (.94)	0.87E–1 (.61)
Multi-Scientific	–0.192 (.26)	–3.896 (.94)	–0.137 (.29)
Multi-Technical	0.305 (.101)	–3.798 (.94)	0.331 (.01)**
Multidisciplinary	–	–3.602 (.95)	–

Notes:
Non linear probit. Dependent variable: Binary. Number Obs. 371.
Truncated regression. Dependent variable: Positive participation. Number Obs. 326.
Coefficient significance between brackets. Marginal effects have the same significance of coefficients.
LL Restricted Probit = –137.08; LL Restricted Truncated = –546.72

Major country fixed effects[35] are present in the truncated regression model. They can be subdivided into three sub-groups. First, the dummy variables for France, Germany, Italy and Spain have negative significant values. Given the size and scientific research performance, universities of these countries had a lower participation rate. Among the many possible explanations, the negative sign of these dummies could be related to the administrative and bureaucratic structure of their national university system. In predominantly public financed systems the novelty of a competitive financing process has constrained the propensity to participate in EU R&D projects. Although their university systems have a high quality, they are extremely bureaucratic and they are not used to external co-operation and competitive fund raising. Moreover, particularly in the case of France and Italy, a large portion of research is realised in public research organisations – for example CNRS (F), Max Planck Society (G), CNR (I), CSIC (S) and other public research centres – thus the research intensity of the university system tends to be lower than in other countries.

Second, the dummy variable for Ireland has positive and significant values. Other factors being equal, this indicates that Irish universities had an advantage in the level of participation. This advantage can be interpreted as the result of the policy objectives of the Commission of the European Communities. As highlighted in Section 6.1, since the First Framework Programme, technological and economical convergence among the member states of the EU is a major policy aim. Especially from the Third Framework Programme a clear technological cohesion policy has been developed. Projects involving partners from less-favoured[36] regions tend to be preferred to projects of the same quality but without members from less-developed regions. Some results show that the cohesion policy probably also has a positive influence on the participation of Greek universities, while the statistical evidence does not support the same conclusion for Portuguese universities.

Third, the dummy variable for Belgium has a positive and significant value. This indicates that, given the size and scientific research productivity, Belgian institutions succeeded in having a higher participation rate. A possible explanation is connected with the fact that the diffusion of information about how, where and when to apply for EU funds has taken a relatively long period of time. Belgian universities benefit from their proximity, and have easier access to information and the possibility of face-to-face contacts with the Commission that increase their rate of success. Moreover, the localisation advantage has allowed them to enter early in the system and, consequently, to develop a 'first entry advantage' that has enabled the creation of 'barriers to entry' to the disadvantage of late comers.[37]

The dummy variable for the scientific field has been used to control the bias inherent in the way the number of publications was collected and to control the different propensity in publishing. In the chosen specification, the technology-oriented institutions have positive and significant values.[38] The high value of their coefficients, on the top of the control meaning, may also indicate the existence of an advantage for technology-oriented universities. However, with the available data, no conclusive observations can be made.

Fixed effects to account for the age of the university have also been included. Four dummies for the founding year have been used as proxies for the reputation effect – that is, the older the university, the higher the reputation. Even if some evidence of a positive coefficient for the universities created in the interim between 1900 and 1945 were found, the test for the restricted against the unrestricted specification rejected the latter.

The results of the estimations of the two-equation model presented above point to the existence of important differences in the significance of the factors when they are used to explain the probability of joining an EU-funded R&D co-operative project or when they are used to explain the actual number of times a university participated in projects. Given other factors, such as differences among countries and scientific fields, the scientific research productivity of the university influences both the probability of taking part in an EU-funded R&D co-operative project and the number of times a university participated in these projects, while the size is only significant when used to explain the latter.

Among other reasons, the different frequency in participation seems to be affected by the characteristics and behaviour of the universities, the behaviour of the funding agency, and the unintended consequences of the selection mechanisms. A possible interpretation of the results of the estimations points to the existence of a set of factors that seem to have a significant influence on the frequency of participation. First, as the large universities tend to have more research groups and, consequently, tend to have more participation in EU R&D co-operative projects, the size distribution of the total population of European universities may influence the skewness of the distribution of participation. Second, the existence of important differences in scientific research productivity and the presence of cumulative and self-reinforcement mechanisms could explain why only a small number of universities have a high level of participation. Third, the differences in the national systems of higher education may have created different incentives for participating in EU R&D projects. Fourth, the priorities of the EU research and development policy, especially as it concerns cohesion policy and technology orientation, may influence the frequency of the distribution of participation. Finally, the localisation and information advantage enjoyed by some institutions may have enabled the creation of barriers to entry, permitting them to have a higher participation rate.

6.5   CONCLUSIONS

A growing share of the income of universities in the EU countries is generated through research grants and contracts from both national agencies and the EU. In a context of increasing internationalisation of the research process and of rising importance of the research network, the participation in EU R&D co-operative projects becomes an issue of crucial importance.

This chapter has examined the determinants of university participation in EU R&D projects. The analysis focused primarily on the selection process. Assuming that the process is driven by the 'quality' principle and acknowledging the fact that quality is not observable, an interpretative framework has been put forward. At its heart lies the importance of signalling mechanisms and the fact that the quality principle is intrinsically linked with various types of cumulative and self-reinforcement mechanisms. An econometric model has been developed to test for the relevance of different factors on both the probability of joining an EU-funded R&D co-operative project and the actual number of times a university participated in these projects.

Evidence has been found to support the idea that scientific research productivity influences both the probability of joining an EU-funded R&D co-operative project and the number of times an institution has participated in these projects, while the research size has a positive influence only on the latter. Given the size and scientific research productivity of the university, other factors are important to explain the different frequency in participation. Among others, the following three factors seem to be consistent with the results of the estimations. First, the bureaucratisation and the lack of practice in competitive fundraising of the university system may have a negative influence on the propensity to take part in EU R&D co-operative projects. Second, the existence of techno-economic convergence aims for the Framework Programmes tends to advantage the participation of institutions located in less-favoured regions. Third, due to the unintended consequences of the selection mechanisms the early entrants in the system tend to have advantages in their repeated participation.

The estimations suggest that the scientific research performance is important in the EU decision process, but some evidence of the influence of the cohesion policy has also been found. The relevance given to the scientific research productivity establishes, through the effect of cumulative and self-reinforcement mechanisms, a repeated selection of a minority of high research quality institutions. This tends to maximise short-term research outcomes. Nonetheless, longer term goals are pursued when, following the guidelines of cohesion policy, universities in less-favoured regions have some advantage in participation.[39] In this way, especially in the case of university research, positive knowledge spillovers may increase the research capabilities of those regions.

Finally, if the consequences of a selection based on the 'quality principle' are reinforced by what has been called the first entry advantage, another short-term versus long-term trade-off should be considered. On the one hand, the characteristic of repeated selection may tend to reinforce the dominant research strategies (scientific paradigms and research programmes), limiting research variety, and consequently decreasing the probability of scientific innovation.[40] On the other hand, the standardisation of scientific knowledge enables an increase in communication, and consequently a rise in the value of current science.

In the context of a policy perspective, a better understanding of the two trade-offs and of the interactions between them is needed. Further analysis is needed to evaluate the implications for the university funding structure of an increasing reliance on EU funding. In particular, improved indicators of scientific research activity, such as publication by scientific fields, publications weighted by their impact factor, and more detailed information on the universities participating in EU-funded R&D co-operative projects, for example at the level of the department, should be used.

NOTES

1. For the development of international scientific collaboration see, among others, Luukkonen, Persson and Silvertsen (1992) and Leydesdorff (1992).
2. For the continuation of co-operation after the end of the project see AXION (1995).
3. The Community reimburses up to 50 per cent of project actual costs to companies or research institutes, and to universities and other higher education establishments it reimburses 100 per cent of additional costs.
4. See Commission of the European Communities (1992a).
5. The participant in a project is required to classify her institution in one of the categories.
6. A collaborative link is a connection established between each of the participants in a research and technological development contract. For the calculation of the number of collaborative links a participant may be the co-ordinator, a contractor or an associate contractor (Commission of the European Communities, 1994a).
7. Due to their specific character the programmes under the headings Improvements to European Scientific and Technological Co-operation, Medical and Health, BCR and Fusion are not included in the analysis.
8. Due to their specific character the programmes under the headings Human Capital and Mobility and Fusion are not included in the analysis.
9. Only Environment among the programmes of the previous group receives a relevant share of funds (16 per cent) in absolute terms.
10. As the Fourth Framework Programme pursues the guidelines of the previous one, and as consistency in the policy behaviour of the Commission can be presumed, one may expect that the trend will be confirmed.
11. Impact and unintended effects of EU funding upon the allocation of national public and private research funding going to higher education institutions – that is, university departments – in the UK are discussed in Chapter 7. A detailed analysis of substitution effects and additionality of EU R&D funding is presented in David, Geuna and Steinmueller (1995).
12. For the importance of pre-contractual informational asymmetries and market signalling see the original contribution of Spence (1974).

13. The funding and in general the management of the European higher education system, in both teaching and research, has been mainly driven by non-competitive criteria. Only recently, in a few countries that is, especially in the United Kingdom, the system is undergoing a profound modification directed towards a more market-oriented approach. For the discussion of the ongoing changes see Chapter 2 and the final part of Chapter 3; see also Geuna (1998b, 1997).

14. A number of national university systems are still characterised, on the one hand, by extremely high entrance costs but, on the other hand, by low competition for research funding when in the system. To obtain tenure the candidate has to go through a rigorous selection process. However, when she has succeeded in being selected, the competition for fundraising tends to be low. In practice, every year each professor is entitled to use a certain amount of research funds independent of her research productivity. However, as described in Chapters 2 and 3, this situation is changing at an increasing pace. Due to budget constraints the national systems are developing a competitive approach to university research behaviour and funding.

15. Taking into account the fact that a university can apply not only to the Commission of the European Communities, but, for example, also to its national funding agency, it is no longer correct to speak of monopsony. Indeed, as Community and national policy objectives are sometimes overlapping one can assume that for an institution to apply to the national agency is a non-perfect, but still possible, substitute for the Community application.

16. The relevance of price as signalling device, does not mean that the other ways of quality signalling, described in the next section, are less important for this kind of contract.

17. The results of Chapter 4 support this view. Only a very small number of new postwar universities are members of the high scientific research productivity, research intensive cluster.

18. For example, in the second call for proposals of the BRITE-EURAM Programme, 207 experts were involved in technical assessment of the proposals.

19. Here the implicit hypothesis that there is a fixed number of places is made.

20. This suboptimality may be mitigated in the long term by a high human capital mobility.

21. Among the 427 HEIs participating in Community Framework Programmes 97 are PSIs. However, each of these PSIs has participated in very few projects, accounting for only 4.3 per cent of the total number of times HEIs participated in EU R&D projects (Geuna, 1996).

22. See for example Malerba et al. (1991).

23. In both the Second and the Third Framework the research concerned with information and communications technologies was under the supervision of DG XIII, therefore it is not included in the data set. Some other small programmes directed by DG VI, DG XIII and DG XIV are also not included. Still, about 55–60 per cent of the funds were administered by DG XII.

24. When the totality of HEIs is considered, the number of institutions taking part in EU R&D projects rises to 427; respectively 69 PSIs, 28 new British universities and 330 universities.

25. See Chapter 4 for their description.

26. For a detailed description of the variables see Chapter 4, Section 4.1.1.

27. For humanities and social sciences there exists the specific Social Science SCI which, however, has not been utilised due to the much lower propensity to publish by researchers in humanities and social sciences. Thus, these data are biased to the detriment of institutions within the humanities or social science departments. However, under the first three Framework Programmes only a minor part of the budget was indirectly committed to socioeconomic studies, so that this is not considered a serious weakness for the purposes of the present analysis.

28. The two towns are only 120 kilometres from one another.

29. In six categories there are no entries.

30. See Cragg (1971) for the original specification of the two-equation model.

31. The nine dummies for scientific fields orientation are the result of a re-categorisation of the original classification in 22 classes given by the variable *Scientific fields*.

32. The dummy variables for The Netherlands, Denmark and Natural and Medicine universities are not included in equation (6.2) because the related universities always have probability 1.

33. The Probit model correctly predicts 90 per cent of the outcomes.

34. See, for example, Commission of the European Communities (1992a, p. 10).

35. The reference country is the United Kingdom.

36. In the last Council Regulation 93/2081/EEC Greece, Ireland and Portugal are still included as entire countries in the less-favoured regions.
37. For evidence on the phenomena in the UK context see Pike and Charles (1995, pp. 20–21).
38. Other more detailed specifications have also been estimated. The coefficients of the institutions focused on medicine were sometimes significant and negative, indicating the presence of an overestimation of the scientific research productivity of these institutions. Also due to the small number of institutions with these characteristics, the test for the restricted against unrestricted specification did not allow the null hypothesis to be rejected. Thus, the nine dummies specification has been chosen.
39. For the development of this problematique in the case of the BRITE-EURAM programme see Gambardella and Garcia-Fontes (1996).
40. For the discussion of scientific paradigms and research programmes see, respectively, Kuhn (1970) and Lakatos (1970).

7. EU and national university research funding: the BRITE-EURAM Programme

In the last chapter, emphasis was placed on university participation in Community Framework Programmes. As revealed, 88 per cent of European universities have taken part at least once in an R&D project financed by the EU. A context of national university research funding stagnation or reduction of the advancement in budgetary scope of the EU's research and development policy made this source of university research funding increasingly important. Although the incomes from EU contracts and services are small compared to total university funding,[1] they represent an important share of the research funds due to specific services. In this chapter the relationships between EU and national university research funding will be analysed.

The expansion in budgetary scope of the EU's research and technological development policy has increased the need for a better understanding of the consistency between Community and national policies. Although the need for a closer integration of the RTD activities in Europe is clearly stated in the Fourth Framework Programme,[2] no clear guidelines have been defined. The most common approach to the understanding of the relationships between EU and national science and technology policies has been based on the definition of boundaries between Community and member state RTD activities. The definition of the respective domains is given by the principle of subsidiarity[3] that dictates that 'the Community should take action on research only if the objectives can be better achieved by the Community than by the Member States acting on their own'. To apply this principle, the objectives that can be better achieved by the Community, need to be clearly defined. One attempt to define the categories by which to restrict Commission funding activities has been made by the House of Lords, Select Committee on the European Communities (1990). Nonetheless, David, Geuna and Steinmueller (1995), discussing the proposed categories, point out that one of the criteria for Commission actions requires that there would be added value in performing them at the Community rather than at the national level. However, the concept of 'added value' may carry a large set of meanings, leaving the definition of the limits of Community action unclear. Consequently, David, Geuna and Steinmueller, acknowledging that rigid boundaries between

Community and member states research objectives cannot be drawn, highlight that the Community RTD policy can be better viewed as a political outcome. If the research objectives of the EU and national actions cannot be clearly separated, the funding priorities of EU RTD policies might diverge from the national funding priorities. This situation gives rise to a complex set of interactions between EU and national initiatives. For example, member states favouring different technological priorities can modify a funding initiative undertaken by the Community augmenting or subtracting national funds for specific technological fields. At the extreme is the case in which the member states substitute EU funding for their own – that is, they deduct national funds from fields that have received EU funds.

The analysis of the interactions between EU and national research funding can be developed either at the country, technology or institution level. For the purpose of this chapter, the focus is on the last. The relationships between EU and national university research funding are studied considering both the deliberate action of government in response to EU funding, and the unintended consequences related to the existence of two overlapping sources of research funds. The analysis is carried out at the level of the university department mainly because it allows one to capture the micro-mechanisms that can explain the conduct of the complete institution.

To obtain the required level of detail, a specific EU RTD programme (BRITE-EURAM) and a single country (in this case, the UK) had to be chosen. With regard to the EU programme selected, BRITE-EURAM was chosen for the following reasons. First, the continuity present in the programme's aims and structure in the successive Framework Programmes allows a sufficiently long period of time to observe effects. Second, considering both the level of participation and funding for shared cost actions, BRITE-EURAM is the second most important EU programme. Third, as pointed out in Chapter 6, BRITE-EURAM is an extremely important source of HEIs' funding. Finally, its sectoral orientation involves not only applied and development work, but also more basic research with industrial applicability allowing for substantial contributions from universities. With regard to the country selection, the UK was chosen for two main reasons. First, as pointed out in Chapter 5, the ratification of the Education Act (HMSO, 1988) led to profound modification within the university funding system in the United Kingdom. Due to these changes, EU funding plays a larger and more important role, both directly – that is, through an increase of the EU share of total HEIs research funding, and indirectly – that is, through a series of cumulative and self-reinforcing mechanisms. Second, the new UK 'market oriented' approach could be used as a blueprint by other continental systems, raising the importance of understanding its development and consequences.

The chapter is organised as follows. The first section describes the BRITE-EURAM innovation system and examines the evolution of its research programmes. Section 7.2 discusses university participation in BRITE-EURAM shared-cost projects. The study of the relationships between EU and national university research funding in the UK for the institutions involved in the BRITE-EURAM programmes is presented in Section 7.3.

7.1 THE BRITE-EURAM INNOVATION SYSTEM

In 1992 non-military R&D expenditures in the EU countries accounted for 45 866 MECUs. Of these, 38 653 were realised at the national level and 7213 at the European level. Four institutional modalities exist for R&D co-operation at the European level: the EU Framework Programme (2812 MECUs), the EUREKA programme (704 MECUs), the European Space Agency (2967 MECUs) and the large scientific research institutions for basic research such as CERN and ESRF (856 MECUs).[4] Table 7.1 illustrates the breakdown by aims of national and EU R&D expenditures. It shows that the EU Framework Programmes are responsible for 6.1 per cent of total non-military R&D expenditures and for 11.3 per cent of the expenditures in support of industrial innovation. The BRITE-EURAM programme is the source of almost the totality of these funds.

Table 7.1   Share of R&D expenditures by aims, 1992[5]

Aims	National		EU frameworks	
	Col. %	Row %	Col. %	Row %
Fundamental research	53.0	94.9	8.9	1.2
Support to public policy	21.3	92.3	24.5	7.7
Industrial innovation	7.9	81.0	15.3	11.3
Spatial	8.4	52.3	0.0	0.0
Aeronautic	2.5	97.2	1.0	2.8
Telecommunications	3.7	51.0	38.1	38.7
Nuclear	3.1	77.8	12.2	22.2
Total	100	84.3	100	6.1
MECUs	38 653		2 812	

Note: The row % does not sum to 100 due to the exclusion of the other three European modalities of R&D co-operation

Source: OST (1996).

Since 1989 three BRITE-EURAM programmes have been financed by the Commission of the European Communities.[6] The overall objective of these programmes is the improvement in the competitiveness of European manufacturing and material processing industries.[7] The priorities of the programme, however, have evolved according to the European economic situation. The passage from the First to the Third Framework Programme saw the relevance of materials-related technologies diminished, and the importance of the technologies for transport means augmented. The BRITE-EURAM programmes apply a transversal approach to the innovation process. Rather than focusing their support on a specific type of technology or on a specific industrial sector, they concentrate their intervention at the level of the production technologies in the broad area of material processing and manufacturing technologies. For example, among the projects financed there are some carrying on research on chemical process but not on chemical products or, alternatively, on electrical materials but not electrical equipment. The European economic situation in the 1980s can explain why this approach has been chosen. On the one hand, to reach a higher level of technological cohesion between the less-favoured regions of the EU, such as Greece and Portugal, and the more advanced, such as Germany and the UK, Community action had to focus not only on leading edge technologies but also on more traditional ones. Moreover, the focus on production technologies allows a general upgrading of the industrial structure of less developed regions through the development of knowledge that can be transferred to the production of other products. On the other hand, the large penetration of Japanese and, to a lesser extent, American products during the 1980s was interpreted as evidence of the existence of lower cost production processes. Hence, there was a need to stimulate process innovations with the ability to lower European manufacturing production costs.

Looking at the projects financed,[8] it is possible to highlight the participation of firms from most industrial sectors. Nonetheless, automobile, machine tool/mechanical engineering, materials processing, aeronautics, electrical materials and civil engineering can be considered the core sectors. At the technology level, particular emphasis has been put on automatism and informatics, design, structural material technologies, and functional material technologies. One must also bear in mind that the most important disciplines are applied mathematics and informatics, applied physics, and material science.

A heterogeneous set of participants took part in the BRITE-EURAM shared-cost projects. In the first and second programmes, big companies are the largest single type of institution in terms of both participation and funding. Small and medium enterprises have a level of participation similar to that of big companies, but their funding is lower, although higher than that for the total of the Framework Programmes.[9] The large participation of SMEs owes much to the special incentives for their participation present in the BRITE-EURAM programmes and to the large presence of SMEs in sectors like textile/clothing and material processing. As discussed below in Section 7.2, even if the BRITE-EURAM programmes have a strong industrial orientation, HEIs are playing a relatively important role accounting for about one-quarter of the total participation and one-fifth of total funding. Their contribution to the projects has been mainly in terms of basic research with industrial applicability.

Given the technological and sectoral foci of the BRITE-EURAM programmes, the distribution of participation by countries mirrors the industrial strengths in manufacturing and materials processing of the European countries. Germany is the country with the highest level of participation, followed by France and the UK. In particular, Germany tends to have a strong involvement in automobiles, machine tools and chemistry; France appears to have an edge in automobiles, aeronautics and instruments; the UK is especially present in civil engineering and electricity/electronics.

7.1.1   The BRITE-EURAM Research Programmes

The first BRITE-EURAM programme was built upon the experience and achievements of both BRITE (Basic Research in Industrial Technologies for Europe) and EURAM (European Research on Advanced Materials) programmes. Under BRITE (1985–88), 215 shared-cost research projects were developed. The Commission of the European Communities allocated to it public funds of about 180 MECUs. The most relevant aim of the programme was to develop the applications of new technologies and new materials in traditional industrial sectors. During the same span of time under the EURAM (1986–89) programme, the Commission of the European Communities approved 91 projects, totalling 30 MECUs. The programme was supported with the goal of stimulating the development of research in new materials (Commission of the European Communities, 1992c, p. 65).

The BRITE-EURAM 1 (1989–92) programme (henceforth B-E I) is hence the aggregation and extension of these two programmes. It was approved by the Council of Ministers on 14 March 1989 and budgeted in the Second Framework Programme for about 500 MECUs. The main aim of this 4-year programme was to improve the competitiveness of European manufacturing and material processing industries in the world market. Also relevant were the following strategic objectives: (i) to foster trans-frontier collaboration in strategic industrial research, (ii) to support the transfer of technology across Community frontiers and between sectors, particularly those with many SMEs, and (iii) to underpin the process of European cohesion (Commission of the European Communities, 1993c, pp. 9–16). Even if the programme was devoted to pre-competitive research, it was characterised, more than the previous two, by a market-oriented activity. The programme covered five R&D areas: (1) Advanced Materials

Technology; (2) Design Methodology and Assurance for Products and Processes; (3) Application of Manufacturing Technologies; (4) Technologies for Manufacturing Processes; (5) Aeronautics. To assist SMEs the programme included not only shared-cost research contracts, but also concerted actions and feasibility awards.[10] The emphasis on SMEs and the more market-oriented kind of research supported distinguish the B-E I programme from the two previous ones. In the four years' lifespan of the B-E I programme, about 1000 different institutions took part in at least one of the 350 shared-costs collaborative R&D projects which have been financed by the Commission of the European Communities.[11]

On 9 September 1991 the Industrial and Material Technology programme – BRITE-EURAM II – (henceforth B-E II) – was approved, within the Third Framework Programme, for the period 1991–94 by the Council of Ministers. The operating budget of the programme was approximately 670 MECUs. This programme resulted from the merging of the two programmes B-E I and Raw Materials and Recycling (1990–92).[12] Following the previous programme, the basis of B-E II was the revitalisation of European manufacturing industry. Its main aims were: (i) to increase the competitiveness of European industry in the face of strong international challenges, particularly in strategic sectors of advanced technology; (ii) to strengthen European economic and social cohesion consistent with the pursuit of scientific and technical excellence; (iii) to increase the implementation of advanced technologies by SMEs; (iv) to increase the involvement of manufacturing SMEs in European RTD thereby developing links with other enterprises (Commission of the European Communities, 1992d, pp. 7–11). Eventually, the programme was characterised by the focus on advanced technology, the relevance given to the process of European economic and social cohesion and by the particular support for the SMEs' participation.[13]

The programme included three main R&D areas: (1) Materials and Raw Materials with the two sub-areas of Raw Materials and Recycling, and New and Improved Materials and their Processing; (2) Design and Manufacturing with the two sub-areas of Design, and Manufacturing and Engineering; (3) Aeronautics. Industrial enterprises, universities, research organisations and other institutions have taken part in the programme through five schemes of support. They are: (1) shared-cost collaborative research projects. In particular, about 90 per cent of the available Community research budget was ascribed to the two sub-categories Industrial Research (80 per cent) and Focused Fundamental Research (10 per cent); (2) concerted actions already implemented in B-E I; (3) accompanying measures, among which the previously mentioned feasibility awards were particularly important; (4) co-operative research action for technology; and (5) targeted research actions.[14] Up to March 1994, about 1050 different institutions had taken part in at least one of the 323 shared-cost collaborative R&D projects financed by the Commission of the European Communities.[15]

Of particular note from the previous description is the continuity present between the two BRITE-EURAM programmes. Indeed, B-E II can be seen as a further step in the process of definition of a European programme. Due also to the Maastricht Treaty and to the feedback from the previous programme, B-E II turned out to be a programme with a clearer strategic orientation and an improved and enlarged variety of schemes of support.

The current research and technological development programme in the field of industrial and materials technologies BRITE-EURAM III (1994–98) (henceforth B-E III) was approved by the Council of Ministers on 27 July 1994. The operating budget of the programme was set at about 1500 MECUs. As with other programmes, the concern with the competitive position of the European manufacturing industry is at the heart of the programme. In particular, competitiveness is seen as the most effective means of maintaining and even increasing employment. Confronted with economic recession and the increased level of pollution, the programme hopes to stimulate the industry's capacity to 'develop technology for a human-centred production system taking account of human factors and based on clean technologies' (Commission of the European Communities, 1994d, p. 7). Three specific objectives are identified: (i) 'in the short term, priority should be assigned to research for the adaptation of existing technologies, or for the development of new technologies . . . particularly in sectors where the level of technology is lower; SMEs in these sectors account for a large proportion of European industry'; (ii) 'in the medium term, research will focus on industries which are already developing innovative technologies and strategies allowing better use of human resources while endeavouring to reduce the adverse environmental impact of production'; (iii) 'in the long term, research will focus on new technologies for the production and the design of products which allow new industries or markets to be created in a context of sustainable growth' (ibid., p. 8).

As for B-E I, the programme is subdivided into three main R&D areas: (1) Production Technologies for Future Industries; (2) Technologies for Product Innovation; (3) Technologies for Transport Means. While the first two technical areas, with different names and different sub-classes, are similar to the first two areas of B-E II, the third one has been broadened to include not only aeronautics but also other technologies for transport means. The programme is implemented through the same schemes of support used in B-E II. The only new tool is the Pre-Normative Research Project, which is linked to the fulfilment of the general goal of the Fourth Framework Programme of supporting the other Community policies through pre-normative research. Finally, the observation made above for the evolution of B-E II in comparison with B-E I, can also be made for the new programme versus the previous one. The various BRITE-EURAM programmes are the result of a process of evolution driven by the change in external economic and non-economic factors. The various modifications, however, take place without affecting a group of consolidated features of what can be defined as the BRITE-EURAM system of innovation.

7.2 UNIVERSITY PARTICIPATION IN BRITE-EURAM

The following analysis focuses on the contracts which were signed between 1989 and 1 March 1994 in the BRITE-EURAM I and BRITE-EURAM II (henceforth in general B-E) programmes.[16] The data regarding the contracts signed in the B-E programmes have been provided by the DG XII (Directorate-General Science, Research and Development) of the Commission of the European Communities.[17] The contracts signed were respectively 352, with 1783 participants in the Second Framework (SF) and 703, with 2056 participants[18] in the Third Framework (TF). For each contract available information included the title of the project, the duration of the contract, the cost and EU contribution, the participants' names and locations, and the participants' position in the network (main contractor, secondary contractor, and so on). Unfortunately, information such as the type of institution (large enterprise, small–medium enterprise, university, research organisation, and so on) and its size were not released. Also, due to their peculiarities, contracts such as feasibility award, first step CRAFT, concerted action, other 'like-grant' action and time amendments have been excluded from the data-set, while the institutions involved in contribution amendments have been considered as normal contractors taking part in the network. The data-set constructed in this way takes into account about 90 per cent of the contracts (of those involving shared-cost actions) signed during the SF, and 80 per cent of the ones signed during the TF.[19]

In relation to the type of cost reimbursement, the participants can be classified into two organisational types. The community reimburses up to 50 per cent of the project's actual costs to companies or institutes that operate a project costing system. Universities, higher education establishments and similar non-commercial bodies receive up to 100 per cent of the additional costs.

Table 7.2   Participants in the two frameworks by organisational type

Organisational type	Second framework	Third framework	Total
HEIs	476 26.8%	441 26.5%	916 26.7%
Other institutions	1 302 73.2%	1 221 73.5%	2 523 73.3%
Total	1 778	1 662	3 440

Source: Elaboration of CEC data.

Table 7.3   Main contractor figure by organisational type

Organisational type	Second framework	Third framework	Total
HEIs	72 20.6%	60 18.6%	132 19.6%
Other institutions	278 79.4%	263 81.4%	541 80.4%
Total	350	323	673

Source: Elaboration of CEC data.

As shown in Tables 7.2 and 7.3, the total population of 3440 participants is distributed among 673 contracts, with 350 contracts in the SF and 323 in the TF. If one looks at the total population, HEIs, with a bit more than a quarter of the participation, play quite a relevant role both in the SF and in the TF, while in the main contractor figure their relevance is less evident and their share decreases from the SF to the TF, indicating that industry plays a more important role in establishing the research effort. Table 7.4 shows the data concerning the EU contribution. While in the SF the share of EU contribution to HEIs and the share of their participation are about the same value, in the TF they are different due to a decrease in the EU contribution of about 4 points.

Table 7.4   EU contribution in the two frameworks by organisational type (in ECU)

Organisational type	Second framework	Third framework	Total
HEIs	101 431 835 27%	87 581 446 23%	189 013 281 26%
Other institutions	275 379 914 73%	292 722 066 77%	568 101 980 74%
Total	376 811 749	380 303 512	757 276 261

Source: Elaboration of CEC data.

To better understand the role played by HEIs in the B-E programmes, the EU contribution structure is analysed in more detail. First, the variable EU contribution has been subdivided into six categories: (1) 0–25 000 ECU; (2) 25 000–100 000 ECU; (3) 100 000–200 000 ECU; (4) 200 000–300 000 ECU; (5) 300 000–500 000 ECU; (6) > 500 000 ECU. Then, the contracts (in this case one each participant) have been classified in relation to these classes. Figure 7.1 shows the allocation of EU total contribution, with each bar representing the number of contracts present in that class. The distribution is very similar in the two frameworks. As expected, the TF usually exhibits lower values than the SF; only in the first and last category does the TF have more contracts.

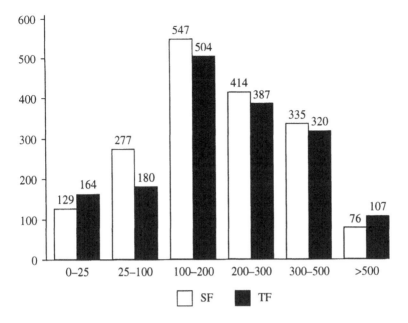

Figure 7.1   EU total contribution contracts count

Turning to Figure 7.2 (allocation of EU contribution to HEIs), one can attest that, going from the SF to the TF, a much larger number of HEIs have participated in projects with a contribution smaller than 25 000 ECU. The number of contracts in the first category is more than double. Minor changes have also occurred in other categories: HEIs decreased their presence in the fifth and sixth categories of contracts and increased their participation in projects of the fourth class. Figure 7.3 presents the allocation of EU contribution to institutions other than HEIs. Enterprises and research organisations have decreased their participation in low budget contracts (class 2 has lost a relevant number of contracts) and they have increased their presence in the top class. Overall, comparing the participation in contracts of HEIs and other institutions, it can be underscored that, although HEIs had a lower level of participation in the high categories, their presence in contracts with an EU contribution higher than 200 000 ECU (classes 4, 5 and 6) stayed unchanged, 47 per cent and 46 per cent respectively in the Second and in the Third Framework Programmes.

Comparing participation and funding figures for HEIs in B-E with the total distribution of participation and funding in the Second and Third Framework Programmes,[20] it can be pointed out that the B-E programmes are characterised by a lower level of HEIs participation than the total of all Framework

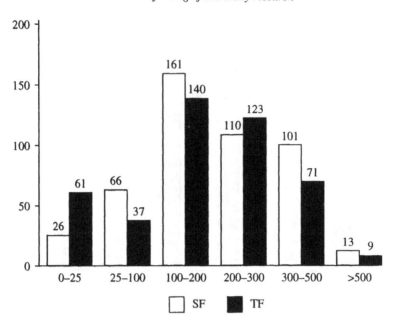

Figure 7.2   HEIs' contracts count

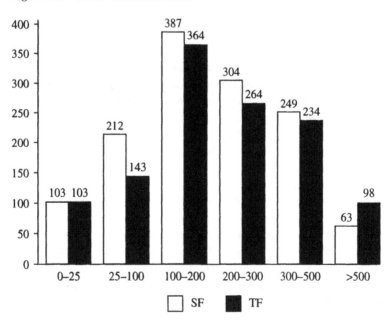

Figure 7.3   Other institutions' contracts count

Programmes. Nonetheless, the share of HEI funding in B-E remains above the HEIs' share in the total of all framework programmes. Furthermore, there is a smaller gap between the share of participation by number (Table 7.2) and by funding (Table 7.4) in B-E relative to the overall EU funding of research programmes. Therefore, even if HEIs have lost their share, they have remained strong players in the B-E programmes compared to other programmes.

7.3   THE PARTICIPATION OF UK UNIVERSITIES IN BRITE-EURAM

To analyse the relationships between EU and national university research funding the case of the United Kingdom is considered.[21] The total participation of UK institutions was respectively 17.5 per cent in the SF and 15.1 per cent in the TF. Table 7.5 shows the participation of UK institutions in the B-E programmes. The share of HEIs' participation, almost equal in the two Frameworks (35.7–35.8 per cent), is about 9 points higher than the aggregate value.[22] Only a subset of the 133 institutions of higher education in the UK (International Association of Universities, 1993) has taken part in the B-E programmes. The UK participation consisted of 49 institutions in 201 projects. Moreover, only four new institutions appear on the roster of HEIs supported by the TF, while 14 institutions that were in the SF did not participate in the TF, leaving 31 institutions that took part in both Framework Programmes. Of the 49 different HEIs participating in either Framework, 40 are 'old' universities. In other words, ex-polytechnics and other higher education institutions rarely succeeded in getting funds from the EU.[23] Of the 40 'old' universities, 26 took part in both Frameworks, while 11 participated only in the SF and 3 in the TF. In total, they account for 174 participations. Finally, if one considers the University of London, rather than the different colleges which form it, one can find 36 'old' university participants in at least one of the B-E programmes, representing 68 per cent of the total population of 'old' UK universities.

Table 7.5   Participation of UK institutions

	Second framework	Third framework	Total
Total participation	311	251	562
HEIs participation	111	90	201
Number of HEIs	45	35	49
'Old' universities	37	29	40

Source: Elaboration of CEC data.

To understand the possible relationships between the EU and the national university research funding, a field study has been carried out. In particular, due to the new market-oriented internal structure of the university, it is most relevant to focus the analysis on the department/research centre. Indeed, to shed light on the interaction among different funding sources, the mechanisms at work at the department level have to be studied. Nevertheless, the university as a whole remains the main actor, the behaviour of which is explained here. The focus on the research centre is then justified, not by the interest in explaining the functioning of the department itself, but by the need to identify the micro-mechanisms that can explain the conduct of the complete institution.

The following analysis focuses on those departments involved in the two B-E programmes. Only Materials Technology, Material Science and Engineering departments have been considered.[24] It can be maintained that each university has only one of the three departments. Thus, the number of 'old' universities can be considered as the population of reference. A sub-sample of 20 departments was contacted, the heads of the departments were interviewed via telephone, and asked to fill in a questionnaire.[25] Of these 20 departments, 16 responded to both the telephone interview and the written survey, representing the 40 per cent of the 'old' universities present in the B-E programmes and accounting for 55 per cent of the times 'old' universities (95) have participated in a contract. It is thus a meaningfully large sample. The original sample of 20 departments were selected according to the financial dimension of their university (11 Large, 6 Medium and 3 Small) and their regional location (15 England, 3 Scotland and 2 Wales). The 16 departments that responded belong to 8 Large, 6 Medium and 2 Small universities; 13 of them are located in England, 2 in Wales and 1 in Scotland.

The survey addresses the changes in the funding structure of the department in the period 1990–93 and the situation in 1994. The questions require rating on a scale of different importance (from 1: Unimportant to 5: Extremely Important) a predefined set of alternatives. The questionnaire is structured in a way that allows respondents to classify the various departments in relation to their type of research involvement (Question 1) and to their financial dimension (Question 5). All the departments have high research intensity. The funds from research council, EU contracts and services, and industry contracts and services tend to be always extremely important, they are valued on average, 4.9, 4.5 and 4.2 respectively. Only one department assesses the three sources of funds as of medium importance. The relevance of fees for the total funding of the department can be used as a proxy for teaching orientation. On average, fees reports a value of about 3.7, that is to say, of medium importance. Fifty per cent of the departments regard fees as medium or less important for the total funding of the department, confirming the strong research orientation of the sample considered. The average budget of the respondents was about £2.4m with a lowest extreme of £0.65m and a highest extreme of £4m. They have been classified as small and medium departments (SMDs) if their annual budget was below £2.9m and as large departments (LDs) otherwise.

The aim of the survey was to assess the existence of relationships between EU and national university research funding. In particular, the telephone interviews and the second, third and fourth questions of the questionnaire try to identify the presence of positive or negative dependence between the two sources of funds in terms of cumulative and self-reinforcement phenomena and substitution effect. The following observations are based on the responses of these 16 surveyed departments.

First, the presence of cumulative and self-reinforcement phenomena in the process of fund raising emerges clearly from both interviews and questionnaires. These are due to the Matthew effect.[26] Research groups that are successful in finding external funding for their research have a higher probability of producing publishable research, which improves their probability of getting funds in the future. When this concept is applied to the EU funding process, it is possible to highlight the presence of a specific 'path dependent' additional mechanism at work. Success in obtaining funds from the EU enhances the ability to raise research funds in the future from both EU and Government sources. This is due to four micro-mechanisms:

1. The level of equipment funding that the department receives from the central administration of the university depends in part upon the value of their external research contracts. EU contracts have a particularly significant weight.
2. The ability to obtain EU funds is regarded as critical for the assignment of high rank in the UK's Research Assessment Exercise. Thus, it affects the share of funds for research received by the university from the exchequer grant and the research council.
3. The international character of the competition for EU funds, and therefore the high quality of the participants, improves the reputation of the winners. Obtaining EU funds is thus reputation-building, which increases the probability that winning institutions will receive future funding both from the EU and the research council.
4. Network creation via EU co-operative projects enables the department/university to form a stable co-operation with industrial partners, which provides a means to generate projects which increase future funding.

The relevance of these micro-mechanisms is confirmed by the results of the survey. Specifically, the receipt of EU funds was judged to have a positive influence on EU sources by 79 per cent of the respondents, while 57 per cent of the respondents also found a positive effect of receipts from industrial funding. In the case of government funds the impact is generally a bit less important. This is perhaps because the Research Assessment Exercise is a relatively novel enterprise, as are the internal university negotiations about the departmental distribution of funds received by the university. Thus only 36 per cent of the responses note a positive influence, while 64 per cent claim that UK government funding had no influence.

Second, when the existence of substitution effects – that is, an increase of funds from one source is linked to a decrease of funds from another – is studied, 63 per cent of all the responses indicate no such substitution. However, if one breaks down the responses by university and by department size, it can be shown that:

- 57 per cent of the SMDs in small and medium universities observe some form of substitution;
- 71 per cent of the LDs in large universities do not notice any form of substitution.

Thus, the funding policy followed by the government appears to be influenced by the size of the department and university, implying the selective application of substitution in a manner that favours the already major research performers.

Third, the impact of government funding policy, and its interaction with the EU funding system, can be better understood when the process of diversification – that is, moving from fewer main sources of funds to more and different funding sources – is considered. In particular the findings of the survey allow the following observations:

- Overall, 56 per cent of the answers indicate an increase in its annual budget, while none indicates a decrease. However, a somewhat smaller number of the SMDs indicate increases rather than no change.
- There has been an increase of EU funds in all the departments surveyed. Their growth is particularly important for SMDs.
- The research council funds have generally tended to decrease, but the effect is more notable among SMDs.
- Industry funds have only undergone minor changes or have decreased mainly in SMDs in small and medium universities.
- The exchequer grant has been cut in all the departments without distinction as to the dimension of the department budgets.

If the department budget size and university budget size are respectively taken as proxy for 'quality' and political power, it can be maintained that, on the one hand, UK government university research funding tends to be additional to EU funding mainly for a small group of high quality/politically strong departments/universities. On the other hand, SMDs, especially when located in small and medium universities, rely for their research money to a larger extent on EU funds which, although highly concentrated, are more broadly distributed across universities. Furthermore, due to the recent economic recession, business enterprises have reduced external funds for research, and high quality departments or universities with long lasting industrial relationships have strengthened their advantage in obtaining contract and grants from industry.

7.4   CONCLUSIONS

The research and development policy of the EU appears to increasingly affect the implementation of national policies. Given the partial overlapping of EU and national actions, a better understanding of their interactions is needed. The analysis of the relationships between EU and national research funding can be developed at different levels of aggregation. Here the interactions between the two sources of funds have been analysed at the level of the university. Although the income from EU contracts and services accounts for only a small portion of total university funding, their relevance becomes much more evident when compared with a similar source of funds – for example, research grants and contracts with the research councils.[27]

Three main conclusions can be drawn from the analysis of the relationships between EU and national university research funding in the UK context. First, the group of universities involved in the B-E programmes tends to be quite large in comparison to the total population of 'old' universities, although it is small compared to the number of HEIs. Second, the analysis at the department level has highlighted a set of mechanisms that, by their intrinsic nature, reinforce the research and grant-servicing capabilities of the players that are in the game. They also increase the cost – that is, the required quality – that a potential new entrant has to pay to gain access to funding. Third, some evidence has been found to support the view that small and medium-sized departments, mainly when they are part of a small or medium university, suffer funding substitution, while for large departments EU funds seem to be accompanied by substantial funds from the UK government.

Whether or not the overall impact of UK government research policies regarding universities gives rise to a substitution of EU funds for national resources, depends not only on the consequence of conscious, deliberate government policy directions but also on the outcome of criteria applied in pursuit of other objectives. The promotion of greater stratification among universities with regard to the conduct of research may cause the addition of the two sources of funds as an outcome of strengthening the already large and elite research institutions. Or, by further handicapping the smaller institutions and weakening them in their ability to compete for funding from government and industry, it might produce such a contraction as to yield, over time, unambiguous evidence of substitution.

Further research evaluating different programmes and countries is required to support the results of this analysis. Nonetheless, the outcome of this study points to the relevance of unintended consequences in policy analysis. Particularly in the case in which there is a lack of or only partial co-ordination between various policy actions, such as in the case of EU and national research funding, the final outcomes of these actions will be determined by their interactions. Hence, the existence of diversified non-co-ordinated competitive funding sources may give rise to effects that were not intended by policy makers.

NOTES

1. See Chapter 5, Section 5.1.1 Table 5.1 for the figures in the UK case.
2. For an analysis of current co-ordination actions see Commission of the European Communities (1994c).
3. See, among others, Commission of the European Communities (1994b) and EIPA (1991) for a discussion of the subsidiarity principle.
4. The source of these figures are estimations made by the OST (1996).
5. Environment, agriculture, transport and infrastructure are included in Support to public policy. Nuclear research financed by the EU Frameworks is mainly carried out in the joint research centres.
6. See Section 7.1.1 for the description of their structure and aims.
7. Pharmaceuticals and electronics are excluded because the research in these sectors is the focus of other Community programmes.
8. For a detailed evaluation of the programmes BRITE, EURAM, and BRITE-EURAM I see Commission of the European Communities (1997b, 1996, 1993d).
9. See Table 6.2, Chapter 6 for the distribution of participation and funding by organisational type in the two Framework Programmes.
10. Concerted actions are projects to support the co-ordination of broad-based, pan-European collaborative research activities in promising new technologies with the benefit of real added value as a result of cross-border collaboration. The Commission supports the co-ordination costs, but not the research costs. Feasibility awards are a special type of contract, available only to SMEs, that cover up to 75 per cent of the costs of research undertaken within nine months (subject to a maximum of 30 000 ECU) to establish the feasibility of a concept, process or material for a collaborative BRITE-EURAM project.
11. See Appendix 1: Network Formation and the Main Hub for the analysis of participation.
12. During the two years of life of the RAW programme, 69 shared-cost research projects for about 23 MECUs were financed.
13. The Co-operative Research Action for Technology (CRAFT) was designed to provide enterprises, especially SMEs not having their own research facilities, with the possibility to contract outside research institutes to carry out research on their behalf (ibid.: p. 13).
14. Targeted research actions were focused on specific subjects of common interest – for example, environmentally friendly technologies and flexible and clean manufacturing. They supported industrial research projects that may be grouped together and be subject to special co-ordination to ensure synergy between the separate projects.
15. See Appendix 1: Network Formation and the Main Hub for the analysis of participation.
16. In Appendix 1 an analysis of the network characteristics of the BRITE-EURAM programmes is presented. For an analysis of the dynamics of research network in BRITE-EURAM see Garcia-Fontes and Geuna (1998).

17. The contracts signed under RAW and AERONAUTICS are not included.
18. Here the participants' number accounts for any type of contractor including also institutions involved in time/contribution amendments. Instead, in the statistics presented in the following analysis only contractors involved in shared-cost actions are considered as participants.
19. The data for the Third Framework were only available up to 1 March 1994, the 80 per cent represents an estimate of the contracts signed up to that date.
20. See Table 6.2, Chapter 6 for the distribution of participation and funding by organisational type in the two Framework Programmes.
21. For a broad analysis of the impact of European Community policies upon science and technology in the United Kingdom see Georghiou et al. (1993). For the analysis of the additionality issue in the UK context see David, Geuna and Steinmueller (1995).
22. See Table 7.2 HEIs' share.
23. An intriguing question is whether these institutions do not have the competence/quality necessary for applying to the EU or if they 'strategically' decide not to apply.
24. These are the three research units that have taken part most frequently in B-E programmes.
25. See the annexed telephone questions and questionnaire (Appendix 2).
26. Chapter 6, Section 6.2 introduced an interpretative framework in which cumulative and self-reinforcement phenomena are influencing the allocation of funds to universities at the European level.
27. In the UK EU funds are, on average, 21 per cent of research council funds, and for about 10 per cent of the institutions they represent more than 50 per cent. One head of department interviewed pointed out that if EU funds had to be cut the department would run the risk of closing down.

APPENDIX 1:   NETWORK FORMATION AND THE MAIN HUB

This appendix presents the analysis of the network structure of B-E programmes. Table 7.A1 shows the distribution of participation according to the position in the network. Going from the Second to the Third Framework two main changes in the network structure can be highlighted. First, there has been an important increase in the number of subcontractors.[1] Networks have become more branched in small components. Therefore, the number of network linkages with different priority level has increased. On the one extreme there are the relationships among contractors at the international level, on the other extreme there are the linkages between contractors and sub-contractors at the local level which were pre-existing to the RTD project. The increase in subcontractors implies an increased probability of having networks composed by parts of already pre-existing networks. Therefore, networks of the TF are characterised by less genuine novelty.

Table 7.A1   Distribution of participation type

Participation type	Second framework	Third framework	Total
Main contractor	350 (19.7) ·	323 (19.4)	673 (19.5)
Second contractor	337 (19.9)	312 (18.8)	649 (18.9)
Third contractor	305 (17.1)	296 (17.8)	601 (17.5)
Fourth contractor	258 (15.5)	196 (11.8)	454 (13.2)
Fifth contractor	178 (10.0)	135 (8.1)	313 (9.1)
Other contractors	130 (7.3)	142 (8.5)	272 (7.9)
Sub contractors	220 (12.4)	258 (15.6)	478 (13.9)
Total	1778	1662	3440

Note: Figures in parentheses are percentages.

Source: Elaboration of CEC data.

Second, up to the third contractor there are no big differences between the two frameworks. Instead, the share of participants identified as fourth contractor has strongly decreased in the TF. Hence, in the last framework the networks are composed by a smaller number of contractors. Typically in the TF there are three contractors and a certain number of subcontractors. In general, the TF's networks are then characterised by a lower number of contractors and a larger number of subcontractors.

Table 7.A2   Network by number of participants

Number of participants*	Second framework	Third framework	Total
1	7 (2.0)	3 (0.9)	10 (1.5)
2	22 (6.3)	7 (2.2)	29 (4.3)
3	44 (12.6)	91 (28.2)	135 (20.1)
4	58 (16.6)	52 (16.1)	110 (16.3)
5	94 (26.9)	54 (16.7)	148 (22.0)
6	61 (17.4)	42 (13)	103 (15.3)
> 6	64 (18.3)	74 (22.9)	138 (20.5)
Total	350	323	673

Notes:
* The number of participants is given by the sum of co-ordinator, contractors, subcontractors and contribution amendments contractors.
Figures in parentheses are percentages.

Source: Elaboration of CEC data.

When one takes into account the average network size, the distinction between contractors and subcontractors becomes less important. Table 7.A2 illustrates the networks' distribution by size (number of partners) in the two frameworks. While the mean number of partners is about five for both frameworks, in the TF slightly less than 50 per cent of the projects are carried out by networks with four or less participants. This is due to the fact that an extremely high number of networks (91) have only three participants. In the SF the networks with five participants are the ones with the highest share. Going from the Second to the Third Framework the size of the network witnesses a contraction, with a polarisation of projects within the three-participants network structure.

In general, without taking into account the participants' position in the network, the most recent B-E programme is characterised by networks of smaller size. Moreover, when the type of participants is considered too, the networks of the TF are not only smaller but they are also characterised by a larger number of subcontractors, then by an increasing number of, probably pre-existing, one-to-one relations.

To shed more light on the structure of participation in the B-E programmes the concentration in the participation is analysed. A name has been assigned to the various participating institutions and they have been identified in the different projects in both frameworks. The result is shown in Table 7.A3. An institution can be involved in RTD projects only once (single participation), or several times (repeated participation). For the latter type of organisation it is possible to calculate how many times, including the first, it has taken part in a project (expanded participation). The analysis of these variables allows us to highlight the following observations.

Table 7.A3   Concentration in the participation

	Second Framework		Third framework		Total	
Single participation (A)	711 (40%)	71.2%	780 (47%)	75.3%	1184 (34.4%)	69.6%
Repeated participation (B)	287	28.8%	256	24.7%	516	30.4%
Total Number of institutions (C) = (A) + (B)	998		1036		1700	
Expanded participation (D)	1067 (60%)		882 (53%)		2256 (65.6%)	
Total participation (E) = (A) + (D)	1778		1662		3440	

Source: Elaboration of CEC data.

First, the average level of participation for the institutions with repeated participation (B) is decreasing, from an average participation in 3.7 projects in the Second Framework to 3.4 in the Third. In other words the institutions with only one participation obtained a higher share of contracts (from 40–47 per cent). Second, when one considers the two frameworks together an increase in the average level of participation (4.4 projects per institution) can be highlighted. That is due to the presence of institutions that are both in the Second and in the Third Framework. Third, there are 334 institutions present at least once in both frameworks. This group of institutions is characterised by an average level of participation equal to 5.4. Moreover, these 334 institutions, after the first participation, are involved another 1474 times in a project. Considering that in the two frameworks there are 1740 contracts with institutions that already had a participation (D − B = 2256 − 516), it means that 334 institutions are responsible for 85 per cent of the repetitions (1474 = 85 per cent of 1740). They represent only 19.6 per cent of the population, but they account for 1808 contracts, that is to say 52.6 per cent of the total contracts signed during the two frameworks. Fourth, the 516 institutions with repeated participation (B) in both the frameworks can be divided into two groups: the first one formed by the 334 institutions with a mean participation of 5.41 and a second group of 182 institutions with an average level of participation equal to 1.46 (266/182, where 266 = 1740 – 1474). Finally, the 1700 institutions present in the two frameworks can be characterised as follows:

- the 'singles' formed by 1187 institutions that got only one contract;
- the 'networkers' formed by 182 institutions that got more contracts, but only in one framework;
- the 'main hub' constituted by 334 institutions that got more contracts in both frameworks.

To conclude, the analysis of the network structure of the B-E programmes highlights the efforts of the Commission to enlarge the population of institutions involved in R&D projects. In the TF there is, indeed, a larger variety; there are more institutions with a single participation. Nonetheless, it is extremely important to stress the relevance of the main hub. If 19 per cent of the institutions succeeded in getting 52 per cent of the contracts it means that more than half of the EU funds were directed to the same group of institutions. Assuming that these organisations have an extremely high research quality, then excluding every kind of bureaucratic inertia and lobbying this implies that the distribution of funds is heavily shaped by the merit criterion and then strongly influenced by cumulative and self-reinforcement mechanisms.

NOTE

1. Each contractor is entitled to subcontract part of his research to other institutions that become his specific subcontractor.

APPENDIX 2:   TELEPHONE INTERVIEWS AND
QUESTIONNAIRE

Telephone Interview, Four Questions:

First, How have the sources of funds for research changed over time in your department?

Second, Is there some kind of positive or negative interrelation among the various sources of funds?

Third, What type of research expenditure have been most influenced by recent funding patterns.

Fourth, Can you say something specific on the role played by the EU funds?

Questionnaire:

QUESTION I

The annual survey on university financing, published by the Universities' Statistical Record, identifies a certain number of income sources. At the most aggregate level the breakdown is among the seven classes we use below.

How important are the following sources/classes for the total funding of your department this year? (*Circle your choice*)

	Unimportant				Extremely Important
1. Exchequer Grant	1	2	3	4	5
2. Research Council	1	2	3	4	5
3. Government contracts and services	1	2	3	4	5
4. EU contracts and services	1	2	3	4	5
5. Industry contracts and services	1	2	3	4	5
6. Fees	1	2	3	4	5
7. Others	1	2	3	4	5

QUESTION 2

Do you think that in recent years (1990–1993) the funding structure of the department has undergone a process of diversification (***Diversification***: moving from fewer main sources of funds to more and different funding sources)? (*Circle your choice*)

YES   NO

If yes, how important was the change (growth or contraction) of the following classes in the years 1990–1993? (*Circle positive* (+) *or negative* (–) *to indicate diversification change*)

	Unimportant						Extremely Important
1. Exchequer Grant	+	–	1	2	3	4	5
2. Research Council	+	–	1	2	3	4	5
3. Government contracts and services	+	–	1	2	3	4	5
4. EU contracts and services	+	–	1	2	3	4	5
5. Industry contracts and services	+	–	1	2	3	4	5
6. Fees	+	–	1	2	3	4	5
7. Others	+	–	1	2	3	4	5

QUESTION 3

Have you noted some form of substitution (*Substitution*: an increase of funds from one source is linked to a decrease of funds from another) among the various form of funding in your department in recent years (1990–1993)? (*Circle your choice*)

YES   NO

If yes, do you agree/disagree that the following forms of substitutions have occurred?

	Strongly Agree				Strongly Disagree
1. Fees have substituted Exchequer Grant	1	2	3	4	5
2. EU contract and services have substituted Research Council	1	2	3	4	5
3. EU contract and services have substituted Government contract and services	1	2	3	4	5
4. Industry contract and services have substituted Research Council	1	2	3	4	5
5. Industry contract and services have substituted Government contract and services	1	2	3	4	5
6. Research Council has substituted Exchequer Grant	1	2	3	4	5
7. Others. (Specify which and how important)					

QUESTION 4

Do you think that EU funds receipt has had either a positive or a negative influence on the following funding sources? (*Circle your choice*)

	Strongly Positive	No Influence			Strongly Negative
1. Exchequer Grant	1	2	3	4	5
2. Research Council	1	2	3	4	5
3. Government contracts and services	1	2	3	4	5
4. EU contracts and services	1	2	3	4	5
5. Industry contracts and services	1	2	3	4	5
6. Fees	1	2	3	4	5
7. Others	1	2	3	4	5

QUESTION 5

Could you please give us an estimate of the annual budget of your department including total salaries and other costs?

£.......................

Has this value changed in the last four to five years? (*Circle your choice*)

    a) Increased   b) Decreased   c) No Change

Could you please tell us the number of BRITE-EURAM projects in which your department has been involved?

PART IV

Summary and Conclusions

8. Conclusions

This book has focused on the economics of European universities and, in particular, on the issue of how the changing structure of research funding influences university research behaviour. Its overall objective has been to evaluate the presence and importance of the unintended consequences of recent changes in the rationale for allocating society's resources to the support of university research and related training activities. In Part I this issue has been examined from a theoretical perspective, introducing an economics approach to university research behaviour that allows one to take into account and evaluate the indirect consequences of the new competitive approach to university behaviour and funding. On the basis of this and an evolutionary account of European universities which defined the unit of analysis of the book, empirical modelling has been used to test some of the behavioural hypotheses in Part II and Part III. This concluding chapter gives an overview of the results of this book and presents some possible directions for further research.

Before turning to review the principal findings, a reminder of the disciplinary perspective on the subject matter and the methodology of this book may be called for. The economics of university research behaviour has been approached in this book not only within the larger framework of public economics complementary to the economics of science, but also it has been related explicitly to the literature on industrial knowledge production and innovation processes. This work therefore may be seen as an effort to provide one necessary building block for the economics of knowledge production and distribution, interpreting the latter to comprise the study of all the various public and private components of the system upon which the modern knowledge-based economy has come to depend.

8.1 SUMMARY OF THE RESULTS

Part I presents European universities as the units of analysis of the book, and develops both a theoretical framework and an historical characterisation of certain functions of these institutions. Chapter 2 introduces an economics approach to the analysis of university research behaviour, which motivates and guides all of the empirical analysis carried out in this book. After showing that the utility-maximising approach to university behaviour is an unsatisfactory framework to study the current changes underway in the university system, an alternative framework is proposed. This seeks to explain university research behaviour as a result of the relevant incentives and constraints. The examination of the impacts, in terms of incentives and constraints, of a diversified funding structure for university research lies at the core of this analysis. Chapter 2 not only yields an analysis of university research behaviour but, linking this to the changes in the rationale for resource allocation to the university, puts forward behavioural hypotheses that are tested in the empirical studies of Parts II and III. In particular, the presence of unintended consequences of the competitive rationale for resource allocation is examined in relation to the following four problematiques: (1) increased concentration of resources; (2) disproportionate incentives for a short-term foreseeable research endeavour; (3) conflicting incentive structures; and (4) exacerbation of the impact of cumulative and self-reinforcement phenomena present in the process of scientific production.

An evolutionary account of European universities is presented in Chapter 3. The historical analysis of the development of the institutions of higher education and research (after the eighteenth century) in Europe reveals that, although important national idiosyncrasies are present, a set of common attributes characterise European universities. Highly diversified modern European universities are the result of a process of incremental institutional innovation. Their governance and organisation derive from the medieval tradition, the approach to scientific discovery developed by the scientific societies, the Humboldtian ideal of university and the postwar rationale of the 'endless frontier'. Hence, contemporary university behaviour is based on operating and decision-making rules that have developed in the adjustment to changes in the environment all along the history of the university.

Since the Second World War a process of rapid growth and diversification has characterised the national university systems of all the EU countries. This process was paralleled by a rise in society's expectations of economic returns from the funding of university research. Chapter 3 examines the impact of these phenomena, discussing the modifications taking place in the university systems of the various EU countries. It suggests that one of the possible outcomes of the ongoing changes is the polarisation of the university system with, at the one extreme, a small group of dynamic research-oriented universities and, at the other extreme, a large group of mainly teaching-oriented institutions.

Part II begins by presenting a statistical analysis of contemporary European universities. The first section of Chapter 4 examines the level and changes in university research funding and publication output at the national level in 1981–95. Then, on the basis of an original database, it presents a detailed analysis of the total population of universities for 11 EU countries in 1992. Approximately two-fifths of the active European universities have been founded within the past 50 years. The total population of universities is characterised by a large number of small–medium-sized institutions, with low scientific research orientation and low scientific research productivity.

The second section of Chapter 4 develops a methodology to describe the university system in terms of its main features. The modelling approach used aims at analysing whether it is possible to identify well-defined clusters of institutions with similar size, research output and foundation period. The results provide robust support for the hypothesis of a stratification (polarisation) of the university system at the European level. In fact, two clearly distinct clusters of institutions have been identified. The first comprises a small group of dynamic research-oriented universities of large size, founded almost exclusively before the Second World War, with a high international scientific reputation and international networks of public and private research partners. The second is composed by a large group of small-sized institutions, mainly founded in the postwar period, which are either involved in technological research or teaching, with a national or local focus. These results suggest that the policies aimed at a more directed allocation of the research effort, and at the creation of quasi-market incentive structures developed during the 1980s and early 1990s, have already produced an extremely high level of concentration of university research.

To better understand the possible consequences of the competitive approach to university behaviour and funding, a still more detailed analysis of the relationships between funding and research output has been carried out in Chapter 5. First, the evolution of the funding structure of 'old' UK universities in the period 1989–93 is examined, showing how the growth of specific incomes has not been sufficient to cover the diminution of general funds for research.[1] Then, the econometric modelling developed in Chapter 4 is applied at the start and at the end of the period considered to evaluate the impact on the scientific publication rate of the changes in the research funding structure and, specifically, of the increased reliance on industrial funding of certain universities. The results of the analysis at the static level (at the start and at the end of the period) indicate that the universities with smaller scientific faculties and with lower scientific research productivity tend to depend more heavily on industrially funded research. Also, the analysis at the dynamic level (changes between the two periods) shows that the universities which were pushed to rely more heavily on industrial funding – that is, the ones for whom the cuts in the general public support were not offset by an increase of public specific funds – have further lowered their average scientific publication rate. The findings confirm the view that, on the one hand, the leading research-intensive UK universities are the most important recipients of industrial support and that, on the other hand, they are among the less dependent on industrial funding.[2] In addition, evidence has been found to support the hypothesis that the universities which have sustained significant cuts in public funding were pushed to do routine contract research for industry, resulting in low publications output (and spillovers) and knowledge that does not lay a basis for further scientific and technological innovations.

Overall, the two chapters in Part II present robust evidence supporting the view that the competitive approach to university behaviour and funding is resulting in the polarisation of the university system with a high concentration of research resources in a few institutions. This process accompanies an increased dependence on industrial funding of the financially weaker universities. In Chapter 5 some evidence validates the hypothesis that the routine contract research carried out for industry by these weaker institutions produces mainly private returns to the firms who support only a part of total cost. Hence it represents a form of public subsidy for particular industries for a kind of research that firms can and have to pay for themselves.

In Part III the analysis focuses on a particular type of competitive funding mechanism, the EU contract for R&D co-operative projects, and its interactions with other sources of funding. Chapter 6 examines university participation in EU-funded R&D co-operative projects. First, it presents a descriptive analysis at the aggregate level of the participation of higher education institutions in the three Framework Programmes of the European Commission. HEIs are the largest single type of institution in terms of the number of times they participated in a project. They have taken part in networks including a large majority of research institutions, but they have also collaborated with industrial partners. Finally, although they are the dominant players in a few programmes such as Step/Epoch and Environment, they also participated in a respectable number of projects in the industrially-oriented programmes.

In the second section of Chapter 6 an interpretative framework explains the different level of university participation in EU-funded R&D co-operative projects in terms of information signalling, and cumulative and self-reinforcement mechanisms. These phenomena may yield a lock-in situation in which a restricted group of institutions are repeatedly granted support from the European Commission. On the basis of this framework and a detailed statistical description of the participation of the 379 European universities in shared-cost actions funded by DG XII of the European Commission, an empirical model is developed. The aim of the two-equation regression model is to test the relevance of size, scientific research productivity, and other fixed factors on both the probability of joining an EU-funded R&D co-operative project and the actual number of times a university participated in these projects. The results of the estimations indicate that scientific research productivity influences both the probability and the level of participation, while research size has a positive influence only on the latter. Among the other results, the analysis of the fixed factors shows that in the case of Irish and Greek universities, the cohesion policy followed by the European Commission exerts some influence on the selection process. Overall, these results suggest that, on the one hand, the relevance given to scientific research productivity in the selection process, through the effect of cumulative and self-reinforcement mechanisms, favours the selection of a minority of high research-intensive institutions. This is efficient in the short term as it maximises current research output, but it may have negative long-term effects. On the other hand, the European Commission pursues long-term objectives attributing advantages in participation to the less-favoured regions (Gambardella and Garcia Fontes, 1996).

The second chapter of Part III, Chapter 7, is one of the first attempts to analyse the possible effects of competitive, non-co-ordinated university research funding from EU and national sources. To obtain the level of detail needed to carry out this type of examination, a specific programme funded by the European Commission – BRITE-EURAM – and a single country – the UK – had to be chosen. First, the chapter presents an analysis of the BRITE-EURAM innovation system, as well as of the institutional participation and network structure of the BRITE-EURAM programmes funded in the Second and Third Framework Programmes. It then studies the relationships between EU and national university research funding for the departments of Material Technology, Material Science and Engineering of the 'old' UK universities. The analysis considers both the unintended consequences resulting from the existence of two non co-ordinated sources of funds, and the deliberate action of the government in response to EU funding. Specifically, a survey and interviews have been made to evaluate the dependence between EU and national sources of research funds in terms of cumulative and self-reinforcement phenomena and substitution effects. The results of this empirical study underscore the presence of micro-mechanisms that unintentionally support a 'path dependent' funding process: success in obtaining funds from the EU enhances the probability of raising research funds in the future from both EU and government sources. These mechanisms not only reinforce the capabilities of the game-players, but also increase the research 'quality' required by a potential new entrant in order to be granted the support. Furthermore, some evidence attests to the presence of a selective application of substitution of funds from the government which favours the already major research performers.

In general, the results of the studies carried out in the two chapters of Part III indicate that, in a diversified funding structure, the criteria applied in granting a source of funds have indirect effects on the allocation of other resources. Given the existence of cumulative and self-reinforcement phenomena, these effects tend to give a disproportionate advantage to the high research-intensive universities.

8.2 OVERALL CONCLUSIONS

Building upon the conclusions emerging from the separate chapters, more general observations and questions are suggested. First, the results of the various studies carried out in this book indicate that universities, rather than presenting a homogeneous behavioural response to the modifications in the university research funding system, react according to their specific characteristics. Moreover, the competitive approach to university behaviour and funding increases differences within the university system. This augmented diversity, in turn, implies an increasingly diversified response to policy actions which leads to important unintended effects. As a result, there is the need for a rethinking of policy action reflecting the diversity present in the system. Policy initiatives should develop an approach that accounts for the heterogeneity of institutional response. In the light of these considerations, the studies developed by the new economics of science (some of them cited in this book) and this book itself can be seen as an attempt to provide a theoretical and empirical framework for understanding university research behaviour that opens the way for further research aimed at the redefinition of policy actions.

Second, although this book does not supply a definitive answer to the question of whether or not the competitive approach to university behaviour and funding causes a shift in university research away from fundamental research, some indications in support of this view have been found. If this is the case, as it seems, it is highly likely that, due to the diversion of money from the funding of exploratory research to the financing of a more applied type of research, the stock of fundamental knowledge will probably increase at a slowing growth rate. With continuously shrinking government funding for fundamental research and increasing public and private spending on targeted research, the stock of general knowledge available as a foundation or enabler of more specialised research will become smaller relative to the demands for its use. To the extent that applied and development research draws on the stock of generic knowledge, and if the stock of knowledge follows the law of diminishing returns, the marginal productivity of applied and development research will tend to decline (Aranson, 1995). Moreover, the increasing propensity to fund research with a clear and predictable output will tend to reinforce the dominant science, limiting research variety and consequently decreasing the probability of scientific innovation (Kuhn, 1970; Lakatos, 1970). This, in turn, is likely to reduce the new knowledge base from which new technological innovations can flow. Both phenomena are reinforced by a competitive research allocation of resources based on *ex-post* evaluation of university research performance. In fact, should publications be used as a primary signal of professional ability, the incentive structure would bias research decisions toward orthodox, low-risk projects (Garner, 1979).

Third, it is widely recognised that the flow of knowledge among the various sites where scientific and technological knowledge is produced, most notably between university and industry, increases social welfare because it allows a wider and more effective exploitation of the knowledge produced. Nonetheless, tighter linkages between university and industry with the aim of increasing the transfer of knowledge may produce unintended negative effects. In fact, the evidence presented in this book suggests that further government push towards a closer interaction between university and industry may have counterproductive effects. This is particularly true for those universities in a weak financial situation. Constrained to accept industrial funds for developing routine contract research, and faced with the impossibility of charging the real cost of the research,[3] their collaboration with industry results not in a contribution of university to the wealth of society, but in an exploitation for private profit of a public investment. This observation has to be related to the diverse level of industrial and government funding of the various EU countries. Whereas some countries such as the UK exhibit a high degree of university involvement in industrial research, others, such as Italy, may have space still for further development. Notwithstanding these different national situations, government policies for the development of university–industry relationships should be shaped taking into account the general point that an advantageous co-operation for both university and industry requires the existence of scientific, technological and cultural complementarities. Different capabilities are present in the various universities; policy actions should encourage university–industry collaborations that enable the building up and further development of these capabilities. A myopic push for short-term economic return may induce changes in the social organisation of the university that could damage either the university's capabilities for knowledge production or its abilities to transmit knowledge.

Finally, this book has examined the unintended consequences of the competitive approach to university research behaviour and funding, leaving the analysis of the benefits of the competitive system in the background. The implicit assumption made is that the use of a competitive funding system can generate positive effects, mainly in terms of efficiency improvements. The evidence presented in the book, however, indicates that the competitive approach also may give rise to important negative effects. Therefore, what is advocated here is a balance between competitive allocation mechanisms that can improve the short-term efficiency of the system, and non-competitive ones that support longer-term societal objectives.

8.3 DIRECTIONS FOR FURTHER RESEARCH

The above discussion underscores a number of interesting results emerging from the economic approach to university research behaviour developed in this book. These are not conclusive, but, on the contrary, they open the way for further research. Different research paths can be followed; a number of them have already been discussed in the various chapters of this book. Two broad issues for further research that seem most promising at this stage may be briefly mentioned.

First, a deeper understanding of the operation of the university as an economic and social institution is needed. Although Chapter 2 acknowledges the need for a general theory of university behaviour, it has only focused on university research behaviour and, specifically, on its response to changes in the external environment. For that reason, a general system theory of the operation of 'the university' which takes into account the multi-product character of the institution and considers both the internal university behaviour and the response of the university to external changes would greatly contribute to the understanding of the process of knowledge production and distribution. Currently, this research path is hindered by the lack of reliable statistics for the implementation of empirical studies to test alternative behavioural hypotheses, and the difficulties posed by the recognised heterogeneity of the population of institutions of higher education.

A second important research path would be to obtain a better understanding of the implications of the collaboration between university and industry. Although a large body of literature has been produced on university–industry collaboration, clear answers have yet to be given to questions such as: What are the economic and social returns of the substitution of industrial funding for public sector support? What are the trade-offs, if indeed any exist? Is there an optimal share of universities' total research budgets that is financed by industry? Having said this, there is the need for both theoretical and empirical studies analysing university–industry collaboration and its implications from the perspective of the university.[4] This research would contribute not only to the rethinking and reassessment of the science and technology framework, but it could facilitate identification of a 'best practice' which could be more widely diffused for implementation through internal university procedures and external regulatory action.

NOTES

1. In particular, while EU funding receipts have risen throughout the period, UK Industry funding receipts, after an initial small increase, have shown negative growth rates.
2. A similar observation is also true for US universities (Baldwin, 1996).
3. This is due both to the organisational structure of the university, and to the use of the results of research funded with public funds to develop private research.
4. A closely related topic, rarely discussed in the literature, is the understanding of the implications for the university structure of different industrial funds raising capabilities of the various disciplines.

Annex A: Data sources

EU Participation: DGXII, Directorate-General Science, Research and Development, Commission of the European Communities.

INDRE: University Statistics. Volume Three: Finance, Universities' Statistical Record, 1991, 1994.

NEWOLD: International Handbook of Universities, International Association of Universities, 1991, 1993.

No. Researchers: International Handbook of Universities, International Association of Universities, 1991, 1993; different national reports on higher education.

No. Students: International Handbook of Universities, International Association of Universities, 1991, 1993; different national reports on higher education.

NSCIRES: University Statistics. Volume Three: Finance, Universities' Statistical Record, 1991, 1994.

Publications: Science Citation Index, CD-ROM version, ISI, 1993.

SPRUPUBS: J.S. Katz and D. Hicks, B.E.S.S. Database, SPRU, 1996.

RETOT: University Statistics. Volume Three: Finance, Universities' Statistical Record, 1991, 1994.

Bibliography

Adams, J.D. and Z. Griliches (1996), 'Research productivity in a system of universities', *NBER Working Papers Series*, no. 5833.

Aldenderfer, M.S. and R.K. Blashfield (1984), *Cluster Analysis*, London: Sage Publications.

Antonelli, C. (1995), *The Economics of Localized Technological Change and Industrial Dynamics*, Dordrecht: Kluwer Academic Publishers.

Aranson, P.H. (1995), 'Normative and positive theories of science and technology policy', in J.W. Sommer (ed.), *The Academy in Crisis*, Oakland, CA: The Independent Institute.

Arora, A. and A. Gambardella (1990), 'Complementarity and external linkages: the strategies of large firms in biotechnology', *Journal of Industrial Economics*, **38**, 361–79.

Arora, A. and A. Gambardella (1997), 'Public policy towards science: picking stars or spreading wealth?', *Revue d'Economie Industrielle*, **79** (1), 63–76.

Arora, A., P.A. David and A. Gambardella (1998), 'Reputation and competence in publicly-funded science: estimating the effects on research group productivity', *Annales d'Economic et de Statistique* 49/50, 163–98.

Arrow, K.J. (1962), 'Economic welfare and the allocation of resources for inventions', in R. Nelson (ed.), *The Rate and Direction of Inventive Activity: Economic and Social Factors*, Princeton, MA: Princeton University Press.

Arrow, K.J. R.W. Cottle, B.C. Eaves and I. Olkin (eds) (1996), *Education in a Research University*, Stanford, CA: Stanford University Press.

Arthur, W.B. (1988), 'Competing technologies: an overview', in G. Dosi et al. (eds), *Technical Change and Economic Theory*, London: Pinter.

Arundel, A., G. van de Paal and L. Soete (1995), *Innovation Strategies of Europe's Largest Industrial Firms*, PACE Report prepared for the SPRINT Programme.

AXION (1995), *The Impact of EC R&D Policy on the European Science and Technology Community 1987–1991 2nd Framework Programme. National Impact Studies Synthesis*, Study conducted on behalf of the European Commission, Interim Report.

Backhaus, J.G. (ed.) (1993), 'The economics of science policy: an analysis of the Althoff system', special issue of *Journal of Economic Studies*, **20**, (4/5).

Baldwin, W.L. (1996), 'The US research university and the joint venture: evolution of an institution', *Review of Industrial Organization*, **11**, 629–53.

Ball, R. and R. Wilkinson (1994), 'The use and abuse of performance indicators in UK higher education', *Higher Education*, **27**, 417–27.

Bania, N., R.W. Eberts and M.S. Fogarty (1993), 'Universities and the startup of new companies: can we generalize from Route 128 and Silicon Valley?', *The Review of Economics and Statistics*, **75**, 761–4.

Baumol, W.J., J.C. Panzar and D.G. Willig (1982), *Contestable Markets and the Theory of Industrial Structure*, New York: Harcourt Brace Jovanovich.

Beasley, J.E. (1990), 'Comparing university departments', *Omega*, **18**, 171–83.

Becker, G.S. (1962a), 'Investment in human capital: a theoretical analysis', *Journal of Political Economy*, **70**, 9–49.

Becker, G.S. (1962b), 'Irrational behaviour and economic theory', *Journal of Political Economy*, **70**, 1–13.

Becker, G.S. (1975), *Human Capital. A Theoretical and Empirical Analysis, with Special Reference to Education*, Second Edition, Chicago: The University of Chicago Press (Midway Reprint, 1983).

Bell, D. (1976), *The Coming of Post-industrial Society. A Venture in Social Forecasting*, New York: Basic Books.

Bird, G. (1992), 'The economics of managing a university', *Studies in Higher Education*, **17**, 265–80.

Blaug, M. (1970), *An Introduction to the Economics of Education*, London: Allen Lane The Penguin Press, reprinted Penguin Books 1976.

Blume, S. (1987), 'The theoretical significance of co-operative research', in S. Blume, J. Blunders, L. Leydesdorff, R. Whitley (eds), *The Social Direction of the Public Sciences*, Sociology of the Sciences Yearbook, Vol XI.

Blume, S. (1990), *Transfer Sciences: Their Conceptualisation, Functions and Assessment*, presented to the conference 'Consequences of the Technology Economy Programme for the Development of Indicators', Paris, 2–5 July.

Borden, V.M.H. and T.W. Banta (1994), *Using Performance Indicators to Guide Strategic Decision Making*, New Direction for Institutional Research, San Francisco: Jossey-Bass.

Borden, V.M.H. and K.V. Bottrill (1994), 'Performance indicators: history, definitions, and methods', in V.M.H. Borden and T.W. Banta, *Using Performance Indicators to Guide Strategic Decision Making*, New Direction for Institutional Research, San Francisco: Jossey-Bass.

Bossard Consultant (1989), *Contract Research Organizations in the EEC*, Study and Directory carried out for the SPRINT Programme, Luxembourg.

Braxton, J.M. (ed.) (1996), *Faculty Teaching and Research: Is There a Conflict?*, New Direction for Institutional Research, San Francisco: Jossey-Bass.

Brinkman, P.T. (1990), 'Higher education cost functions', in S.A. Hoenack and E.L. Collins (eds), *The Economics of American Universities. Management,*

Operations, and Fiscal Environment, Albany, NY: State University of New York Press.

Brinkman, P.T. and L.L. Leslie (1986), 'Economies of scale in higher education: sixty years of research', *The Review of Higher Education*, **10**, 1–28.

Brizzi, G.P. and J. Verger (eds) (1990), *Le Università dell'Europa: La Nascita delle Università*, Milano: Amilcare Pizzi Editore.

Brizzi, G.P. and J. Verger (eds) (1991), *Le Università dell'Europa: Dal Rinascimento alle Riforme Religiose*, Milano: Amilcare Pizzi Editore.

Brizzi, G.P. and J. Verger (eds) (1992), *Le Università dell'Europa: Dal Rinnovamento Scientifico all'Età dei Lumi*, Milano: Amilcare Pizzi Editore.

Brizzi, G.P. and J. Verger (eds) (1993), *Le Università dell'Europa: Gli Uomini e i Luoghi*, Milano: Amilcare Pizzi Editore.

Broadbent, J and R. Laughlin (1997), 'Contracts and competition? A reflection on the nature and effects of recent legislation on modes of control in schools', *Cambridge Journal of Economics*, **21**, 277–90.

Brocke von, B. (1991), 'Friedrich Althoff: a great figure in high education policy in Germany', *Minerva*, **29**, 269–93.

Buchbinder, H. (1993), 'The market oriented university and the changing role of knowledge', *Higher Education*, **26**, 331–47.

Bush, V. (1945), *Science the Endless Frontier*, United States Government Printing Office, www.physic.uiuc.edu/ysn/docs/html_articles/vBush1945.html

Callon, M. (1991), 'Techno-economic networks and irreversibility', in J. Law (ed.), *A Sociology of Monsters: Essays on Power, Technology and Domination*, London: Routledge.

Callon, M. (1994), 'Is science a public good?', Fifth Mullins Lecture, Virginia Polytechnic Institute, 23 March 1993, *Science, Technology and Human Values*, **19**, 395–424.

Callon, M. and D. Foray (eds) (1997), 'L'economie industrielle de la science', Numéro Spécial of the *Revue d'Economie Industrielle*, **79**.

Carnoy, M. and D. Marenbach (1975), 'The return to schooling in the U.S., 1939–1969', *Journal of Human Resources*, **10**, 213–32.

Carpenter, M.P., F. Gibb, M. Harris, J. Irvine, B.R. Martin and F. Narin (1998), 'Bibliometric profiles for British academic institutions: an experiment to develop research output indicators', *Scientometrics*, **14**, 213–33.

Catalano, P.A. Mori, P. Silvestri and M. Todeschini (1993), *Chi Paga l'istruzione Universitaria? Dall'esperienza Europea una Nuova Politica di Sostegno agli Studenti in Italia*, Milano: Franco Angeli.

Cave, M. and M. Weale (1992), 'The assessment: higher education: the state of play', *Oxford Review of Economic Policy*, **8**, 1–18.

Cave, M., R. Dodsworth and D. Thompson (1992), 'Regulatory reform in higher education in the UK: incentives for efficiency and product quality', *Oxford Review of Economic Policy*, **8**, 79–102.

Cave, M., S. Hanney, M. Henkel and M. Kogan (1997), *The Use of Performance Indicators in Higher Education*, London: Jessica Kingsley.

Chapman, B. (1997), 'Conceptual issues and the Australian experience with income contingent charges for higher education', *The Economic Journal*, **107**, 738–51.

Charle, C. and J. Verger (1994), *Histoire des Universités*, Paris: Presses Universitaires de France.

Clark, B.R. (ed.) (1984), *Perspectives on Higher Education. Eight Disciplinary and Comparative Views*, Berkeley: University of California Press.

Clark, B.R. and G. Neave (eds) (1992), *The Encyclopedia of Higher Education*, Oxford: Pergamon Press.

Cobban, A.B. (1975), *The Medieval Universities: Their Development and Organization*, London: Methuen & Co. Ltd.

Cohen, W. and R. Florida (1996), *For Knowledge and Profit: University–Industry Research Centers in the United States*, New York: Oxford University Press.

Cohen, W. and D. Levinthal (1989), 'Innovation and learning: the two faces of R&D', *Economic Journal*, **99**, 569–96.

Cohen, W., R. Florida and R. Goe (1992), *University–Industry Research Centres in the United States*, Report to the Ford Foundation, Center for Economic Development, Carnegie Mellon University, Pittsburgh.

Cohendet, P., M. Ledoux and E. Zuscovitch (1988), *New Advanced Materials*, Berlin: Springer-Verlag.

Cohn, E., S.L.W. Rhine and M.C. Santos (1989), 'Institutions of higher education as multi-product firms: economies of scale and scope', *The Review of Economics and Statistics*, **71**, 284–90.

Cole, J. and S. Cole (1973), *Social Stratification in Science*, Chicago: Chicago University Press.

Cole, J. and S. Cole (1972), 'The Ortega hypothesis', *Science*, **178**, 368–75.

Commission of the European Communities (1992a), *EC Research Funding. A Guide for Applicants*, catalogue no. CD-NA-14122-EN-C.

Commission of the European Communities (1992b), *Evaluation of the Second Framework Programme for Research and Technological Development*, SEC (92), 675.

Commission of the European Communities (1992c), *BRITE & EURAM: Evaluation Study of Finished Projects. Projects Completed by December 1991*, Report EUR 14541.

Commission of the European Communities (1992d), *A Universe of Possibilities: Industrial and Material Technologies*, Information package.

Commission of the European Communities (1993a), *Catalogue of Research Projects in the Third Framework*, Report EUR 14937, EN.

Commission of the European Communities (1993b), *Working Document of the Commission Concerning the S&T content of the Specific Programmes*

Implementing the 4th Framework Programme for Community Research and Technological Development (1994–1998) and the Framework Programme for Community Research and Training for the European Atomic Energy Community (1994–1998), COM (93), 459.

Commission of the European Communities (1993c), *Evaluation of the BRITE/EURAM Programme (1989–1992) – (areas 1 to 4)*, Report EUR 15070, EN.

Commission of the European Communities (1993d), *Economic Evaluation of the Effects of the BRITE/EURAM Programmes on the European Industry*, Report EUR 15171, EN.

Commission of the European Communities (1993e), *Second Commission Working Document Concerning RTD Policy in the Community and the Fourth Framework Programme (1994–1998) of Community RTD Activities*, COM (93), 158.

Commission of the European Communities (1994a), *The European Report on Science and Technology Indicators 1994*, Report EUR 15897, EN.

Commission of the European Communities (1994b), *Report to the European Council on the Application of the Subsidiarity Principle*, COM (94), 533.

Commission of the European Communities,(1994c), *Research and Technological Development Achieving Co-ordination Through Co-operation*, COM (94), 438.

Commission of the European Communities (1994d), *Proposal for a Council Decision Adopting a Specific Research and Technological Development Programme in the Field of Materials Technologies*.

Commission of the European Communities (1996), *Evaluation of the Economic Effects of the Programmes EURAM, BRITE and BRITE-EURAM I*, Report EUR 16877, EN.

Commission of the European Communities (1997a), *Second European Report on S and T Indicators 1997*, Report EUR 17638 EN.

Commission of the European Communities (1997b), *Evaluation and Analysis of the Technological Transfer Generated by the Programmes EURAM, BRITE and BRITE-EURAM I*, Report EUR 16878, EN.

Commission Jacques Attali (1998), *Pour un Modèle Européen d'Enseignement Supérieur*, at http://www.education.gouv.fr/forum/attali.htm.

Contzen, J. (1991), 'European integration and university research: an overview', *Higher Education Management*, **3** (2), 137–44.

Cox, A. (1994), 'Derogation, subsidiarity and the single market. The case of energy exploration and extraction under the EU utilities procurement rules', *Journal of Common Market Studies*, **32** (2), 126–47.

Cozzens, S. (1989), 'What do citations count? The rhetoric-first model', *Scientometrics*, **15**, 437–47.

Cragg, J. (1971), 'Some statistical models for limited dependent variables with application to the demand for durable goods', *Econometrica*, **39**, 829–44.

Culyer, A.J. (1970), 'A utility-maximising view of university', *Scottish Journal of Political Economy*, **17**, 349–68.

Cyert, R.M. and J.G. March (1963), *A Behavioral Theory of the Firm*, Englewood Cliffs, NJ: Prentice Hall.

Daalder, H. and E. Shils (eds) (1982), *Universities, Politicians and Bureaucrats: Europe and the United States*, Cambridge: Cambridge University Press.

Dasgupta, P. and P.A. David (1987), 'Information disclosure and the economics of science and technology', Chapter 16, in G. Feiwel (ed.), *Arrow and the Ascent of Modern Economic Theory*, New York: New York University Press.

Dasgupta, P. and P.A. David (1994), 'Toward a new economics of science', *Research Policy*, **23**, 487–521.

David, P.A. (1985), 'Clio and the economics of QUERTY', *American Economic Review*, **75**, 332–7.

David, P.A. (1994), 'Positive feedbacks and research productivity in science: reopening another black box', in O. Granstand (ed.), *The Economics of Technology*, Amsterdam: Elsevier Science.

David, P.A. (1997a), 'Reputation and agency in the historical emergence of the institutions of "open" science', University of Oxford Discussion Papers in Economic and Social History.

David, P.A. (1997b), 'From market magic to calypso science policy. A review of Terence Kealey's *The Economic Laws of Scientific Research*', *Research Policy*, **26**, 229–55.

David, P.A. and D. Foray (1994), *Accessing and Expanding the Science and Technology Knowledge-base*, Working Group on Innovation and Technology Policy, DSTI/STP/TIP 94(4), Paris: OECD.

David, P.A. and W.E. Steinmueller (1995), *A Productive Tension: University–Industry Research Collaboration in the Age of Knowledge-Based Economic Development*, Stanford, CA: Stanford University Press, forthcoming 1999.

David, P.A., D.C. Mowery and W.E. Steinmueller (1994), *University–Industry Research Collaborations: Managing Missions in Conflict*, presented at the conference CEPR/AAAS 'University Goals, Institutional Mechanisms, and the "Industrial Transferability" of Research', 18–20 March, University of Stanford.

David, P.A., A. Geuna and W.E. Steinmueller (1995), *Additionality as a Principle of European R&D Funding*, A study carried out for the STOA Programme of the European Parliament, MERIT's Research Memoranda 2/95-012.

David, P.A., D. Foray and W.E. Steinmueller (1998), 'The research network and the new economics of science: from metaphors to organisational behaviour', in A. Gambardella and F. Malerba (eds), *The Organisation of Inventive Activity in Europe*, forthcoming July 1999 from Cambridge University Press.

Diamond Jr, A.M. (1996), 'The economics of science', Special Issue of *The International Journal of Knowledge Transfer and Utilization*, **9**, 3–49.

Dill, D.D. (1997), 'Higher education markets and public policy', *Higher Education Policy*, **10**, 167–85.

Dolton, P.J., D. Greenaway and A. Vignoles (1997), '"Whither Higher Education?" An economic perspective for the Dearing Committee of Inquiry', *The Economic Journal*, **107**, 710–24.

Dosi, G. (1996), 'The contribution of economic theory to the understanding of a knowledge-based economy', *Employment and Growth in the Knowledge-based Economy*, Paris: OECD.

Dosi, G., C. Freeman, R. Nelson, G. Silverberg and L. Soete (eds) (1988), *Technical Change and Economic Theory*, London: Pinter.

Dresch, S.P. (1995), 'The economics of fundamental research', in J.W. Sommer (ed.), *The Academy in Crisis*, Oakland, CA: The Independent Institute.

Dunteman, G.H. (1989), *Principal Component Analysis*, London: Sage Publications.

Edquist, C. (ed.) (1997), *System of Innovation. Technologies, Institutions and Organizations*, London: Pinter.

EIPA (1991), *Subsidiarity: The Challenge of Change*, Proceedings of the Jacques Delors Colloquium, European Institute of Public Administration, Maastricht.

Eliasson, G., S. Folster, T. Lindberg, T. Powette and E. Taguaz (1990), *The Knowledge-based Information Economy*, Stockholm: Almqvist & Wiksell.

Etzkowitz, H. (1997), 'The entrepreneurial university and the emergence of democratic corporatism', in H. Etzkowitz and L. Leydesdorff (eds), *Universities and the Global Knowledge Economy*, London: Pinter.

Etzkowitz, H. (1993), 'Enterprises from science: the origins of science-based regional economic development', *Minerva*, **XXXI** (3), 326–60.

Etzkowitz, H. (1993), 'Redesigning "Solomon's House": the university and the internationalization of science and business', in E. Crawford, T. Shinn and S. Soerling, *Denationalizing Science*, Dordrecht: Kluwer Academic Publishers, 263–88.

Evans, R. (1990), 'Le università di Oxford e Cambridge', in G.P. Brizzi and J. Verger (eds), *Le Università dell'Europa: La Nascita delle Università*, Milano: Amilcare Pizzi Editore.

Fairweather, J. (1988), 'Reputational quality of academic programs: the institutional halo', *Research in Higher Education*, **28**, 345–55.

Faulkner, W. and J. Senker (1995), *Knowledge Frontiers. Public Sector Research and Industrial Innovation in Biotechnology, Engineering Ceramics, and Parallel Computing*, Oxford: Oxford University Press.

Feller, I. (1990), 'Universities as engines of R&D-based economic growth: they think they can', *Research Policy*, **19**, 335–48.

Ferrone, V. (1992), 'Le accademie scientifiche', in G.P. Brizzi and J. Verger (eds), *Le Università dell'Europa: Dal Rinnovamento Scientifico all'Età dei Lumi*, Milano: Amilcare Pizzi Editore.

Flam, F. (1992), 'Japan bids for US basic research', *Science*, **258**, 1428–30.

Foray, D. (1994), *University–Industry Research Relations: Institutional Problems, Organization and Contractual Tools in France*, presented at The CEPR/AAAS conference 'University Goals, Institutional Mechanisms, and the "Industrial Transferability" of Research', Stanford University, 18–20 March.

Foray, D. and B.-Å. Lundvall (1996), 'The knowledge-based economy: from the economics of knowledge to the learning economy', *Employment and Growth in the Knowledge-based Economy*, Paris: OECD.

Frank, R.H. and P.J. Cook (1995), *The Winner-Take-All Society*, New York: Martin Kessler Books, The Free Press.

Freeman, C. (1987), *Technology Policy and Economic Performance: Lessons from Japan*, London: Pinter.

Freeman, C. and L. Soete (1997), *The Economics of Industrial Innovation*, London: Pinter.

Frijhoff, W. (1992), 'Universities: 1500–1900', in B.R. Clark and G. Neave, *The Encyclopedia of Higher Education*, Oxford: Pergamon Press.

Gambardella, A. and W. Garcia-Fontes (1996), 'Regional linkages through European research funding', *Economics of Innovation and New Technologies*, **4**, 123–38.

Garcia-Fontes, W. and A. Geuna (1998), 'The dynamics of network in BRITE/EURAM', in A. Gambardella and F. Malerba (eds), *The Organisation of Inventive Activity in Europe*, forthcoming July 1999 from Cambridge University Press.

Garner, C.A. (1979), 'Academic publication, market signalling, and scientific research decisions', *Economic Inquiry*, **XVII**, 575–84.

Garvin, D.A. (1980), *The Economics of University Behaviour*, New York: Academic Press.

Geiger, R.L. (1985), 'The home of scientists: a perspective on university', in B. Wittrock and A. Elzinga (eds), *The University Research System. The Public Policies of the Home of Scientists*, Stockholm: Almqvist & Wiksell International.

Geiger, R.L. (1993), *Research and Relevant Knowledge. American Research Universities Since World War II*, Oxford: Oxford University Press.

Gellert, C. (ed.) (1993), *Higher Education in Europe*, London: Jessica Kingsley Publishers.

Georghiou, L. et al. (1993), *The Impact of European Community Policies for Research and Technological Development upon Science and Technology in the United Kingdom*, Report prepared for the DGXII of the Commission of the European Communities and for the Office of Science & Technology, HMSO, London.

Geuna, A. (1996), 'The participation of higher education institutions in Community Framework Programmes', *Science and Public Policy*, **23**, 287–96.

Geuna, A. (1997), 'Allocation of funds and research output: the case of UK universities', *Revue d'Économie Industrielle*, **79** (1), 143–62.

Geuna, A. (1998a), 'Determinants of university participation in EU-funded R&D cooperative projects', *Research Policy*, **26**, 677–87.

Geuna, A. (1998b), 'The internationalisation of European universities: a return to medieval roots', *Minerva A Review of Science, Learning and Policy*, **XXXVI**, 253–70.

Getz, M., J.J. Siegfried and Hao Zhang (1991), 'Estimating economies of scale in higher education', *Economics Letters*, **37**, 203–8.

Gibbons, A. (1992), 'Biotechnology, Japanese in for American expertise', *Science*, **258** (November), 1431–3.

Gibbons, M. and B. Wittrock (eds) (1985), *Science as a Commodity: Threats to the Open Community of Scholars*, Harlow: Longman.

Gibbons, M., C. Limoges, N. Nowotry, S. Schwartzman, P. Scott and M. Trow (1994), *The New Production of Knowledge. The Dynamics of Science and Research in Contemporary Societies*, London: Sage Publications.

Gieysztor, A. (1992), 'Management and resources', in W. Rüegg, (ed.), *A History of the University in Europe. Vol.I Universities in the Middle Ages*, Cambridge: Cambridge University Press.

Gilmore, J.L. and D. To (1992), 'Evaluating academic productivity and quality', in C.S. Hollins (ed.), *Containing Costs and Improving Productivity in Higher Education*, New Directions for Institutional Research, San Francisco: Jossey-Bass.

Giorello, G., T. Regge and S. Veca (1993), *Europa Universitas*, Milano: Feltrinelli.

Glass, J.C., D.G. McKillop and N. Hyndman (1995), 'Efficiency in the provision of university teaching and research: an empirical analysis of UK universities', *Journal of Applied Econometrics*, **10**, 61–72.

Glennerster, H. (1991), 'Quasi-markets for education?', *The Economic Journal*, **101**, 1268–76.

Goff Le, J. (1990), 'Introduzione', in G.P. Brizzi and J. Verger (eds), *Le Università dell'Europa: La nascita delle Università*, Milano: Amilcare Pizzi Editore.

Gornitzka, Å., S. Kyvik and I.M. Larsen (1998), 'The bureaucratisation of universities', *Minerva A Review of Science, Learning and Policy*, **XXXVI**, 21–47.

Goudriaan, R. and H. de Groot (1993), 'State regulation and university behavior', *Journal of Economic Behavior and Organization*, **20**, 309–18.

Griliches, Z. (1996), 'Education, human capital, and growth: a personal perspective', *NBER*, Working Paper 5426.

Groot de, H., W.W. McMahon and J.F. Volkwein (1991), 'The cost structure of American research universities', *The Review of Economics and Statistics*, **73**, 424–31.

Guerzoni, L. (1997), 'L'azione del governo per la riforma dell'università: sintesi delle linee guida', MURST, contributo per la discussione, at www.murst.it/progprop/riformal.htm

Guston, H. and K. Keniston (eds) (1994a), *The Fragile Contract*, Cambridge, MA: The MIT Press.

Guston, H. and K. Keniston (1994b), 'Introduction: the social contract for science', in H. Guston and K. Keniston (eds), *The Fragile Contract*, Cambridge, MA: The MIT Press.

Hague, D. (1991), *Beyond Universities. A New Republic of the Intellect*, Hobart Paper 115, IEA London.

Hall, A.R. (1983), *The Revolution in Science, 1500–1750*, London: Longman.

Hanham, H.J. (1991), 'The funding of university research. The role of overheads', *Higher Education Management*, **3**, 107–13.

Hansen, W.L. (1970), 'Income distribution effects of higher education', *American Economic Review*, **60**, 335–41.

Hare, P. and G. Wyatt (1988), 'Modelling the determination of research output in British universities', *Research Policy*, **17**, 315–28.

Hare, P. and G. Wyatt (1992), 'Economics of academic research and its implications for higher education', *Oxford Review of Economic Policy*, **8**, 48–66.

Harris, G. and G. Kaine (1994), 'The determinants of research performance: a study of Australian university economists', *Higher Education*, **27**, 191–201.

HEFCE, *The Impact of the 1992 Research Assessment Exercise on Higher Education Institutions in England*, Ref. M 6/97, http://www.niss.ac.uk/education/hefce/pub97/

HEFCE, *Annual Report 1992–93, 1993–94*.

Hicks, D. (1995), 'Published papers, tacit competencies and corporate management of the public/private character of knowledge', *Industrial and Corporate Change*, **4**, 401–24.

Hildenbrand, W. (1989), 'Facts and ideas in microeconomics theory', *European Economic Review*, **33**, 251–76.

Hippel, E. von (1988), *The Source of Innovation*, Oxford: Oxford University Press.

HMSO (1988), *Education Reform Act 1988 Chapter 40* (Reprinted 1989) ISBN 0 10 544088 4.

HMSO (1991), *Higher Education. A New Framework*, CM 1540.

HMSO (1993), *Realising our Potential. A Strategy for Science, Engineering and Technology*, CM 2250.

Hoare, A.G. (1995), 'Scale economies in academic excellence: an exploratory analysis of the United Kingdom's 1992 research selectivity exercise', *Higher Education*, **29**, 241–60.

Hoare, A.G. (1991), 'Reviewing the review: the geography of university rationalisation', *Higher Education Quarterly*, **45**, 234–53.

Hoenack, S.A. (1990), 'An economist's perspective on costs within higher education institutions', in S.A. Hoenack and E.L. Collins (eds), *The Economics of American Universities. Management, Operations, and Fiscal Environment*, Albany, NY: State University of New York Press.

Hoenack, S.A. and E.L. Collins (eds) (1990), *The Economics of American Universities. Management, Operations, and Fiscal Environment*, Albany, NY: State University of New York Press.

Hopkins, D.S.P. (1990), 'The higher education production function: the theoretical foundations and empirical findings', in S.A. Hoenack and E.L. Collins (eds), *The Economics of American Universities. Management, Operations, and Fiscal Environment*, Albany, NY: State University of New York Press.

House of Lords, Select Committee on the European Communities (1990), *A Community Framework for R&D*, London: HMSO.

Hughes, D., L. Griffiths and J.V. McHale (1997), 'Do quasi-markets evolve? Institutional analysis and the NHS', *Cambridge Journal of Economics*, **21**, 259–76.

Hurst, E.R. (1991), 'Cost calculation and cost management of multinational research projects', *Higher Education Management*, **3**, 114–27.

International Association of Universities (1991), *International Handbook of Universities*, New York: Stockton Press.

International Association of Universities (1993), *International Handbook of Universities*, New York: Stockton Press.

Jaffe, A. (1989), 'Real effects of academic research', *American Economic Review*, **79**, 957–70.

James, E. (1978), 'Product mix and cost disaggregation: a reinterpretation of the economics of higher education', *The Journal of Human Resources*, **13**, 157–86.

James, E. (1986), 'The private nonprofit provision of education: a theoretical model and application to Japan', *Journal of Comparative Economics*, **10**, 255–76.

James, E. (1990), 'Decision processes and priority in higher education', in S.A. Hoenack and E.L. Collins (eds), *The Economics of American Universities. Management, Operations, and Fiscal Environment*, Albany, NY: State University of New York Press.

James, E. and E. Neuberger (1981), 'The university department as a non-profit labor cooperative', *Public Choice*, **36**, 585–612.

James, E. and S. Rose-Ackerman (1986), *The Nonprofit Enterprise in Market Economics*, Fundamentals of Pure and Applied Economics, Chur: Harwood Academic Publishers.

Jílek L. (ed.) (1984), *Historical Compendium of European Universities*, Geneva: CRE.

Johnes, G. (1988), 'Determinants of research output in economics departments in British universities', *Research Policy*, **17**, 171–8.

Johnes, G. (1990), 'Measures of research output: university departments of economics in the UK 1984–8', *Economic Journal*, **100**, 556–60.

Johnes, G. (1992), 'Performance indicators in higher education: a survey of recent work', *Oxford Review of Economic Policy*, **8**, 19–34.

Johnes, G. (1997), 'Costs and industrial structure in contemporary British higher education', *The Economic Journal*, **107**, 727–37.

Johnes, G. and J. Johnes (1993), 'Measuring the research performance of UK economics departments: an application of data envelopment analysis', *Oxford Economic Papers*, **45**, 332–47.

Johnston, R. (1994), 'Effects of resource concentration on research performance', *Higher Education*, **28**, 25–37.

Jongbloed, B.W.A. and D.F. Westerheijden (1994), 'Performance indicators and quality assessment in European higher education', in V.M.H. Borden and T.W. Banta (eds), *Using Performance Indicators to Guide Strategic Decision Making*, New Direction for Institutional Research, San Francisco: Jossey-Bass.

Jorgenson, D.W. (1986), 'Econometric methods for modelling producer behavior', Chapter 31 in Z. Griliches and M.D. Intriligator (eds), *Handbook of Econometrics*, Amsterdam: North-Holland.

Kaiser, F., J.G.M. Florax, J.B.J. Koelman and F.A. van Vight (1992), *Public expenditures on higher education: a comparative study in the member states of the European Community, 1975–1990*, Higher Education Policy Series, **18**, London: Jessica Kingsley.

Karady, V. (1986), 'Les universités de la Troisième République', in J. Verger (ed.), *Historie des Universités en France*, Toulouse: Bibliothéque Historique Privat.

Katz, J.S. and B.R. Martin (1997), 'What is research collaboration?', *Research Policy*, **26**, 1–18.

Katz, J.S., D. Hicks, M. Sharp and Ben R. Martin (1995), *The Changing Shape of British Science*, STEEP Special Report No 3, SPRU.

Kells, H. (ed.) (1993), *The Development of Performance Indicators for Higher Education: A Compendium for Twelve Countries*, Programme on Institutional Management in Higher Education, Paris: OECD.

Kerr, C. (1995), *The Uses of the University*, Cambridge, MA: Harvard University Press.

Kersbergen van, K. and B. Verbeek (1994), 'The policy of subsidiarity in the European union', *Journal of Common Market Studies*, **32**, 215–36.

Kesselring, R.G. and C.T. Strein (1986), 'A Test of the Williamson hypothesis for universities', *The Journal of Behavioral Economics*, **15**, 103–12.

Kirman, A.P. (1992), 'Whom or what does the representative individual represent?', *Journal of Economic Perspectives*, **6**, 117–36.

Kuhn, T.S. (1970), *The Structure of Scientific Revolutions*, 2nd edn, Chicago: University of Chicago Press.

Kuznets, S. (1966), *Modern Economic Growth: Rate, Structure, and Spread*, New Haven, CT: Yale University Press.

Kyvik, S. (1995a), 'Are big departments better than small ones?', *Higher Education*, **30**, 295–304.

Kyvik, S. (1995b), 'Department size and resources for administration', *Tertiary Education and Management*, **1**, 107–8.

Kyvik, S. (1997), 'Funding university research in Nordic countries', *Science and Public Funding*, **24**, 233–44.

Lakatos, I. (1970), 'Falsification and the methodology of scientific research programmes', in I. Lakatos and A. Musgrave (eds), *Criticism and the Growth of Knowledge*, Cambridge: Cambridge University Press.

Lambert, G. and M. Willinger (1994), *Status Quo Preservation and Organisational Inertia*, presented at the EUNETIC conference 'Evolutionary Economics of Technological Change' European Parliament, Strasbourg, 6–8 October.

Larédo, P. (1994), 'Les politiques européennes de R&D au milieu de gué', in F. Sachwald (ed.), *Les defis de la mondialisation innovation et concurrence*, Masson, Paris.

Larédo, P. (1995), *The Impact of Community Research Programmes in France*, Press Ecole des Mines de Paris.

Lee, Y.S. (1996), '"Technology transfer" and the research university: a search for the boundaries of university–industry collaboration', *Research Policy*, **25**, 843–63.

Le Grand, J.L. (1991), 'Quasi-markets and social policy, *The Economic Journal*, **101**, 1256–67.

Leydesdorff, L. (1992), 'The impact of EC science policies on the transnational publication system', *Technology Analysis and Strategic Management*, **4**, 279–98.

Lloyd, P.J., M.H. Morgan and R.A. Williams (1993), 'Amalgamations of universities: are there economies of scale or scope?', *Applied Economics*, **25**, 1081–92.

Lotka, A.J. (1926), 'The frequency distribution of scientific productivity', *Journal of the Washington Academy of Sciences*, **16**, 317–23.

Lowe, J. (1993), 'Commercialization of university research: a policy perspective', *Technology Analysis and Strategic Management*, **5**, 27–37.

Lundvall, B.-Å. (ed.) (1992), *National System of Innovation: Towards a Theory of Innovation and Interactive Learning*, London: Pinter.

Luukkonen, T., O. Persson and G. Sivertsen (1992), 'Understanding patterns of international scientific collaboration', *Science, Technology, and Human Values*, **17**, 101–26.

Maassen, A.M., C.J. Goedegebuure and D.F. Westerheijden (1993), 'Social and political conditions for changing higher education structures in the Netherlands', in C. Geller (ed.), *Higher Education in Europe*, London: Jessica Kingsley.

Machlup, F. (1982), *Knowledge: Its Creation, Distribution, and Economic Significance*, Vols.1–3, Princeton, NJ: Princeton University Press.

Malerba, F., A. Morawetz and G. Pasqui (1991), *The Nascent Globalization of Universities and Public and Quasi-Public Research Organisations*, FAST Research in the framework of the MONITOR Programme.

Mansfield, E. (1991), 'Academic research and industrial innovation', *Research Policy*, **20**, 1–12.

Mansfield, E. (1995), 'Academic research underlying industrial innovations: sources, characteristics, and financing', *The Review of Economics and Statistics*, **LXXVII**, 55–65.

Mansfield, E. and J.Y. Lee (1996), 'The modern university: contributor to industrial innovation and recipient of industrial R&D support', *Research Policy*, **25**, 1047–58.

Mantovani, A. (1991), 'Accademie scientifiche e letterarie', in G.P. Brizzi and J. Verger (eds), *Le Università dell'Europa: Dal Rinascimento alle Riforme Religiose*, Milano: Amilcare Pizzi Editore.

Martin, B.R. (1994), 'British science in the 1980s – has the relative decline continued?', *Scientometrics*, **29**, 27–56.

Martin, B.R. and J. Irvine (1983), 'Assessing basic research: some partial indicators of scientific progress in radio-astronomy', *Research Policy*, **12**, 61–90.

Martin, B.R., D.M. Hicks, E.N. Ling, J.E.F. Skea (1993), *The Effect of Size and Other Factors on the Research Performance of University Departments*, University of Sussex: SPRU.

Martino, J.P. (1992), *Science Funding. Politics and Porkbarrel*, New Brunswick: Transaction Publishers.

Massit-Folléa, F. and F. Epinette (1992), *L 'Europe des Universités. L'Enseignement Supérieur en Mutation*, Paris: La Documentation Française.

Massy, W.F. (ed.) (1996), *Resource Allocation in Higher Education*, Michigan: The University of Michigan Press.

Masten, S.E. (1997), *The Internal Organization of Higher Education; Or Why Universities, Like Legislatures, are not Organized as Markets*, mimeo, University of Michigan Business School.

Matteucci, N. (ed.) (1991), *L'Università nel Mondo Contemporaneo*, Milano: Bompiani.

McBrierty, V. (1993), 'The university–industry interface: from the lab to the market', *Higher Education Management*, **5**, 75–94.

McClellan, J.E. III (1985), *Science Reorganised: Scientific Societies in the Eighteenth Century*, New York: Columbia University Press.

Meek, V.L. and F.Q. Wood (1997), 'The market as a new steering strategy for Australian higher education, *Higher Education Policy*, **10**, 253–74.

Merton, R.K. (1968), 'The Matthew effect in science', *Science*, **159**, 56–63.

Merton, R.K. (1973), *The Sociology of Science: Theoretical and Empirical Investigations*, Chicago: Chicago University Press.

Miller, H.D.R. (1995), *The Management of Change in Universities*, Buckingham: SRHE and Open University Press.

Moed, H.F., W.J.M. Burger, J.G. Frankfort and A.J.F. van Raan (1985), 'The use of bibliometric data for the measurement of university research data', *Research Policy*, **14** (3), 131–49.

Murphy, P.S. (1995), 'Benchmarking academic research output in Australia', *Assessment and Evaluation in Higher Education*, **20**, 45–57.

National Committee of Inquiry into Higher Education (1997), *Higher Education in the Learning Society: Report of the National Committee*, Norwich: HMSO.

National Science Board (1982), *Industry–University Research Relationships*, 14th report of the NSB, Washington, DC.

Neave, G. and F. Van Vught (eds) (1991), *Prometheus Bound. The Changing Relationship Between Government and Higher Education in Western Europe*, Oxford: Pergamon Press.

Nederhof, A.J. and A.F.J. van Raan (1993), 'A bibliometric analysis of six economics research groups: a comparison with peer review', *Research Policy*, **22**, 353–68.

Nederhof, A.J. and E.C.M. Noyons (1992), 'Assessment of the international standing of university departments' research: a comparison of bibliometric methods', *Scientometrics*, **24**, 393–404.

Nelson, R.R. (1959), 'The simple economics of basic scientific research', *Journal of Political Economy*, **67**, 297–306.

Nelson, R.R. (ed.) (1993), *National Innovation System: A Comparative Analysis*, Oxford: Oxford University Press.

Nelson, R.R. and N. Rosenberg (1994), 'American universities and technical advance in industry', *Research Policy*, **23**, 323–48.

Nerlove, M. (1972), 'On tuition and costs of higher education: prolegomena to a conceptual framework', *Journal of Political Economy*, **80**, 178–s218.

OECD (1981), *The Measurement of Scientific and Technological Activities. R&D Statistics and Output Measurement in the Higher Education Sector*, Paris: OECD.

OECD (1984), *Industry and University: New Forms of Co-operation and Communication*, Paris: OECD.

OECD (1987), *Universities under Scrutiny*, Paris: OECD.

OECD (1990a), *University–Enterprises Relations in OECD Member Countries*, Paris: OECD.

OECD (1990b), *Financing Higher Education. Current Patterns*, Paris: OECD.

OECD (1992), *Public Educational Expenditure, Costs and Financing: An Analysis of Trends 1970–1988*, Paris: OECD.

OECD (1995), *Education at a Glance*, Paris: OECD.

OECD (1996), *Employment and Growth in the Knowledge-based Economy*, Paris: OECD.

OST (1994), *Science & Technologie Indicateurs 1994*, Paris: Economica.

OST (1996), *Science & Technologie Indicateurs 1996*, Paris: Economica.

OST (1998), *Science & Technologie Indicateurs 1996*, Paris: Economica.

Palombara, J. (1991), 'Gli usi strumentali dell'università: riflessioni sull'esperienza degli Stati Uniti', in N. Matteucci, *L'Univeristà nel Mondo Contemporaneo*, Milano: Bompiani.

Pavitt, K. (1995), 'Academic research, technical change and government policy', in J. Krige and D. Pestre (eds), *Science in the 20th Century*, Amsterdam: Harwood Academic Publishers.

Pavitt, K. (1993), 'What do firms learn from basic research?', in D. Foray and C. Freeman (eds), *Technology and the Wealth of Nations: The Dynamics of Constructed Advantage*, London: Pinter.

Pavitt, K. (1991), 'What makes basic research economically useful?', *Research Policy*, **20**, 109–19.

Peacock, A. (1991), 'Economics, cultural values and cultural policies', *Journal of Cultural Economics*, **15**, 1–18.

Perkin, H. (1984), 'The Historical Perspective', in B.R. Clark (ed.), *Perspectives on Higher Education*, Berkeley, CA: University of California Press.

Pestre, D. (1997), 'La production des savoir entre académies et marché – une relecture historique du livre: *The Production of Knowledge*', in M. Gibbons (ed.), *Revue d 'Économic Industrielle*, **79** (1), 163–74.

Peters, M. (1992), 'Performance and accountability in 'post-industrial society': the crisis of British universities', *Studies in Higher Education*, **17**, 123–39.

Phillimore, A.J. (1989), 'University research performance indicators in practice: the university grants committee's evaluation of British universities, 1985–1986', *Research Policy*, **18**, 255–71.

Pike, A. and D. Charles (1995), 'The impact of international collaboration on UK university–industry links', *Industry and Higher Education*, **9**, 264–76.

Price de Solla, D.J. (1963), *Little Science, Big Science*, New York: Columbia University Press.

Price de Solla, D.J. (1976), 'A general theory of bibliometric and other cumulative advantage process', *Journal of the American Society of Information Science*, **27**, 292–306.

Raan, R.T.H. van (ed.) (1988), *Handbook of Quantitative Studies of Science and Technology*, Amsterdam: North Holland.

Ramsden, P. (1994), 'Describing and explaining research productivity', *Higher Education*, **28**, 207–26.

Rashdall, H. (1936), *The Universities of Europe in the Middle Ages*, Oxford: Oxford University Press.

Robbins Report (1963), *Higher Education*, HMSO.

Rose-Ackerman, S. (ed.) (1986), *The Economics of Nonprofit Institutions*, New York: Oxford University Press.

Rosenberg, N. (1994), 'Science–technology–economy interactions', in O. Granstrand (ed.), *Economics of Technology*, Amsterdam: Elsevier Science.

Rothblatt, S. (1976), *Tradition and Change in English Liberal Education*, London: Faber and Faber.

Rothblatt, S. and B. Wittrock (eds) (1993), *The European and American University since 1800*, Cambridge: Cambridge University Press.

Rothschild, M. and L.J. White (1991), 'The university in the marketplace: some insights and some puzzles', *NBER Working Papers Series*, no. 3853.

Rudy, W. (1984), *The Universities of Europe, 1100–1914. A History*, Cranbury: Associated University Press.

Rüegg, W. (ed.) (1992a), *A History of the University in Europe. Vol. I Universities in the Middle Ages*, Cambridge: Cambridge University Press.

Rüegg, W. (1992b), 'Themes', in W. Rüegg (ed.), *A History of the University in Europe. Vol. I Universities in the Middle Ages*, Cambridge: Cambridge University Press.

Sanderson, W. (1974), 'Does the theory of demand need a maximum principle?', in P.A. David and M.W. Reder (eds), *Households and Nations in Economic Growth*, London: Academic Press.

Samuelson, W. and R. Zeckhauser (1988), 'Status quo bias in decision making', *Journal of Risk and Uncertainty*, **1**, 1–59.

Santambrogio, M. (1997), *Chi Ha Paura del Numero Chiuso?*, Roma: Laterza.

Schmitt, C. (ed.) (1985–1994), *History of Universities*, Vols. V–XIII, Oxford: Oxford University Press.

Schultz, T.W. (1960), 'Capital formation by education', *Journal of Political Economy*, **68**, 571–83.

Scott, P. (1984), *The Crisis of the University*, London: Croom Helm.

Scott, P. (1997), 'The changing role of the university in the production of new knowledge', *Tertiary Education and Management*, **3**, 5–14.

Senker, J., P. Senker and M. Grossman (1997), *Effects of TCS on Academia*, SPRU Report, University of Sussex, Falmer.

Shapley, D. and R. Roy (1985), *Lost at the Frontier. US Science and Technology Policy Adrift*, Philadelphia: ISI Press.

Simon, H.A. (1955), 'A behavioral model of rational choice', *Quarterly Journal of Economics*, **69**, 99–118.

Simone, R. (1993), *L'Università dei Tre Tradimenti*, Roma: Saggi Tascabili Laterza.

Slaughter, S. and G. Rhoades (1996), 'The emergence of a competitiveness research and development policy coalition and the commercialization of academic science and technology', *Science, Technology, and Human Values*, **21**, 303–39.

Smith, A. (1976), *An Inquiry into the Nature and Causes of the Wealth of Nations*, London: Oxford University Press (1st edn, 1776).

Soete, L. and A. Arundel (eds) (1993), *An Integrated Approach to European Innovation and Technology Diffusion Policy: A Maastricht Memorandum*, SPRINT, Commission of the European Communities, Publication no. EUR 15090, Brussels.

Sommer, J.W. (ed.) (1995), *The Academy in Crisis*, Oakland, CA: The Independent Institute.

Spence, A.M. (1974), *Market Signalling. Information Transfer in Hiring and Related Screening Processes*, Cambridge, MA: Harvard University Press.

Spinner, H.F. (1993), 'Althoff and the changing constitution of science: bureaucratic, economical or cognitive?', *Journal of Economic Studies*, **20**, 134–66.

Stahler, G.J. and W.R. Tash (1994), 'Centers and institutes in the research university', *Journal of Higher Education*, **65**, 540–54.

Stankiewicz, R. (1986), *Academics and Entrepreneurs: Developing University–Industry Relations*, London: Frances Printer.

Staropoli, A., B.M. Kehm, U. Teichler, G.L. Williams, D. Sorace, F. Merloni and R. Moscati (1995), *Modelli di Universita' in Europa e la Questione dell'Autonomia*, Torino: Fondazione Giovanni Agnelli.

Steindl, J. (1965), *Random Processes and the Growth of Firms*, London: Griffin & Co. Ltd.

Steinmueller, W.E. (1994), 'Basic research and industrial innovation', Chapter 5 in M. Dodgson and R. Rothwell (eds), *The Handbook of Industrial Innovation*, Aldershot: Edward Elgar.

Stephan, P.E. (1996), 'The economics of science', *Journal of Economic Literature*, **34**, 199–235.

Stiglitz, J.E. (1988), *Economics of the Public Sector*, New York: W.W. Norton & Co.

Sutton, J. (1997), 'Gibrat's legacy', *Journal of Economic Literature*, **XXXV**, 40–59.

Tapper, E.R. and B.G. Salter (1995), 'The changing idea of university autonomy', *Studies in Higher Education*, **20**, 59–71.

Teichler, U. (1988), *Changing Patterns of the Higher Education System: The Experience of Three Decades*, London: Jessica Kingsley.

The Economist (1997), 'The Knowledge Factory', 4 October.

The Times Higher Education Supplement, Various issues.

Tornquist, K.M. and L.A. Kallsen (1994), 'Out of the Ivory Tower. Characteristics of Institutions Meeting the Research Needs of Industry', *Journal of Higher Education*, **65**, 523–39.

Trow, M.A. (1984), 'The analysis of status', in B.R. Clark (ed.), *Perspectives on Higher Education*, Berkeley, CA: University of California Press.

Turner, S. (1996), 'Comments on the economics of science, special issue The Economics of Science', *The International Journal of Knowledge Transfer and Utilization*, **9**, (Summer/Fall), 99–105.

Tversky, A. and D. Kahneman (1991), 'Loss aversion and riskless choice: a reference-dependent model', *Quarterly Journal of Economics*, **106**, 1039–61.

UNESCO Statistical Yearbook, various editions.

Universities' Statistical Record, *University Statistics. Vol. 1 Students and Staff*, Various issues.

Universities' Statistical Record, *University Statistics. Vol. 3 Finance*, Various issues.

Valigra, L. (1994), 'Academic biotech deals offer more promise than product', *Science*, **263**, 168–9.

Vavakova, B. (1998), 'The new social contract: governments, universities, and society. Has the old one failed?', *Minerva A Review of Science, Learning and Policy*, **XXXVI**, 209–28.

Veblen, T. (1918), *The Higher Learning in America. A Memorandum on the Conduct of Universities by Business Men*, reprinted 1994 London: Routledge/Thoemmes Press.

Vereeck, L.M.C. (1992), *The Economics of Science and Scholarship: An Analysis of the Althoff System*, Maastricht: Universitaire Pers Maastricht.

Verger, J. (ed.) (1986), *Histoire des Universités en France*, Toulouse: Bibliothéque Historique Privat.

Verger, J. (1992a), 'Patterns', in W. Rüegg (ed.), *A History of the University in Europe. Vol. I Universities in the Middle Ages*, Cambridge: Cambridge University Press.

Verger, J. (1992b), 'Teachers', in W. Rüegg (ed.), *A History of the University in Europe. Vol. I Universities in the Middle Ages*, Cambridge: Cambridge University Press.

Vught van, F.A. (1997), 'Combining planning and the market: an analysis of the government strategy towards higher education in The Netherlands', *Higher Education Policy*, **10**, 211–24.

Vught van, F.A. (1991), 'The Netherlands: from corrective to facilitative governmental policies', in G. Neave and F. Van Vught, *Prometheus Bound. The Changing Relationship Between Government and Higher Education in Western Europe*, Oxford: Pergamon Press.

Weale, M. (1992), 'The benefits of higher education: a comparison of universities and polytechnics', *Oxford Review of Economic Policy*, **8**, 35–47.

Webster, A. (1994), 'UK Government's White Paper (1993): a critical commentary on measures of exploitation of scientific research', *Technology Analysis and Strategic Management*, **6**, 189–201.

Weghtman, P. (1991), 'Collaborative scientific research in a European context. A University of Liverpool case study', *Higher Education Management*, **3**, 145–53.

Williams, G. (1992), 'An evaluation of the new funding mechanisms in British higher education: some micro-economic and institutional management issues', *Higher Education in Europe*, **17**, 64–85.

Williams, G. (1992), *Changing Patterns of Finance in Higher Education*, Buckingham: SRHE and Open University Press.

Williams, G. (1984), 'The economic approach', in B.R. Clark (ed.), *Perspectives on Higher Education*, Berkeley, CA: University of California Press.

Williamson, O.E. (1967), *The Economics of Discretionary Behaviour: Managerial Objectives in a Theory of the Firm*, Chicago: Markham Publishing Co.

Wittrock, B. (1993), 'The modern university: the three transformations', in S. Rothblatt and B. Wittrock (eds), *The European and American University since 1800*, Cambridge: Cambridge University Press.

Wittrock, B. and A. Elzinga (eds) (1985), *The University Research System. The Public Policies of the Home of Scientists*, Stockholm: Almqvist & Wiksell International.

Wood, P. (1994), 'Science, the universities, and the public sphere in eighteenth-century Scotland', in *History of Universities*, Vol. XIII, Oxford: Oxford University Press.

Wood, F.Q. (1997), *The Peer Review Process*, National Board of Employment, Education and Training, Australian Research Council, Commissioned Report No.54.

Wood, F.Q. (1995), *Issues and Problems in the Public Funding of University Basic Research*, PhD Thesis, University of New England, Armidale NSW.

World of Learning (1995), London: Europa Publications.

Ziman, J. (1994), *Prometheus Bound. Science in a Dynamic Steady State*, Cambridge: Cambridge University Press.

Zuckerman, H. (1977), *The Scientific Elite: Nobel Laureates in the United States*, New York: The Free Press.

Index